Successful Energy Sector Investing

Successful Energy Sector Investing

Every Investor's Complete Guide

JOE DUARTE

PRIMA VENTURE
An Imprint of Prima Publishing

Published by Prima Publishing, Roseville, California. Member of the Crown Publishing Group, a division of Random House, Inc.

PRIMA VENTURE and colophon are trademarks of Random House, Inc. PRIMA PUBLISHING and colophon are trademarks of Random House, Inc., registered with the United States Patent and Trademark Office.

Library of Congress Cataloging-in-Publication Data
Duarte, Joe.
  Successful energy sector investing : every investor's complete guide to . . . / Joe Duarte.
    p.   cm.
  Includes index.
  ISBN 0-7615-3564-0
  1. Petroleum industry and trade—Finance. 2. Energy industries—Finance.
3. Investments. I. Author name. II. Title.
  HG6047.P47 D8   2002
  332.63'22—dc21   2002019084

02 03 04 05 HH 10 9 8 7 6 5 4 3 2 1
Printed in the United States of America

First Edition

Visit us online at www.primapublishing.com

To my family and friends, who endure with me the ups and downs of the financial markets and of an author's life, with a great deal of understanding and grace under pressure; and also to the subscribers and supporters of www.joe-duarte.com. I couldn't do this over and over again without your support. And to the U.S. armed forces who protect all of us, selflessly, thank you.

Contents

Acknowledgments

Special thanks go to:

The Duarte family. To Sal, Lib, Reneé, and Amanda at "the office," Frank "Webmaster" Kollar, John "King of the Road and Appendixes" Duke, James Williams at *www.energyeconomist.com,* Steve Barakis at BP, Bill Carroll at OXY, David Richardson, Andrew Vallas, and everyone at Prima and Random House. Very special thanks to Thom Hartle for all his help and encouragement, and to Grace F. for excellent guidance and continued interest.

Preface

The events of September 11, 2001, changed our world forever. As free people, none of us will ever feel the same again about the things we once took for granted. But as investors, we have all been handed a whole new set of variables to deal with, from the increasingly uncertain politics of a new world to the complexities of what economies and markets will have to do to continue moving ahead. At the center of all the possibilities is the energy sector, for without it there is no progress, and society, as we know it, would be greatly and permanently changed.

This book is for individuals who want to make money consistently in energy stocks. My goal is to provide a clear and concise treatise for investors in a rapidly evolving and potentially profitable sector of industry. It is intended for a broad investor audience and includes a great deal of detail for those interested in technical and fundamental analysis. I firmly believe that investors who combine the best of both these disciplines will consistently make money in energy. This book provides a snapshot of the energy sector, which is composed of several subsectors, beginning with the integrated oil companies and ending with the slowly rising, but increasingly important, alternative energy sources. Along the way, I use company profiles, as well as fundamental and technical analysis, to give investors several methods with which to explore their investment opportunities.

We live in a new world—as investors and as human beings—with new buzzwords being added to our lexicon on a daily basis. Where germs like anthrax were once the province of microbiologists, physicians, and scientists, they are now as likely to be featured on the nightly and 24-hour news feeds as any other story of common interest. And where OPEC was once considered the only source for long-term global oil production, China and Russia have now emerged as major potential producers and marketers of fossil fuels. These two major powers could redesign their own futures—not as military powers, but as commercial powers.

I consider myself a long-term investor, because I expect to be investing actively until the day I die. But long-term investing, if not tempered by judicious portfolio monitoring and management, is the recipe for disaster. As a result, I approached this book with a lifetime commitment to prudent principles of portfolio management. We'll be looking not only at what stocks to buy, but also at which ones to avoid and when it is best to sell a winner or a stock that has not done what we expected.

We will explore methods for shorter and intermediate-term trading. The book contains sections on limited partnerships and on how to pick dividend yielding long-term stocks. And there are plenty of opportunities to learn how to read charts and understand technical analysis. I paid special attention to answering questions about which type of investor is best suited for each sub-sector, how much of your portfolio should be invested in energy, and how to make the best use of the methods described in the book within those contexts.

But this is not a book on financial planning. Nor is it a book for those who are most interested in geology, physics, chemistry, or any of the other scientific aspects of the energy sector. The aspects of the science that are crucial to investing are included and explored as necessary, but are not the main course.

The best way to use the book is to read each chapter individually and make notes. If you are not a chart reader, this will give you a chance to learn the basics. With practice, you could make money consistently by using these great visual aids. I suggest that when a stock is mentioned in the book, you get online, look at the chart, and try to find similar characteristics to those described herein. If you read the information and try it out immediately, it will likely make a longer-lasting impression.

Any repetition in the book is meant to be reinforcing. The more often you see something, the more likely it is to be imprinted on your brain, and the more likely you are to use it successfully. The chapters flow into one another and are to be used as cross-references.

And finally, no strategy will work every time. But as a professional money manager, I can attest that I use these methods in managing my clients' money and my own account. Good luck in your journey through the world of successful energy sector investing.

1

Introduction to the New Oil Order

When the price of gasoline hit $2.00 per gallon at the height of the spring 2001 California energy crisis, the story blazed at fever pitch in the national news media. To the average observer and especially to West Coast residents, this seemed like a crisis of epic proportions. Even those of us who lived elsewhere and whose gas prices rose to lesser levels found it extremely unpleasant. But that spike in gasoline prices really started brewing in the 1850s with the Pennsylvania oil rush. And the fires were rekindled in 1973, when the United States imposed price controls on domestic oil production. The ebb and flow between supply and demand reached extremes due to the tug of war between politics and the marketplace. The net result of the 150-year struggle was that consumers had to pay higher prices for imported oil, while domestic U.S. producers received less for their product. This led to a severe decline in domestic oil production and increasingly tough policies in the oil industry, both of which will likely change as a result of the September 11, 2001, attacks on the World Trade Center.

Thus, the seed of the problem was planted when market forces, politics, and the industrial revolution began to pull at three sides of an ever-shifting triangle of influences. Here, the fundamentals of the oil game are found. And this is where we will search for investment insights and profits.

Did oil prices truly rise that much in 2001? And was it really price gouging when we paid $2.00 per gallon? As history shows, such dramatic price spikes, and the inevitable attention from the press, often mark the top in prices. This happened in the summer of 1990, when Saddam Hussein invaded Kuwait and oil prices topped $40 per barrel. It happened again in early 2001, when oil prices topped $30 per barrel and sunk to the high teens as the year progressed, once again signaling a significant change in trend in the midst of media-fueled hysteria.

According to the *Energy Economics Newsletter (www .energyeconomist.com),* the average price of a barrel of oil after World War II, as measured in 1996 dollars, was $19.27 a barrel, while the median price was $15.27 per barrel. History shows that each spike in crude oil prices since the 1970s was caused by a Middle East crisis—until 1998, when the California energy shortage and the robust economy, fueled by the Internet bubble, took the blame. But what truly underlies the price of crude oil, and has throughout history, is the relationship between supply and demand, which in turn affects the price of gasoline at the pump and of heating oil, especially in the northeastern United States. The events that trigger the drama are usually part of the equation, but are usually little more than catalysts and not the main cause for changing prices in the energy market. Price change is due to the nuances of supply and demand.

What made the spring 2001 price hike different was that the crisis did not occur in the Middle East. Instead, the central events happened in California, where years of political pressure applied by environmental groups in response to unfortunate events such as those portrayed in the movie *Erin Brockovich* led to the state's over-reliance on natural gas to produce electrical power. The situation was worsened by two major factors. At the time the crisis came to a head, the Internet economy was still en vogue, and servers and PCs were increasing power consumption. The dynamic was aggravated by several years of the state's reluctance to build new power generation plants. So, the California energy crisis was really a classic supply-and-demand story of economics. This perfect storm also evolved from a decrease in U.S. oil refining capacity and low levels of drilling for oil and gas, as a result of 1998 oil prices falling to $11 a barrel. The resulting crisis and subsequent aftermath were worsened by the World Trade Center catastrophe on September 11, 2001, which changed our lives forever and which was partially responsible for the other shoe falling in the energy sector—a worsening economic recession that hastened the fall of the already-vulnerable U.S. energy-trading company Enron.

The United States' subsequent retaliation on Afghanistan after the September 11 attacks set in motion a series of events that will have long-term repercussions on the socioeconomic well-being of all Americans and other peoples around the world. In essence, the terrorist event brought to a head several festering and seemingly unrelated situations that until that point were little more than fodder for the button-down-shirt academic crowd (of which I am a card-carrying member) that favors political talk shows. The upshot was that the entire energy sector came to the forefront of an international debate between major global powers and forms the basis for a new way of looking at the energy markets, as featured in this book.

This *new oil order* is a central concept in the structure of my book, as it establishes fundamental new parameters with which to explore global energy markets. I introduced the term in an interview with Thom Calandra on *CBS Marketwatch,* on November 29, 2001. Simply stated, the new oil order means that the days of OPEC wagging the world's tail have been drastically altered by the emergence of Russia, the world's second largest oil supplier (behind Saudi Arabia) and now a roadblock to OPEC strategies.

In the article, Thom quoted U.S. Energy Secretary Spencer Abraham as having described Russia as "a separate nucleus of the energy equation." Translating the sentence into economic terms, we can see that the secretary was sending a message to OPEC, one that said: You have competition, and we won't be shy about making deals with them.

Nowhere was this clearer than in the fall and early winter of 2001, when the headlines featured pictures of Presidents Bush and Putin entangled in friendly dialogue. Their negotiations will almost certainly have significant consequences over the next few decades, but in the short term the talks served to keep oil and natural gas prices relatively low, while at the same time squeezing the OPEC economies and making Russia a preferred provider of energy to Europe and the United States.

So, now that the world has a new set of dynamics filtering through the energy markets, it is important to understand where we stood prior to this new paradigm. First, the Internet economy is here to stay. Although the dot-com bubble has burst, the effects of the new dynamic it spawned did not fade. Businesses and individuals now depend more than ever on computers, the Internet, and wireless devices for communication and even leisure. PCs, servers, routers, and the warehouses and office buildings where they are stored and maintained require 24-hour-a-day, 7-day-a-week climate control, as well as electrical power. Second, the increased risk of doing business in the Middle East and, to some degree, Latin America has turned U.S. and North American oil fields—even those protected by the National Park statutes—into prime exploration sites. And third, it will be years before California builds enough power plants to meet the demand for power, even after hundreds of technology companies have gone out of business. Finally, the California energy crisis and the demise of Enron may have dealt deregulation of the energy business a near death blow for the foreseeable future.

What it all adds up to is a world in which the demand for energy—and fossil fuels—will remain steady or more likely will increase over the next few decades. At the same time, the supply is to some degree on a long-term downward spiral, creating a classic economic setup for a long-term price squeeze in this commodity. And although the latter is an extremely general statement, it is vi-

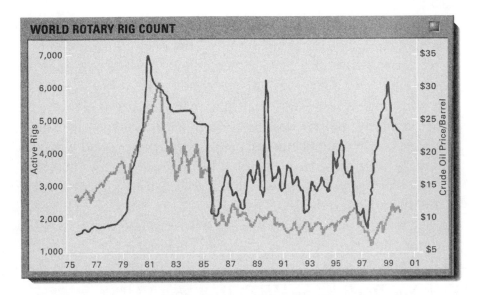

Figure 1.1: *Supply and demand as measured by the world rotary rig count from 1975–2001, courtesy of WTRG Economics/Baker Hughes/ Energy Information Administration.*

able as long as it is qualified and adjusted for periods of slowing economic growth, as well as for the rising curve that represents increased fuel efficiency in homes and vehicles.

The clear and unambiguous understanding of those dynamics and adjustments will give investors an edge. Those who can sort through the ever-shifting supply-and-demand equation and transfer this information to an analysis of companies at the forefront of executing their business plans while tapping into the new dynamics of the market will be successful energy sector investors. This book provides an analysis of the fundamentals—the market trends of leading companies and those that stumbled in the ever-changing new oil order.

Figure 1.1 clearly shows the industry cycle in the oil market: As the price of oil rises, so does the number of active rigs. At some point, the number of active rigs produces too much oil for the market, there is a glut, and the price corrects. Eventually, the number of active rigs falls, and the cycle begins once again. The rise and fall in oil prices tends to lead the rise and fall in the number of active rigs. But what paints a more sobering picture is that the number of active rigs has not risen to 1970 levels; thus, the price of oil has been kept at a higher average than if all those rigs had remained active. If all the rigs were still active, consumers would be paying much lower prices at the pump. And while this sounds like a conspiracy theory, it is important to note that many rigs either went dry or became too expensive to operate during this period. Nevertheless, the statistics are very compelling and suggest that the oil industry learned its lesson in the early 1970s about excessive levels of supply.

What You Don't Know Won't Hurt You

Anyone who has ever watched a Boston Red Sox game on television or been to the historic Fenway Park has seen the CITGO sign above the "Green Monster," the high left-field fence at the fabled stadium where every game takes on World Series proportions, no matter what the participants' standings. Those who see the sign don't realize that CITGO is a privately held subsidiary of Petroleos de Venezuela S.A. This in itself is quite interesting, because Venezuela is a member of OPEC and had a left-leaning government in power in 2001. In subsequent chapters, I will expand on the topic of Venezuela, a country that as of this writing has begun to govern by decree (especially pertaining to the oil industry), yet it maintains a large enterprise in the most democratic of all nations.

For now, it is important to understand that the Venezuelan government was the only government in the Americas that condemned the U.S. attacks on Afghanistan and that when the price of oil fell in 2001, Venezuelan President Hugo Chavez traveled the world for three weeks, trying to convince OPEC and non-OPEC oil producers to cut back on oil production, in order to prop up the price of oil.

As long as the Chavez government is in place, it could present a source of controversy and volatility for both oil markets and the U.S. oil supply, of which Venezuela is a significant source. Thus, I found it ironic and perfectly illustrative of the oil market's multiple personalities that as the Venezuelan government condemned U.S. retaliation for the September 11 terrorist attacks and decreed stringent cutbacks on private enterprise in its own country, the CITGO sign is a Boston landmark that was once defended by crowds of protesters when the city government wanted to tear it down.

The CITGO Web site *(www.citgo.com)* is an excellent source of information because not only does it provide interesting facts, its focus is quite partisan. Thus, it encapsulates the essence of the oil industry. It is an industry that is international, highly political, often misunderstood, and so much a part of our culture that most of us would not be able to function without many of the products and services it provides.

The Web site also expands on the concept of why the California energy crisis came about, and why the historically low gasoline and energy prices of the 1970s are not likely to return in the near future, barring a worldwide depression. This isn't to say that the price of gasoline in the United States might not occasionally reach or fall below the $1.00 per gallon mark. But the days of 29 cents per gallon and the price wars of the early 1970s, when every available rig was drilling at full tilt, are likely gone forever. According to the Web site, the United States had 265 oil refineries in 1976. By 2001, the number had come down to 152. At the same time, petroleum and gasoline demand increased by 15 percent and 20 percent, respectively, while refining capacity increased by only 11 percent. This means that now fewer rigs are at work, and fewer refineries are producing the finished products, such as gasoline and heating oil. The evidence suggests that long-term demand is not really outstripping supply, but that supply is being adroitly managed by the industry. Thus, the oil industry has created a unique environment by adjusting the basic laws of economics.

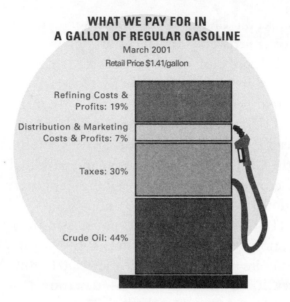

**WHAT WE PAY FOR IN
A GALLON OF REGULAR GASOLINE**
March 2001
Retail Price $1.41/gallon

Refining Costs &
Profits: 19%

Distribution & Marketing
Costs & Profits: 7%

Taxes: 30%

Crude Oil: 44%

Figure 1.2: *What we pay for in a gallon of regular gas as of March 2001,* *courtesy of* CITGO (www.citgo.com).

But before anyone labels me a conspiracy theorist, which I am not, I suggest that you read on, as there is more to the story.

As we see in figure 1.2, aside from the cost of crude oil itself, the most important component in the price of a gallon of gas is taxes. If we look at the price of gas in March 2001, according to CITGO, 42.3 cents of that price was taxes, while 62 cents was the price of oil itself, 27 cents was refining costs, and 9.87 cents was marketing costs. This is a perfect example of government's some-times-confusing role in the energy market and why the industry has closely controlled where it drills and to what degree.

This huge tax on energy—along with imbalanced government intervention, as in California—can lead to terrible consequences. The government's battle cry is for lower energy prices for con-sumers at all costs. But it makes no sense to have a purported market-based economy at the same time that the government is levying huge taxes, instituting stringent price controls, and limit-ing the construction of power plants—all events that took place in

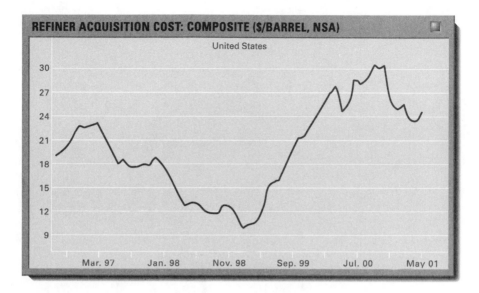

Figure 1.3: *Refiner Acquisition Cost: Composite. Courtesy of the* Dismal Scientist (www.dismal.com) *and Economy.com.*

California at some point during the energy crisis. If taxes are 30 percent of the cost of a gallon of gas or, for the purpose of illustration, a unit of electricity, then by controlling prices at a high level, either directly or indirectly, the government still gets its cut by collecting taxes; however, the oil and power companies suffer because their inability to raise prices to meet rising expenses cuts into their profit. Worse, the consumer only gets an illusion of relief, because even if prices stop rising for a while, chances are that once the price controls are lifted, the oil and power companies will raise the price of a gallon of gas and a unit of electric power, in order to make up for the lost profits and costs.

Figures 1.3 and 1.4 illustrate another significant factor in the price of a gallon of gasoline: the cost of acquisition for refiners. This means that the price of oil itself, the transportation costs, and other costs of doing business are extremely important contributors toward what we pay for at the pump. The relationship is simple: Gasoline prices rise and fall based on the costs of refining,

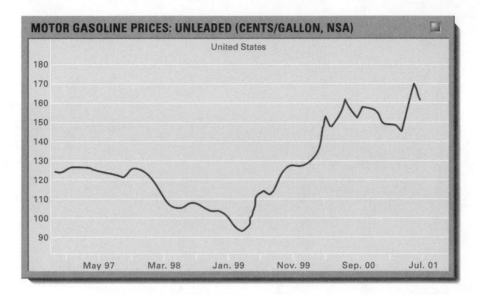

Figure 1.4: *Unleaded Gasoline Prices for United States, courtesy of the* Dismal Scientist (www.dismal.com) *and Economy.com.*

which are directly tied to the price of crude oil. The nearly perfect correlation between the two charts is as important a piece of information as you'll find in this book.

As investors, we must understand the ins and outs of this complex exercise, for they affect the prices not just of commodities such as gasoline, heating oil, and crude itself, but also the price of the underlying stocks. As the chart of Valero Energy (figure 1.5), a leading refiner of clean-burning fuel, shows, the costs of refining and the cost of a gallon of gas are near-perfect predictors of the price of the company's stock. Savvy money managers and traders buy and sell the stock as they project the company's profit margin and as it in turn corresponds to rises and falls in acquisition costs. The subtle point here is that the price of Valero rose and fell in nearly direct correlation to the price of a gallon of gas, which in turn moved in nearly direct correlation to the refiner's acquisition costs. So this means that contrary to what may seem sensible,

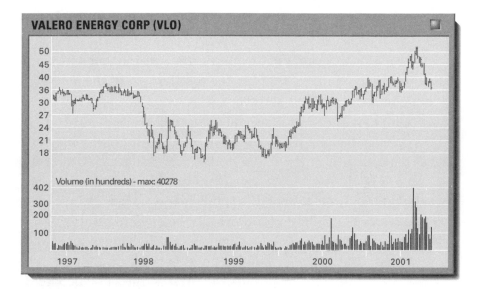

Figure 1.5: *Valero Energy Corp. (NYSE:VLO), courtesy of Telescan.*

lower oil prices are not much help to refiner's profits, because refiners can't raise gasoline prices when oil prices are low.

Therefore, the best time to own refining stocks is when gasoline prices are rising, as that is when companies can pass on costs
to consumers. This also shows how savvy oil companies are. They
back-load price increases when the price of oil rises, in order to
blame oil producers for the high price of gas at the pump. That is
an efficient market.

I wrote this book because I believe that the California energy
crisis is just the tip of the iceberg of what's coming in the energy
sector—certainly, as long as George W. Bush is president of the
United States. For Mr. Bush is a man of principle. And whether
you like him or not, he is not going to budge much from his oil-
drilling roots. Mr. Bush and Vice President Cheney both have the
insight of oilmen. They understand the nuances of how the ebb
and flow of supply and demand in this market work. They know
that each of the players involved in this tug of war also know this

chess game. And they are not afraid to play. As long as the Bush team is in place, energy will be a hot issue, which will provide excellent money-making opportunities for well-informed investors. And this book aims to decipher the puzzle, to lead the investor to both consistent analysis and the best potential for profit.

Note how the world has changed after the September 11 catastrophe, and along with it, the subtle perceptions of policy makers changed. Just in the few months after the attacks, interested observers could see the new dynamics at play, with the Bush team in the center. By December 2001, the energy debate changed from not *whether* the Gulf of Florida would be open to drilling and exploration, but to *how much* of the previously banned area would be opened. And although Congress was not talking about it in late 2001, by the time this book hits the presses, the same debate will focus on Alaska.

Note how, during the same period, Russia came out of nowhere to single-handedly stop OPEC's bullying in the oil market, and how the United States gently and quietly made its former enemy a "separate nucleus in the energy equation." And note how, during this same period, the United States announced that it would unilaterally stop adhering to the Anti-Ballistic Missile Treaty crafted in the 1970s with the then "evil empire" of the Soviet Union. And all the while Mr. Putin quietly disagreed, calling the U.S. departure from the treaty "a mistake." But on the other hand, the two countries gave themselves six months to come up with an agreement that would allow both sides to keep their people satisfied, while the United States could begin to work on its vaunted Star Wars project and Russia could tend to the oil fields. This is not a conspiracy theory, but an example of the kind of analysis that must be undertaken for us to understand the seismic changes in global politics and the energy markets.

And this also is not a book about partisan politics. It is partly a chronicle of how we got to where we are today and what to expect in the future, for the Bush legacy will set the tone for the next administration. It is, above all, a wake-up call to investors who want to participate in what could be one of the most exciting sectors and profit centers for the next decade or even longer.

In a sense, Mr. Bush is a lightning rod, an intangible factor in the sea of history and a man whose legacy as president—regardless of his merits or failures outside of energy policy and its consequences—will likely be judged on the price of a gallon of gasoline or the price of heating oil. And although Mr. Bush is a focal point in the energy sector's future, because of his high visibility and profound influence as president of the United States and as the man who spearheaded the "War on Terrorism," he will also serve as a reference and a focal point along our journey, for his moves will shape the new oil order in the first decade of the 21st century. He is, however, only one in a group of individuals and corporations that really sets the stage for what happens at the gas pump.

Thus, Mr. Bush is not the reason that the energy equation is where it is today. He is merely the guy who had an interesting situation handed to him, at a very critical time in history, and who may actually make some rather drastic and long-lasting changes. As I stated earlier, the real problems in the U.S. energy market are the low refinery capacity, low drilling activity, and occasional events, such as California's policy blunders, at a time when the high-tech economy increased the demand for energy. This is compounded by an increasing dependence on foreign oil, which as I write is slowly beginning to change, but which will remain in place for at least the first decade of this century. And this foreign dependence is not going away altogether, as Russia will become an ever more important part of the U.S. oil supply, while OPEC's role will likely decline or stabilize. First, Mr. Bush will fight for the rights of the oil industry and will champion the U.S. crusade for energy independence. His endeavors will cause actions and reactions that in turn will create activity in the oil sector, which will result in opportunities for savvy investors.

And second, whatever he accomplishes, no matter how watered down it becomes after congressional debate, and regardless of how controversial or contentious his fights with Congress and political and environmental action groups become, Mr. Bush's actions and their results will set the stage for the next several decades in the U.S. and global energy sector.

A Little Background on the Oil Industry

"Texas Tea," "Black Gold," and other names are applied to the precious resource that, along with money and sometimes love, makes the world go round: petroleum. For no modern, or nearly modern, society on this planet is independent of petroleum and its cousins: natural gas, gasoline, diesel, propane, kerosene, and heating oil. And the potential for a global energy crisis, or at least a severe test of the supply-and-demand equation, could well be on its way, even as you scan this introductory paragraph. It follows that the economic, social, and environmental implications of such a crisis—if, indeed, it materializes on a global basis—could lead to catastrophic results on many levels, as well as to a wealth of possibilities for well-informed investors.

I have been blessed with the opportunity to write this, my third, book. And for that, I am eternally thankful to the Fates and to my publisher. In my first two books, *After-Hours Trading Made Easy* and *Successful Biotech Investing,* I tackled two critical topics in the ever-changing story of financial markets, but felt that I still had work left to do.

I am an avid observer of human behavior, and beyond just helping you improve your investment knowledge, one of my goals as a writer is to guide you to think, to introspect, and to interpret what the market says—as, for example, in the previous section where we explored some factors that cause refinery stock prices to rise.

In *Successful Biotech Investing,* I noted how the demise of the technology sector during the year 2000, as measured by the Philadelphia Semiconductor Index (SOX), was coincident to the relative stability of the biotechnology sector, as measured by the Amex Biotechnology Index (BTK). I also suggested that the biotechnology sector would be a leader in the first decade of the 21st century, a prediction that I am willing to extend for at least another decade. I based my analysis on the fact that investors put their money behind a dream, in expectation that it would be fulfilled and, in many cases, exceeded. And the promise of the eradication of disease and the lengthening of life are still powerful draws.

History and chart analysis suggested to me that the 10-year bull market in technology was vulnerable, due to the loss of the dream quality of the sector. How small can a chip get? And how fast can we make a PC? Well, at some point, the size will decrease, and the chip will move faster, but the changes would be so subtle that the naked eye won't be able to tell the difference. As of the early part of 2001, we may have gotten very close to that point. What's the next step? How about the implantation of Net-enabled software into the brain? At present, that is the realm of science fiction and way beyond anything that Wall Street's day-trading crowd will likely start talking about for a few years.

In *Successful Biotech Investing* I did not suggest that biotechnology stocks would rise in a straight line over the first quarter of the century. It is nearly certain that costly setbacks will occur along the way for most sectors in the stock market, including biotechnology. This will be the result of normal market movements and the rapid speed with which the external forces that govern our world continually vie for attention and predominance. For external events are increasing their influence on the financial markets, and as time moves faster, due to speed-of-light communication, market volatility will be the rule, not the exception.

So, as in my previous works, I will not make any outrageous predictions or give market index targets for the rest of the 21st century. Instead, I will provide a foundation from which to analyze the increasingly important energy and power-generating sector of the stock market, a sector that I believe has the potential to change the mechanical side of our lives every bit as much as biotechnology can change the organic side.

What made me decide to next tackle the topic of energy? I have always invested in oil stocks, both for my clients and myself.

And being from Texas, I can't avoid the cultural influences of the oil industry. But the combination of politics, market forces, and the supply-and-demand equation rising to a different level made the topic irresistible, both from an investment point of view and academically.

But more important, I believe that the diversity of this sector offers investors of all temperaments and time horizons the opportunity to participate. This sector provides both the income-generating opportunity of a blue-chip stock like Exxon-Mobil, with its high dividend yield, and the huge potential for capital gains that can erupt in the oil-drilling sector when it hits its stride. This means a potential for a total-return long-term investment, as well as intermediate and short-term trading profits.

According to OPEC's own Web site and the U.S. Department of Energy, the supply of oil in non-OPEC countries will run out by the middle of the second decade of the 21st century, although it is not clear if that projection included Russia, in its newfound place at the top of the non-OPEC heap. Common wisdom also suggests that OPEC's own supply could run out by the end of the century. Humanity has apparently used up a significant portion of its available supply of fossil fuels in less than 200 years, after the first gush of oil stained the lucky men whose faces got splashed.

But the truth could well be that the world's oil supply may not run out as quickly as people are saying. The interest in drilling for as much oil as possible certainly seems to have waned, given the historically low active rig count shown earlier. And this suggests that oil companies are not interested in drilling for oil in wells where it costs more to get the oil out than the profit to be made on the market.

So the true dynamic is not so much a question of supply, as it is being able to extract the supplies that are already known to be there and to do so profitably. The key factors are in two separate arenas. From a producer's standpoint, the dynamic has changed after the September 11 attacks. Oil companies, which in the past might have been willing to search for oil in politically unfriendly territories, are now more likely to be interested in braving Siberian winters, as Russia's political climate and willingness to exploit its vast supplies may outweigh most other factors.

From the industry's point of view, the greatest effect on profitability will be the efficiency with which the oil is extracted, as well as the efficiency with which the fuel is refined and delivered to the public. For utilities and power producers, the main dynamic beyond the efficiency with which energy is produced will be the ease with which business can be transacted in any given region. Thus, some of the greatest advances in the oil and energy sector may come not only from finding more oil, but from technological advances that will improve a company's ability to extract every drop of oil and gas from the ground, to squeeze every available drop of gasoline at the refinery, and to generate every possible megawatt at the power plant. Those companies that can operate most efficiently will be the winners.

I found it quite interesting, while researching this book, that the energy sector has expanded beyond petroleum to an increasing dependence on natural gas and other alternative fuels. Most investors are under-invested in the sector, as a result of increased reliance on technology stocks for portfolio growth. But as the Nasdaq Composite and the classic tech stocks continued to falter in 2001, technology itself evolved and offered investors a chance to invest in applied technology. An important future focus of technology will likely shift from pure technology, as measured by PC and cell phone sales, to applied technology, as it is related to energy exploration, generation, and the phenomenon of trading energy itself in the open market. As the Enron story grew, this new dynamic became increasingly important in the global marketplace—not just as an investment vehicle for individuals, but as a sector whose antics will be explored as a pivotal area that could move the noninvestment world, such as Congress.

Thus, the California energy crisis may have been the tip of the iceberg, as the convergence of environmental, political, and market forces promises to lead this sector into a market leadership role, both in its growth potential and in its ability to capture head-lines, with Wall Street as the focal point. My goals for this book are to:

1. Provide a historical perspective

2. Fully catalog the present state of the sector, beginning with a global picture and working toward a full explo-ration of the main subsectors in the energy area

3. Project the current dynamics into the future

4. Apply the principles of technical and fundamental analy-sis of stocks to the energy sector

Intellectual Inclusion, a Small Course in the Dynamics of Thought

I believe that an investor who knows how to think will be more successful than one who uses luck, dartboards, or stock tips. Thus, before I delve into the energy sector, I would like to offer a short course on thought organization, which I think will help you get more out of this book than you might have expected.

Think and Grow Rich is a book that changed my life. As the book clearly states, just by the mere act of reading the words on those pages, a whole set of interesting events occurs in the sub-conscious mind. When I read the book, I began to formulate and implement a plan that has brought me to what I've always wanted: to be a writer. And my goal as a writer is to produce a body of work that stimulates you to think, make changes, and move ahead.

These changes, which in my opinion occur at the chemical and molecular level of the mind, are possible in all people who can read and let their minds work unhindered. That is why I began this book with the Valero Energy example, a simple set of graph-ics that clearly shows that if you know what to look for, organize it, and retrieve it in a timely fashion, you can make intelligent investment decisions. If you let this example work its way into your memory bank, it will serve as a template.

I let my mind work at its own pace, and on a subconscious level, for that's when it works best. Subconsciously, it searches for all the "files" that might have the answer. Subconsciously, it organizes and edits what it searches for. And when the information is ready, your subconscious mind brings it up for discussion with the conscious. I suggest that you do this when reading this book. Let your mind do its work.

Call it what you will, but this is the essence of thinking: the constant search for answers and responses to what the environment throws at us. And I call this thinking process Intellectual Inclusion, or the profitable use of the interaction between experience, personality, and our daily give-and-take with the environment. The key words are *thought process*. And the goal is to learn the process, correctly. Once you learn the process, you can adapt it to all situations, and it will do its job automatically, as is natural.

So, why is this so important? Because few sectors of industry are as predictable and cyclical as oil and energy. Knowledge of what worked in past cycles, when properly organized and retrieved in a timely fashion, is the key skill required for successful energy-sector investing. What has just happened in energy will in some way likely happen again in the future and will likely have similar factors affecting it. OPEC may be diminished, but its demise is still far into the future. And I suspect that Russia and the United States will find something to disagree about along the way. Most important is that even though their number is shrinking, undemocratic countries are still out there, and they are likely to have large oil supplies. That means that political instability will always be a factor to contend with in the energy sector.

Thus, Intellectual Inclusion is a key concept. By learning to think efficiently, you can encapsulate the basic premises ruling the energy sector and use what you already know largely by reflex, if you can recognize the patterns. Furthermore, successful investing is the direct result of the mind's ability to recognize the patterns of successful management in corporate behavior, which is then recognized by the market and reflected in stock prices. In *Successful Biotech Investing,* I described the pattern of corporate success that, when implemented by research-stage biotechnology companies, will allow them to make the transition to full-fledged and, it is hoped, profitable pharmaceutical companies.

The concept worked well in the biotech rally of March to June 2001, where my benchmark biotech company, Genzyme, did all the right things and remained near the top of the performance ladder, while the rest of the sector rallied initially, but then faded. That concept, when translated to the energy sector, can serve you just as well, when you decide which stocks to buy and sell.

We will use Intellectual Inclusion for two purposes. First, to learn what drives the energy cycle, a topic I've already touched upon, but will expand on further. Then, we want to apply those variables to each subsector and eventually to the companies in the subsector. More important, we want to find the companies in each sector that are best at both executing their business plan and communicating those plans to the marketplace in order to be recognized. The recognition part is as important as the execution side, because only when enough big-money players recognize success does a stock rise.

When we identify a company in a sector that is successful and that remains successful, both in execution and in its ability to communicate, we should learn all about its methods and use them as benchmarks with which to measure other companies. There is usually one best way to succeed in a particular sector, and those companies that can customize that approach to their own personalities will be the leaders.

What's the bottom line about Intellectual Inclusion? The mind is a two-way filter that processes information brought in by the senses and then formulates a response. The mind is also the storehouse and processing plant of genetic and environmental information that makes us who we are.

The filter may malfunction because it receives flawed or erroneous information, because it makes an error in processing, or both. The end result is an inappropriate answer and its consequences. Therefore, miscommunication—and thus the majority of all the world's problems—come from a bad filter.

Don't let your filter misguide you when making investment decisions. Learn the basic concepts before moving on in this book. Use your own experience to customize what you learn here. And don't be afraid to think about the markets in an unorthodox fashion. Because I used Intellectual Inclusion, I was one of the first analysts to publicly note Russia's effect on the oil markets and was able to coin the phrase "the new oil order," along with Thom Calandra. If you take your time, do your analysis, and work efficiently, you will make money in the energy sector.

Where the U.S. Economy Is in 2001, in Terms of Energy Dependence

The final point in this introduction concerns the present status of the U.S. economy regarding its energy efficiency. By understanding this important aspect of the energy equation, we will be able to make better forecasts and improve our ability to dissect the inevitable media scrutiny of the energy sector.

In a July 12, 2001, article entitled "The State of Energy in the U.S.," Thorsten Fischer, an economist and columnist at the *Dismal Scientist,* suggested that the United States has become more energy efficient since the oil crisis of the early 1970s, reducing its reliance on energy as a generator of gross domestic product (GDP). He suggested that this was a major reason for the economic slowdown not being worse in 2001.

Figure 1.6 shows that the energy intensity of the United States continues to decrease. This is measured by the amount of energy (thousands of BTUs) required to produce a dollar of gross domestic product. The chart shows that the United States is now twice

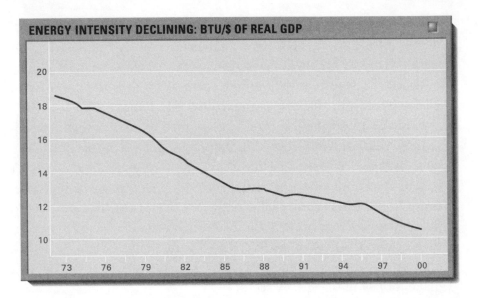

Figure 1.6: *Energy Intensity Declining, courtesy of the* Dismal Scientist (www.dismal.com) *and Economy.com.*

as efficient in its production of goods and services as it was in 1973. At the current pace, we could make a rough projection that by the year 2011, the figure could be near 5, which would factor in more advances in technology and perhaps an acceleration of the trend.

Figure 1.7 shows that the decade of the 1990s, when much of the energy efficiency developed, was also a period of rising economic output for the United States, as measured by GDP in dollars. If we look at both of these charts simultaneously, we see that the U.S. economy could quite possibly grow in leaps and bounds over the next decade, even if the efficiency of energy usage dropped to a slower rate of efficiency. We could adjust our growth expectations slightly, due to the recession of 2001, but over the long term, the trend for U.S. growth is likely to remain upward.

As I will expand on in the next chapter, demand for energy will likely continue to increase or, at worst, stabilize at a higher level than where it was a decade earlier. This is a direct result of

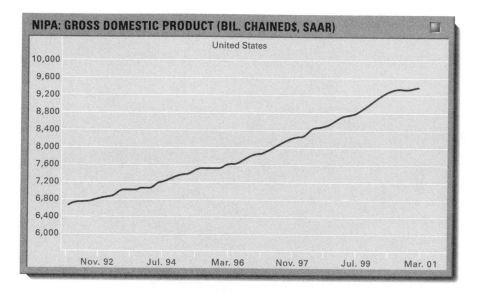

Figure 1.7: *Gross Domestic Product, courtesy of the* Dismal Scientist (www.dismal.com) *and Economy.com.*

technology acting as a significant driver of energy consumption. Furthermore, rising demand, tempered by increased efficiency in extraction methods and power production, will likely keep energy prices either steady or rising, although perhaps not at rates that will threaten economic growth to the degree experienced in the 1970s. The intangible in all of this analysis is the global political situation. Were a major local war between Israel and the Arab world to erupt and perhaps eventually pit the Middle Eastern OPEC countries against the West, it would have very negative consequences, despite the new presence of Russia as an alternate source of fossil fuels.

Finally, we note that Fischer's article ends on a sobering note, as figure 1.8 indicates. Unless something radically changes in U.S. domestic energy policy—as it well could if domestic drilling is more aggressively pursued, which is likely after the September 11 attacks—oil imports will continue to increase, while domestic production has begun to flatten out of a decade-long downward

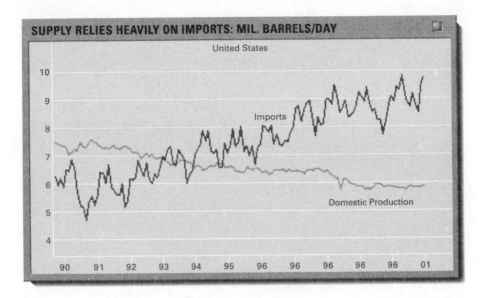

Figure 1.8: *Rising dependence on foreign oil, courtesy of the* Dismal Scientist (www.dismal.com) *and Economy.com.*

trend. This means that even though the U.S. economy is more efficient than ever in energy use, it is also increasingly dependent on foreign oil. And despite more aggressive domestic drilling, that's where politics comes in.

Although the United States is the world's greatest economy and depends on the price of oil to a great degree for ease of doing business, we want to look at the impact of oil prices on other global economies. A direct contrast is provided by the economies of OPEC countries, according to a study at energyeconomist.com by James Williams. His data show that in most cases, the rise and fall of the gross domestic products of OPEC countries are directly tied to the price of oil. This dependence on one source of income is the root of the problem in the interactions between the producer and the consumer sides of the equation. However, OPEC is interested not in price swings, but in keeping the price of oil in a trading range that in 2001 was quoted as being $20 to $25 per barrel.

When the price of oil falls below the band, political and social problems tend to erupt in OPEC countries. The countries most economically vulnerable to swings in the price of oil are Qatar, the United Arab Emirates, Kuwait, and Saudi Arabia. Kuwait and Saudi Arabia also suffer from huge and noticeable discrepancies in the distribution of wealth, a situation that many in the intelligence community suggest is responsible for both the rise of terrorist activity and Saudi Arabia's apparent lack of cooperation with the United States during the war in Afghanistan. The second tier of vulnerable countries is made up of Venezuela and Libya, whereas Iran, Algeria, and Indonesia show less volatility.

Perhaps OPEC countries' singular dependence on oil revenues to run their economies sets up the predictable trading and investing environment of the energy market. This dependence also holds OPEC hostage to indirect influence or even straight blackmail by terrorists, as well as vulnerable to the ever-present threat of social upheaval, which is why they remain undemocratic and discourage other forms of freedom that the Western world takes for granted. And it is also the same reason why Venezuela began to turn to the left in 2001. Where there are limited socioeconomic resources, governments usually turn to undemocratic measures.

My aim is not to deride people's choice of how they govern themselves, but merely to explore the background that sets up the dynamics of the energy markets.

Finally, it makes sense to conclude that the ever-present threat of social unrest in the OPEC cartel set up a vicious cycle that, when coupled with the events of September 11, was pivotal in leading the United States to increase its interest in participating with Russia in the ever-changing new oil order.

Summary

The energy sector is cyclical and is most influenced by the supply-and-demand equation related to crude oil. Supply and demand are affected by political and economic forces. When the demand exceeds supply, political forces such as environmental groups and Congress tend to stay quiet. When supply begins to shrink, OPEC and the oil-producing countries tend to cut back production. When production levels fall far enough, then prices begin to stabilize and eventually rise. When prices rise far enough, political pressure begins to intensify, until it reaches levels in which the oil industry increases its activity and eventually prices begin to fall.

The California energy crisis is just one of many events that have led to higher oil prices and the ensuing political pressure, which eventually led to an easing of oil prices. What makes this event slightly different is that refining capacities are not keeping up with demand for gasoline and California still lacks enough power plants to supply its high-tech and high automobile–use economy; thus, the cycle may not lead to historically low oil prices. As a result, this is one of the best times in history to reap profits from energy stocks.

Furthermore, even though the U.S. economy is more efficient than ever in its use of energy, it is increasingly dependent on foreign oil. This, of course, sets up the potential for political leverage from abroad and tends to make life quite interesting for investors.

We want to learn to recognize the key turning points in the oil cycle and partner that knowledge with patterns of success, in companies and in stocks.

CHAPTER

2

History

The ever-changing political landscape can be confusing to investors who try to make buying and selling decisions about their energy stocks. But history shows the energy sector to be ruled by a fairly predictable behavior pattern, based on supply and demand. This chapter will describe the history of the major companies influencing today's oil industry and how they got where they are today. The focus will be on events and on repercussions of those events, rather than on business models, successes, or failures. That will come later. For now, we want to understand the behavior pattern of the industry and the influences that have shaped it into what it is today. Armed with that information, we can then explore business models and individual companies.

Petroleum is one of the key commodities in the world, along with food and water. Without it, life as we know it would not exist. Thus, to understand what the future will likely hold for the energy sector, we should take a good look at the past and look for repeating patterns and results, as well as key differences and instances of major divergence from the past that are likely to shape the future. We are not looking for precise cycles with which to build a black box that will generate buy and sell signals. Although that would be wonderful, especially if it worked, life is not that simple. Instead, this chapter's goal is to develop a method to analyze daily developments in the energy sector.

I will refer quite often to two kinds of history. First, the written history, or the annals of the industry sector. Much of that history will deal with government decisions, global politics, and key developments, in terms of how business was conducted and of technological events that changed the landscape. I will highlight the key events, in a conventional sense, and also will describe how I see them having influenced the current state of affairs and how they may affect the future. But you should already be applying the principles of Intellectual Inclusion and allowing the facts and patterns to seep into your subconscious mind.

The second kind of history, and one that I briefly mentioned in chapter 1, is the history of price action in the energy sector. I will expand on that concept by looking at long-term charts and, where appropriate, will describe key moments of past history that have been repeated with similar results. A prime example was the effect on energy markets of the supply and demand crisis of the 1970s and the events that preceded it, which to a great degree seem to have repeated themselves in the late 1990s and early 21st century. This is a point that Fed Chairman Greenspan supported with his remarks in a satellite conference to central bankers in June 2001, when he pointed out that each economic recession since 1970 has been preceded by a spike in energy prices.

This is a central tenet of our model in the prediction of what can happen in the energy sector. Our job as investors is to constantly scour the available information in order to predict and to prepare for events that will lead to a spike in crude oil prices. For after that spike, a very high probability exists that shock waves will occur in the economy and financial markets.

The Anatomy of an Energy Crisis

And while Mr. Greenspan clearly noted the true relationship between oil prices and economic activity, my own analysis goes further. I discovered a pattern that continues to repeat itself and whose latest incarnation will likely spawn the greatest change in the energy sector since the oil gushers in Texas first erupted. This new dynamic will change the way that oil and energy market analysis is conducted in the future, as old, irrelevant players are replaced by a new crop of actors and circumstances.

In the early 1970s, the United States had just come out of the huge bull market in technology of the late 1960s. The great engines of that time were Xerox and IBM, whose products greatly influenced society and the ways of business. This huge bull market was powered by cheap oil. But, as often happens, great technological advances in the West failed to trickle down to the underdeveloped world, much of which just happens to have the oil the West depends on. So, as the technological revolution of that period reached its zenith, thus began the energy crisis and the subsequent decline of the stock market in the United States, culminating in the 1973–1974 bear market.

In the late 1980s, the PC made its presence known, launching new Wall Street darlings like Dell and Microsoft. The stock market crashed in 1987, but the economy didn't until 1990, when Saddam Hussein invaded Kuwait and oil prices rose, topping at $40 per barrel. Again, the connection between technology, progress, the maldistribution of wealth, and an energy crisis is quite notable.

In the late 1990s, the Internet changed the world. But once again, as the West basked in its new technological glory, the underdeveloped world, with the largest portion of the world's oil, failed to participate to the same degree. Some of the more developed countries in South America and parts of Asia, though, as well as other select parts of the globe, did enjoy at least a small economic bounce, as telecom companies, eager to expand their empires beyond the saturated Northern Hemisphere, poured money into them for a few years. But due to the telecom companies' miscalculation of the bureaucratic snags involved in building new infrastructure in these relatively underdeveloped countries and the bursting of the Internet bubble, the money flow dried up.

In many ways, this was worse for the emerging markets, because the potential for hope was quickly extinguished before it had a chance to cement itself into a permanent infrastructure.

At the same time, huge productivity gains in the United States led to increased wealth creation, and an increased maldistribution of global wealth ensued. The rich got richer and the poor were once again disappointed, except this time they had begun to taste the elixir of success and progress, only to have it removed from their lips before they could truly appreciate it. So the damage to the underdeveloped world when the Internet bubble burst was worse, emotionally and psychologically.

The crash and burn of California's energy sector and the subsequent dot-com devaluation were the responsible events this time that led to the familiar pattern of a dramatic rise in oil prices, followed by recession and a dramatic fall in the price of oil, with its repercussions around the globe: rising unemployment in the Northern Hemisphere and the threat of political unrest in the emerging and underdeveloped nations.

And just as gasoline prices in the United States went from 23 cents a gallon to over $1 in the 1970s and 1980s, the energy crisis of the early 21st century manifested itself in rising oil prices, a doubling of natural gas prices, and U.S. gasoline prices at nearly $2 per gallon by the summer of 2001. The result was predictable: A recession began to take shape, which was officially proclaimed in December, but really began in March.

The New Face of an Old Dynamic, and How the World Changed After September 11, 2001

Oil crises, of which there have been several since the 1950s, have usually been punctuated by, or closely associated with, violence in the Middle East, given that region's strategic and influential role in the market due to its rich oil reserves. But this time was different, as self-proclaimed Islamic militants crashed two airplanes full of passengers into New York's World Trade Center and one plane into the Pentagon on September 11, 2001, killing thousands of civilians in the process. The obvious difference is that in 2001, in contrast to previous crises, the violence was exported from the Middle East to the United States, which changed everything in international politics and the world energy market. The organization responsible for the attacks was known as Al Qaeda, and the body of evidence against it and its leader—a Saudi exile and multimillionaire named Osama bin Laden, with a long history of terrorist activity—was overwhelming and included a controversial videotape aired in December 2001 by global broadcasters, to a mixed and predictable reaction around the world. The tape was reportedly obtained by U.S. intelligence during a raid in Afghanistan during the U.S. invasion.

The events that unfolded after the attacks on the World Trade Center were multiple and significant, and I will expand upon them as the book progresses. But historians will argue for decades about how the world changed on that day, much as it did when Enola Gay dropped its cargo over Japan in 1945. For just as World War II changed its course as a result, so did the dynamics of U.S. and global foreign policy—and its close relative, economic policy—drastically change. Many political winners and losers forged their long-term fates on that and following days, as international leaders either joined or ignored the U.S. call to action when it declared its "War on Terrorism."

The first call of condolences and nearly unconditional assistance to the United States came from Russia. And that phone call may well have been the watershed event that changed the way the energy sector works for the next 20 to 30 years, and perhaps beyond. For as I will discuss later, the newfound closeness between Presidents Putin and Bush led to a series of economic and political developments whose outcome was unequivocal. On that day, Russia suddenly became the pivot point of the world oil market, dethroning Saudi Arabia as the swing producer and clearly weakening OPEC. The cartel suddenly found itself a necessary liability, not the staunch partner that, at least on the surface, it had been.

In the months following the attack, OPEC was very quiet until the price of oil began to fall below $20. As I noted in chapter 1, oil is OPEC's only source of income. When the price of oil falls below a certain price—such as $20, in this instance—receipts fall, and so do the economies of OPEC countries. When economies in OPEC countries falter, the chances for social unrest increase. And so began, quite predictably, OPEC's campaign to raise the price of oil back to its intended range through its tried and true method—cutting supplies.

But what OPEC did not count on this time was the resistance it got from Russia and the significant cost of the battle for the cartel, as Russia's stature in the West rose significantly. This led to an increasingly benign stance from international lending agencies and a sudden interest from Western oil companies in resurrecting their interests in Russia's technically archaic, but richly supplied, oil fields.

In a spellbinding report on December 11, 2001, the international intelligence Web site Stratfor.com *(www.stratfor.com)* featured an analytical piece entitled "Saudi Stability on Borrowed Time." In this insightful account, Stratfor, a service that continually exhibits an uncanny ability to get to stories—and to be correct—before the mainstream media, noted that Saudi Arabia expected a $12 billion budget shortfall for fiscal 2002 (its 17th deficit in 18 years, running back to 1982), which had amassed a public debt for the kingdom of $168 billion. It also noted that the Saudi government was potentially having trouble finding external financing sources and was considering the issuance of bonds, privatizing its utilities, and reducing state subsidies as well as taxes.

Saudi's social problems, according to Stratfor, ran deep, with up to 30 percent male unemployment estimated in a population of 16.2 million. More interesting is the fact that 65 percent of the workforce in the kingdom is foreign, and that Saudi's plans for privatization of utilities would run into problems due to the difficulty for foreign investment created by Saudi laws.

Stratfor noted that the cuts in public spending would lead to social unrest, because the royal family would no longer be able to "buy the public's support." But the most chilling conclusion of the report was Stratfor's expectation of Saudi Arabia becoming the "champion of the Islamic world," in an attempt to win the hearts and minds of the public.

Thus, it made sense that when Saudi Arabia's power in the oil markets was on the ropes, the United States and Russia would take the opportunity to forge an alliance based on mutual needs and beliefs. Russia's vast oil resources and need for foreign capital were the perfect fit for an America in need of oil and natural gas, as well as an American energy industry that faced a rising risk of political problems—if, indeed, political problems were to surface in Saudi Arabia, as well as in other places in OPEC, the most likely of which was Venezuela.

Finally, Stratfor cautiously noted that although Saudi Arabia was likely to take some very unpopular steps in the view of Washington, the Saudis still believed that American troops stationed on their territory would protect the Saudi government against any popular uprising. At the same time, Stratfor noted that the Saudi government would likely be forced to review the American military presence on its own soil, a move that the report called "contradictory" to the Saudi kingdom's strategic needs.

What this report did was encapsulate a significant problem for the U.S. oil supply, prior to Russia's change of heart. But it also tells us that the West is walking a rather loose tightrope when it comes to its energy needs. Thus, the clear path for the United States and its energy companies is to start looking for diversification, away from Saudi Arabia and unfriendly members of OPEC.

This report leads to many potential lines of thought, ranging from the sublime to the fantastic. But the bottom line—if Stratfor were to be correct, as its analysis often is—is that we could then project a scenario into the middle of the first decade of the 21st century in which increased politically induced volatility occurs in the oil market. This potential volatility was already being factored into domestic energy policy in the United States, as laws that had prevented drilling for oil and natural gas in the public lands of the

United States were being relaxed. But perhaps the biggest surprise of all could be how relations with Iraq, Syria, and Iran warm up over this period, as Saudi Arabia embarks on its new direction, dictated by its own internal problems.

As I write these paragraphs, I must note that I am only a student, reporter, and interpreter of history as it applies to the financial markets. I undertake this kind of analysis on a daily basis, to make decisions about investing in the energy sector. In this forum, I am only interested in delivering information and interpretation to you, the reader, about how world events affect the energy markets. My own religious beliefs and practices are private, as are those of others whose beliefs I unconditionally respect, although do not necessarily condone or agree with—including those who are called "terrorists" by governments and the media, although they may refer to themselves as soldiers, brothers, liberators, or otherwise. It is important for you, the reader, to understand that I am not in any way attempting to vilify, glorify, or judge any one particular group or individual. I am presenting you with information obtained from credible sources, analyzing it, and applying it to the subject at hand, which is to make money by investing in the stocks of oil, natural gas, utilities, oil service, and other forms of energy companies. I will let the words and the deeds of all mentioned in this treatise speak for themselves and will allow you the privacy of making your own judgments in these matters, as they pertain to other aspects of life beyond investment.

The Connection Between High Tech and Oil Prices

The relationship between technological advances, with their ability to fuel economic growth, and the price of oil—and thus the behavior of the economies in the oil-producing countries—is a crucial concept and one that has both political and industrial components. And although in chapter 1 I described in great detail the vulnerability of OPEC to the business cycle, I noted that the U.S. economy has greatly removed itself from the effect of oil prices in a very

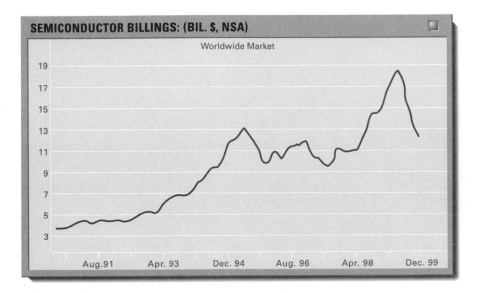

Figure 2.1: *Semiconductor Billings 1990–2000, courtesy of the* Dismal Scientist (www.dismal.com).

long-term sense. This is the primary reason why a garden-variety recession in the United States does not lead to social unrest.

Now that we've established some political guidelines, we should look at the connection between technology and the energy sector from an industrial viewpoint. Earlier in this chapter, I noted that the unraveling of the Internet economy was partly responsible for the situation in the energy markets that unfolded in 2001. And just as the Nifty Fifty technology stocks of the late 1960s mostly collapsed, except for a handful of survivors like IBM, so did the majority of the Internet stocks, except for the true innovators like America Online—which became AOL–Time Warner—and other likely survivors, such as EBay and Amazon.com.

Figure 2.1 shows the activity in semiconductor billings for the 10-year period between 1991 and June 2001. This 3-month moving average, courtesy of *www.dismal.com*, smoothes out the monthly gyrations of this volatile indicator and provides the picture of a bull market in technology for most of the period. But

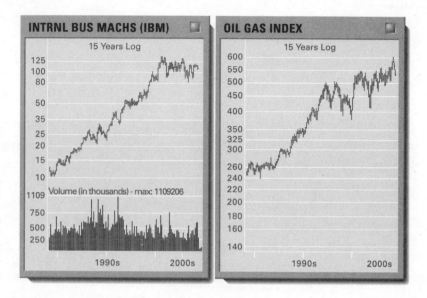

Figure 2.2: *Comparing oil stocks (XOI; right) to IBM (NYSE:IBM; left) in the 15-year period from 1986 to 2001.*

when the Internet bubble burst, we see that the billings, which are a representation of the health of the chip sector—and by default, the technology industry—fell apart.

Next, in figure 2.2, we see that in the 15-year period from 1986 to 2001, IBM had a huge bull market, which corresponded to a significant move in the Amex Oil Index. The charts point to the fact that IBM topped out in 1999, very close to the time that the semiconductor billings saw their top, while the oil stocks had one more rally before finally breaking down in 2001. The chart of XOI also shows that the oil stocks were still in a long-term bull market, while IBM looks to be in a long-term consolidation pattern.

Again, these charts support the notion that growth in the rate of technological advance in the Northern Hemisphere and more advanced countries is closely followed by an increase in energy prices, as a result of the increased demand for oil that technological growth engenders. As a market analyst, I find this relationship quite compelling and central, from both an economic point of view and a technical analysis standpoint.

This relationship is related, in my opinion, to the political, as well as the economic, aspects that govern the energy cycle. As Northern Hemisphere economies thrive, they take the OPEC countries along for the ride. But due to the economic diversity of the Northern Hemisphere, especially the United States, when the technology cycle breaks down, it leads to lower economic growth, which results in lower oil demand and then to a lowering of the price of oil. This in turn causes a great deal of discomfort to the OPEC economies, whose main source of income is oil. When this happens, a flurry of political problems can often erupt, especially when less-developed members of OPEC feel the pinch of lower oil prices.

But history shows that gasoline and power prices eventually stabilize. The cycle will bottom when the economy, especially the technology sector, begins to show signs of improvement and the global economies pick up steam. The key factor will be how fast the recovery is driven by new technology and its increasing demand for power. Newly introduced political problems as a result of the September 11 events will likely delay both the scope and the speed of the recovery, as well as perhaps limit the geographical range, as North American companies, wary of terrorist risk around the world, pick and choose their projects more carefully.

Oil, energy, and politics are all connected, and investors need to understand the history before making decisions. History's pattern is quite clear. The developed countries, usually led by the United States, will embark on a new era of technology. The technology increases power consumption. The technology bubble eventually bursts, and OPEC gets caught unaware with too much supply on the markets. There is usually a crisis, such as the California energy crisis, that makes the news coverage quite sensational. The United States eventually reaches a crisis stage due to this imbalance of the supply-and-demand equation. And the rest of the world takes the opportunity to push its agenda ahead in the UN, at the expense of the United States.

Investing and speculating are nonpatriotic occupations. And in a world where anyone can wire money to a discount broker and trade online 24 hours per day, in a very real sense there are no countries, just the ebb and flow of funds from one place to another along the information superhighway.

So why is history so important? Because by combining your knowledge of history—which in fact is about human behavior—with knowledge of technical and fundamental analysis, you could improve your investment results significantly. Without an understanding of the history of the sector and the fundamentals that rule the way it works, it would be impossible to anticipate significant moves in the sector. The bottom line is that if you don't have a good grasp of the history of the sector in which you invest, you won't have a good feel for why the sector behaves the way it does.

The History of the Oil Sector

The first two sections of this chapter grounded us in a modern setting, with historical proportions. But the traditional view of the history of the oil sector is a fascinating exploration, which we are about to undertake.

The history of the modern energy sector—from here on, this will mean oil, natural gas, gasoline, and other products, unless specifically stated—really begins with petroleum and the first oil well, drilled in 1859 by Edwin L. Drake, a retired railroad conductor. There will be a separate section on nuclear energy.

But before Drake's oil well, the real history starts in biblical times, when Noah was described as using pitch, a solid form of petroleum, in building the Ark before "The Great Flood." Those who built the streets and walls of Babylon in 600 B.C. also used pitch in their construction.

Missionaries in the American frontier described Native Americans using crude oil for fuel and medicine in the 1600s. And there are accounts and evidence of such use by the Native Americans for hundreds of years before missionaries arrived.

By 1750, colonists in Pennsylvania and West Virginia found oil seeping out of the ground as they dug for salt mines. A major development came in 1840 when Canadian geologist Abraham Gestner discovered kerosene, which could be distilled from oil or coal and which became the leading fuel for lamps. And in 1857, Samuel M. Kier, a Pittsburgh pharmacist, used oil medicinally. As a result, the price of oil may have enjoyed its first bull market.

But the true watershed event came in 1859, when Edwin L. Drake drilled a well near Titusville, Pennsylvania, using a steam engine to power the drill. This triggered an oil rush, which turned into an oil boom. Supplies increased, and the price of oil dropped from $20 to 10 cents a barrel. By the 1860s, Pennsylvania was in the throes of an oil boom. Railroads were built to carry the oil. And in 1865, the first oil pipeline was built, which carried the oil for 5 miles. Within 10 years, the pipeline was 60 miles long and ran to Pittsburgh.

By the 1880s, there was production in Kentucky, Ohio, Illinois, and Indiana. By the 1890s, California, Oklahoma, and Texas had joined the oil-producing states. And in 1901, the Spindletop field in Texas produced the first gusher in North America. Production boomed to 64 million barrels per day in 1900.

Italy began production in 1860, followed by Canada, Poland, Peru, Germany, Russia, Venezuela, India, Indonesia, Japan, Trinidad, Mexico, and Argentina. Iran was the first Middle Eastern country with an important oil find, in 1908. Iraq came on in 1927, and Saudi Arabia in 1938, to be followed by other Gulf states.

The Key Players and How They Got There

Now that we know that today's oil industry had a rather humble and disorganized start, the next step is to see how we got today's behemoth oil companies and how their past actions may actually give us a hint about the future.

The Standard Oil Company begins our first leg of development. The formation of Texaco is the second major leg. And the development of Europe's Royal Dutch-Shell, British Petroleum, and Total Fina Elf is the third leg.

The history is fascinating on its own and warrants its own major text, doused with commentary from those who are still alive and were there to see the development of this incredible phase of human history. My visits to company Web sites during the research phase left me feeling as if I had been transported into an Indiana Jones movie, as I read tales filled with adventure, hardship, politics, and great triumphs of human effort.

Standard Oil—The First Monopoly

The original Standard Oil Company was established in 1870 by John D. Rockefeller, whose rise to fame and fortune was quite similar to those of other industrial-age icons like Andrew Carnegie, the steel magnate; Charles Schwab, the original owner of the brokerage firm that still bears his name; and William Wrigley, whose chewing gum is still being chewed; as well as Thomas Alva Edison and Henry Ford, whose contributions to capitalism and modern society are well documented.

Rockefeller started working at age 16, and by age 23 he entered the oil business. Just like other early entrepreneurs, he thought and grew rich. This means that he formulated his plan, formed his team, and set out to organize the oil industry by buying refineries, building tank cars, developing a pipeline system, buying oil fields, and developing a distribution network. In 15 years he had standardized the flow of oil from producers to consumers through his company.

The Standard Oil Trust was established in 1882, centralizing control of 90 percent of the oil industry in the United States. But since 1870, many of the same complaints plagued Standard Oil that were leveled at the Bell System/AT&T's monopoly in phone service and Microsoft's hold on the software industry. In 1892, the Supreme Court of the United States ordered the separation of Standard Oil of Ohio from the Standard Oil Trust. In 1899, Standard Oil Company of New Jersey became the holding company for 37 subsidiary companies of the old Standard Oil Trust.

And in 1906, the United States sued Standard Oil of New Jersey, leading to the Sherman Antitrust Act that justified the breakup of the company in 1911. Among the leading reasons for the breakup, besides the huge glut of power controlled by a single entity, were the business tactics employed by Rockefeller, which included rebates and other types of privileged treatments to his preferred customers.

Already, we see precedents and similarities, as the long arm of the government, spurred on by populist forces, moved in to curb a monopoly. As often happens, with government intervention the results are controversial. Take the California energy problem, as many of the same forces that led to the breakup of Standard Oil cajoled the California state government to simultaneously enact incomplete deregulation policies and place moratoriums on power plants, while the Silicon Valley economy continued to increase its demand on power. Of course, the results were predictably disastrous, with Pacific Gas & Electric's power-generating subsidiary declaring bankruptcy. More important is that the state of California was forced to sign a 10-year deal with another utility, Calpine, for guaranteed energy, which cost the state a great deal of money.

Thus, even modern history clearly illustrates that well-meant central planning in a market-based economy can yield disastrous results. This relationship is a central concept that will crop up countless times in this book. The interplay between governments, entrepreneurs, and investors is the key equation to monitor because, as investors, we are dependent on the actions of the other two. When the government and the entrepreneurs don't get along, crises erupt, which usually affect the value of our investments.

Unfortunately, many casual investors are not aware of this relationship and fail to factor it into their analysis, which can lead to losses, as the energy sector marches to the beat of the news climate on a regular basis. As the world moves, albeit in fits and starts, toward a global, tariff-free enterprise zone, many cultural and regional issues come to the forefront, which eventually lead to market volatility and cause what has been a fairly common occurrence since 1987: financial market crises. The U.S. government's main goal, California notwithstanding, is to turn the whole world into a market-based trading zone, with supply and demand as the primary reasons for market movements. The implied results of this goal are to reward innovation and persistence or to grant the greatest portion of the potential riches to those who learn how to work the system, whether as businesspeople, investors, or both.

But the United States faces tough ideological competition, as many global governments—even though communism has been totally discredited, and regardless of the propaganda otherwise—want to keep power and money in the hands of the ruling elite. As a result, although the United States generally tends to deregulate industries and fight monopolies (despite the consequences, as I will explore later), much of the world tends to close its markets and create state-owned monopolies. And as history shows over and over again, too much government intervention in the business world doesn't work. The proof is in the devastating results that occur—such as the California crisis—whenever the United States turns back toward a socialist-type model. In the information age, when billions of dollars can change hands in a few minutes, the role of central planning by governments has been diminished, while the role of the markets has been increased. Once governments realize this, they will benefit greatly.

I also note that the next potential California-like problem could come in the Northwest and the Gulf states of the United States. The latter include the Southwest and Southeastern areas, including Florida. The same dynamics are beginning to emerge there, as the balance between environmental preservation and economic growth will once again be challenged and the debate over oil drilling in Alaska and in the Gulf of Mexico heats up. As I write, the government is slowly but surely opening up the Gulf of Mexico, as well as the Rocky Mountain area, to oil and gas exploration. This is a prelude to what will likely be a heated debate about Alaska's public lands.

More interesting is that the beginning of the 21st century has brought the merger of six major oil companies, forming three even larger entities. Exxon merged with Mobil, British Petroleum merged with Amoco, and Chevron and Texaco merged. Exxon, Mobil, Amoco, and Chevron were all members of the Standard Oil Company prior to its breakup in 1911. This is no accident, given that these companies are responsible for dealing with another monopoly, over which the U.S. government has no jurisdiction but can wield considerable pressure: OPEC. The relationship of these major oil companies with the cartel will be severely affected by the events of September 11, 2001.

One of the most important developments in the key period of 1870–1911 came in 1909, when British Petroleum was formed to develop a major find in Iran (called Persia at the time). This was a prelude to what would happen in 1938, when Standard Oil of California—today's Chevron—discovered oil in Saudi Arabia. The world has never been the same since, as the balance of power based on supply began to slowly shift toward the producing countries.

Chevron spent five years and $5 million, during a very difficult economic time, to discover what the company describes as "oceans" of oil. A total of 52 oil fields were discovered by Chevron, including the Ghawar field, the biggest oil field in the world. Ghawar is 150 miles long by 25 miles wide and holds 60 billion barrels of oil, six times more than North America's largest field, Alaska's Prudhoe Bay. One quarter of the world's current oil reserves are found in the original 320,000 square miles first discovered by Chevron.

But here today's world becomes clearer. As the scope of the find became evident to Chevron, the company realized that it could not do all of the required work on its own. Thus, it formed a partnership with Texaco, whose history is quite interesting. This partnership led to the formation of the Arab American Oil Company, known as Aramco, which still operates today as Saudi Aramco and which is now wholly owned by the Saudi Arabians, who bought out their American partners. More interesting is that Exxon and Mobil joined the alliance after World War II, again bringing together pieces of the old Standard Oil.

So, even after Rockefeller's Standard Oil companies had been broken up in 1911, three of them found their way back together, albeit on foreign soil, along with a relative outsider, Texaco—a firm that joined the club as it merged with Chevron. No conspiracy—just good sound business practices, as far as I'm concerned.

On Saudi Aramco's Web site, Standard Oil is referred to historically as a "major oil company," whereas Texaco, Exxon, and Mobil are called "other oil companies." This is a perfect example of the nationalistic fervor with which the oil producers treat their most precious resource, and it serves as a subtle, but nevertheless omnipresent, hint at the somewhat stressed relationship between oil producers and oil consumers, a relationship that will likely be tested during the first decade of the 21st century, as the events I described in the prior section begin to play out.

It is also a hint about how OPEC operates in a similar fashion to Rockefeller's monopoly. But despite all the rivalry, all ended well, because Aramco is the world's largest oil producer, and its former partners have merged into two of the largest oil companies in the world. The more things change, the more they stay the same. Once again, history repeats itself and gives us clues about what may come in the future: the world's oil supply in the hands of a few large entities that find it difficult to get along with each other. The trump card is what shape the new set of difficulties will take as the new oil order continues to consolidate its position. What's my view? Their conflict is our opportunity, as investors. Conflict creates volatility, and volatility translates to movement in price.

Texaco—Independent As the Lone Star State

Texaco's tale is a true Texas-style jaunt, complete with colorful characters and grit and representative of the state's colorful Wild West heritage. The tale starts on March 28, 1901, with the first gusher logged in the fabled Spindletop field in East Texas. Founder "Buckskin Joe" Cullinan had learned the oil craft in Pennsylvania and enlisted the aid of cofounder Arnold Schlaet, a financier. Together, they formed the Texas Fuel Company, with the goal of extracting the oil in Spindletop and selling it to refineries on the East Coast of the United States.

"Buckskin Joe" used Intellectual Inclusion, although he may have called it something else. He had learned the oil trade in Pennsylvania and was fully awake, relating to his environment, when he saw the Spindletop opportunity. He immediately seized it, assessed his strength (he knew the business) and his weakness (he was not a financial wizard). He then formed his team, with the first key player being Schlaet, a financier.

The company expanded by an acquisition and was once again blessed when its newly occupied headquarters turned out to be 20 miles away from Sour Lake, a region 20 miles south of Beaumont, Texas, where another significant find was made. By 1902 the Texas Company was formed, and the company laid down the first pipeline from the Spindletop field. It measured 6 inches in diameter. Later that year the company opened its New York City office and made its first sale. By August 1902, the Texas Company had bought its first vessel, a barge to transport oil from Texas to Louisiana. And by the end of 1902 the company had changed its name to Texaco, by accident, as a cable was addressed to them with the word either misspelled or intentionally changed. They noticed it and knew they had a brand name.

By 1903, thanks to the company's foresight, the Sour Lake find began to produce, saving the firm from bankruptcy. In 1903 the company built its first refinery and began to sell asphalt, a by-product. The year 1904 brought the company's first research laboratory and its first international business center in Belgium. By 1908 the company had moved to Houston.

In 1910 Texaco began publicly trading on the New York Stock Exchange and in 1911 opened its first filling station in Brooklyn, New York.

Texaco's first filling station in Houston was the prototype for today's convenience stores. Texaco called it a service station, which meant that value-added services were available for customers. This is a key innovation, given where the bulk of Texaco's business comes from in the 21st century—refining and retailing oil and related products and services. In 1918 Texaco developed the first continuous commercial process for deriving gasoline from heavy oil.

Texaco continued its expansion into research and marketing, constantly tweaking the processes, and in 1931 bought the Havoline brand of motor oil, which remains a world leader in its field. In 1934 Texaco began operation of the first submersible drilling rig.

In 1940 Texaco began to sponsor opera broadcasts and in 1941 supported the war effort by building radar equipment at one of its research labs. In 1943 Texaco and seven other oil companies operated a fleet of tankers on a nonprofit basis to support the war effort.

In 1950, Texaco built the Trans-Arabian pipeline, the first pipeline across Saudi Arabia. In 1954 Texaco developed a process that allowed the production of large quantities of hydrogen. In 1959, the Port Arthur refinery became the first computer-operated refinery in the United States.

In 1984 Texaco bought Getty Oil, increasing its strategic reserves by 1.9 billion barrels. In 1988, Texaco and Saudi Aramco formed Star Enterprise, a joint venture to refine and market oil products to the East Coast of the United States.

Along the way, the road has been littered with lawsuits, including those alleging environmental and racial problems at Texaco, as well as a bankruptcy that resulted from Texaco's battle with Pennzoil over Getty Oil and Pennzoil winning a lawsuit. Texaco went bankrupt in order not to pay Pennzoil. According to legal reviews of the Texaco case, the company owed Pennzoil $10 billion after an appeals court decreased the initial court award. But at the time, the company had $37 billion in assets. The court allowed the bankruptcy because Texaco's lawyers convinced the judge that to pay the $10 billion would be impracticable. Reviewers of the case were amazed that the company successfully pled "poverty," despite its huge financial assets.

While it is beyond the scope of this book, I would like to note that in the past, and to a certain degree in the present, there is a negative side to the global natural resources industry: its environmental record. This has to be considered from a social standpoint, as demand for energy increases in an ever-tougher political climate and at a time when natural resources continue to dwindle. Thus, as energy investors, we need to be prepared for occasional shocks to the system, as we will likely hear more about environmental impact from the news media, as well as from environmental and other groups that oppose the oil industry. I like clean air and water as much as anyone and just point this out to provide a balanced picture.

From a business point of view, legal challenges cost money and hurt profits. It is within this framework and this understanding that I have written this book. I present the facts and the company histories, with emphasis on the business side of the equation. And I do so with the knowledge that company Web sites and literature will predict the best possible outcome and present the facts in the best possible corporate light. I have no public political agenda to promote, as my only interests lie with investors and helping them profit from the world and its existing and evolving circumstances. Now, we can move on without anyone being offended.

Texaco's history is quite significant because it illustrates several key points. First, the company was not the first major oil company in the world to be formed. But now that it has merged with Chevron, it is part of the remnants of the old Standard Oil.

Texaco's other contributions include its involvement with technology that is related to energy, but is usable outside of the energy sector, such as hydrogen. Hydrogen was initially used for fertilizers, but may be an excellent fuel source, with cleaner emissions than gasoline. BMW has had nitrogen-burning prototypes on European roads for some time now, which suggests that we may be on our way to alternative fuels. And therein lies the main lesson in how Texaco runs its business—by thinking ahead and by acting quickly on opportunities.

Now, we've looked at a macro view of the American experience in relation to two very distinct oil companies: Standard Oil, the monopoly, and Texaco, the southern upstart that hit the ground running and never looked back. Along the way, both companies had setbacks. Both discovered significant finds in Saudi Arabia. And both had or now have significant business ties to Saudi Aramco. Finally, the two competitors merged over a century after the industry got its start.

Obviously, a pattern is developing. Texaco tends to be more of a maverick, putting a great deal of emphasis on its marketing, while Chevron is a very traditional company in the mold of its founders. Texaco was the first company to have a nice tiled service station and was among the first to sell food, drinks, and other convenience products at its stations. Texaco also put money into research and, after having environmental and racial discrimination problems and bankruptcy, now goes to great lengths to put forth its ethics and racial policies on its Web site. It also promotes a safe environment policy.

Texaco, in its ever progressive mold, owns a 25 percent stake in Dynegy, a small, but aggressive, new world utility company whose presence and stature in the business changed dramatically after the demise of Enron.

The lesson to learn from this brief glimpse into the American oil industry concerns how these companies continued to move forward during difficult times. Standard Oil had to dismantle its empire—and yet the surviving subsidiaries are still at the top of the game. Texaco obviously has always known a good deal. That's why it agreed to merge with Chevron. Next, we will explore the European experience.

Royal Dutch/Shell Group— A Marriage of Convenience and Common Sense

Just as the American experience was colorful and full of drama, the European experience was and remains an interesting story in its own right. First, we'll explore the action in the Royal Dutch/ Shell group, which is a partnership run jointly by two independent companies, making it a fairly unique business arrangement that has been in place since 1903.

The Shell portion came from London's East End, where Marcus Samuel Sr. opened a small shop to sell seashells (not by the sea-shore) to nature enthusiasts. The shop turned into a prosperous im-port-export business. Marcus Junior discovered oil exporting in a visit to the Caspian Sea coast and saw a profit opportunity in the export of kerosene to Japan. According to the story, Marcus discov-ered that Standard Oil had a monopoly on the business and realized that he needed to find a way to compete.

So, like a good thinking man, Marcus noted that the Suez Canal offered a way to deliver kerosene for a lower price. And in 1892 he commissioned the first special oil tanker and was able to deliver 4,000 tons of Russian kerosene to Singapore and Bangkok.

Once again, we see the familiar pattern of success emerging. An alert young man traveling around the world noted a situation that could be improved and, as a result, could be profitable. He knew there was demand and knew there was supply. He also knew that he needed to contend with well-established and very powerful competition. He surveyed the available technology and found a way around his problem, thus establishing himself and his company in a special niche of the emerging oil industry.

In 1890, a Dutch company named N. V. Koninklijke Neder-landsche Maatschappij tot Explotatie van Petroleum-bronnen in Nederlandsch-Indie was formed to develop oil fields in Sumatra, in the Southeast Asia region. And in 1896, the company built its own fleet of tankers to compete with the British. This became the Royal Dutch side of Royal Dutch/Shell in 1903, when the two companies merged into the Asiatic Petroleum company, once again proving that on both sides of the Atlantic there was the urge to merge, since size does matter in the oil business. Four years later, the Royal Dutch/Shell group merged globally.

Today's Royal Dutch/Shell group owns 60 percent of Royal Dutch Petroleum and 40 percent of Shell Transport and Trading Company.

The group expanded into Romania, Russia, Egypt, Venezuela, and Trinidad. Again, it's easy to see that expansion is the key to survival, as a European company spread its wings across Europe and across the Atlantic Ocean, proving that globalization is not a new idea at all. In fact, the main resistance that underdeveloped countries have to globalization was greatly influenced by the expansion of the oil companies around the world and its negative consequences. Here again, history shows that business strategies employed in most industries follow a previously seen pattern. I will expand on this theme later and show how this fits into company analysis.

World War I was not kind to Shell, as much damage was done to its European properties, delaying expansion. But that didn't happen in the United States, where Shell formed the Shell Company in California. In 1922 Shell Union Oil Corporation was formed when Shell merged with the Union Company of Delaware, while expansion continued in Turkey and Asia. Shell entered the chemical business in 1929 and launched the first liquid rocket fuel. Then Shell moved its operations to the Caribbean island of Curaçao. Shell also aided the Allies in World War II.

In the 1950s, Shell was among the first to develop super-tankers and was instrumental in the development of natural gas, discovering one of the largest natural gas fields in the world in Groningen, the Netherlands, which by 1970 was producing almost half the natural gas consumed in Europe. Shell discovered many more significant natural gas sites around the world, especially in the North Sea, where the company concentrated a great deal of effort, with handsome payoffs in the early to mid-1970s as significant finds were made.

The strategy and luck paid off, when natural gas demand increased in Europe as a result of OPEC's aggressive pricing in the 1970s, which led to the now well-known energy crisis of the 1970s. Shell also developed an interest in coal and metals during that period, which again showed a great deal of foresight. In 1974 Shell formed Shell Coal International and bought a well-established metals firm, opening the way to diversification and expanding its role in chemicals.

Shell was an aggressive provider and developer of unleaded gasoline in the 1980s. And in the 1990s it began to focus on renewable energy sources. In 2001 Shell made a bid for Barrett Resources, an American company with vast fuel reserves in the Southwestern United States, but in uncharacteristic fashion failed to close the deal by undervaluing Barrett's assets. We will explore this event later as we go into business practices and models in the energy industry.

It's quite obvious from the history of these major companies that each one has a distinct personality. Exxon-Mobil continues to carry the classic stance of the Rockefeller empire, due to its size and power. Chevron combines the old and new world, with its merger with Texaco, a company that has a more lively, maverick-type personality. And Shell's history has a very European, almost cerebral, feel—especially its ability to operate competitively in the present, while preparing for the future.

BP-Amoco—A Right Proper Combination of Old and Really Old Money

This is another combination of Standard Oil and Europe, as Amoco was originally known as Standard Oil of Indiana. But the road to BP-Amoco began in Persia (now called Iran), when in 1901 William Knox D'Arcy, with the permission of the Shah of Persia, began to explore for oil. As with Texaco, D'Arcy was the financier and the brains behind the operation. The task of finding and exploiting the oil fell to engineer George Reynolds, whose job was extremely difficult, due to bad weather and labor problems. Costs mounted, and a financial infusion was procured from the Burma Oil Company in 1905. And in 1908, the company finally struck oil in commercial quantities, the first significant find in the Middle East.

The Anglo-Persian Oil Company was formed in 1909, with 97 percent of the shares being owned by the Burma Oil Company.

D'Arcy became a director after the pioneering stage, with the initial chairmanship of the company falling on the shoulders of Lord Strathcona, who was succeeded by Sir Charles Greenway in 1914.

Greenway did not want to fall into the clutches of the always-acquisitive Royal Dutch/Shell and sought capital from the British government; he was supported by Winston Churchill, who was the First Lord of the Royal Navy. Just prior to the outbreak of World War I, Anglo-Persian contracted to provide fuel to the Royal Navy in exchange for an injection of 2 million pounds sterling into the company. The government also received majority shareholder status and the right to appoint two directors to the board.

This was a novel approach to financing and a clear departure from policies of other major companies in the world, which were all privately funded. What it accomplished, however, was the almost-certain survival of the company as long as the British government stayed in business. It also showed that Winston Churchill was someone to take seriously in matters of global military and diplomatic affairs.

The British government reduced its shareholder status over the years and ended most of its participation in 1987.

The company continued to expand after WWI, growing along its consumer lines by introducing gas pumps and marketing its products in Iran and Iraq, as well as establishing fueling stations aimed at both sea and air routes. Refineries were established in Wales and Australia, while exploration was expanded into Canada, South America, Africa, Papua, and Europe.

BP did not expand into the United States in its early days, whereas Royal Dutch/Shell did. This interesting nuance is likely to have been directly related to the fact that BP was essentially a government-controlled company and its expansion into major markets like the United States might have been limited by the political implications of such a move.

Greenway retired in 1927, having accomplished his goal of establishing the company as a major global player in the oil industry.

After WWII, the company continued to grow, expanding the role of Iran as a leading oil producer in the world and branching out into the chemical industry. But by 1951, the Iranian government was increasingly interested in running operations; it nationalized Anglo-Iranian's assets and brought operations to a halt.

Yet the truth is a little deeper here and goes beyond nationalism, because in 1953 Britain boycotted Iranian oil, due to a global oil glut. Because of the boycott and the glut, Iran was unable to sell oil in the world market and suffered severe financial problems. The central figure in this drama was Mohammad Mossadegh, who eventually replaced the prime minister of Iran and exiled the shah.

The shah enlisted the aid of the CIA and returned to power, and by 1954 a consortium of companies was created, with the newly renamed British Petroleum holding a 40 percent stake. As a result of the Iranian crisis, BP was forced to diversify its oil producing to Kuwait and Iraq, as well as its refining capacity to Europe.

In 1965, following the lead of Royal Dutch/Shell, BP discovered oil in the North Sea, which it followed with a major find in 1970. Perhaps the most significant development in BP's history, as well as its foothold in America, came when it struck oil in Prudhoe Bay, Alaska, in a find that turned out to be the biggest oil field in the United States. BP then made a deal with Standard Oil of Ohio and eventually became the main shareholder of the venture.

The 1970s were not kind to BP, with oil crises in 1973 as OPEC took control of its oil supplies and technologies. And in 1979 the Iranian revolution led to another disruption in oil supplies. But—as with Texaco's example earlier, in which the company was saved by a new discovery in its early history—BP's Alaska and North Sea finds came online and allowed the company to survive.

The company also diversified into the animal feed business and other consumer products. BP had a significant presence in metals mining, as well as in coal, chemicals, and even information technology.

In 1987 BP bought the 45 percent of Standard Oil that it did not already own, a pact that resulted from the Prudhoe Bay find, and also bought Britoil, a major U.K. exploration firm. BP America was established as a result of the Standard Oil transaction. And finally, BP bought out the British government. By the early 1990s, BP had sold its food, technology, and minerals businesses. In 1998 BP bought Amoco and formed BP-Amoco, once again proving that Standard Oil lives on in the big time, even if the names have changed.

Amoco was formed in 1889 and was originally known as Standard Oil of Indiana; it was formed to refine oil from a field in Lima, Ohio. Immediately after the 1911 breakup of Standard Oil, Amoco scientists developed the thermal cracking process of refining gasoline. The process doubled the yield of gasoline from a gallon of crude oil and allowed for the development of cleaner-burning fuels.

Amoco formed its own exploration company in the 1930s and by 1935 had discovered the Hastings field in Texas. The company expanded into chemicals and developed all-purpose motor oils for the military effort in World War II.

But Amoco returned to its strength in exploration after the war and was the first company to drill a well out of sight of land in the Gulf of Mexico, off the Louisiana coast. Again, in 1947, it introduced a new method of refining that increased the yield of oil and natural gas. Also in the 1940s, the company expanded into Canada.

In 1958, Amoco scientists improved the method of polyester production, a chemical process with wide business impact for many industries beyond energy, and built upon its presence in synthetic fibers in 1968 when the company expanded into carpet fiber. In the 1970s, Amoco introduced self-service stations and consolidated its operations to improve efficiency and cut costs. The trend toward efficiency and partnering led to the merger with BP in 1998.

Total Fina Elf—Late to the Party, but Not Forgotten or Diminished

In 1924, a French consortium formed the Compagnie Francaise des Petroles (CFP), with the goal of developing an oil industry for France, which has no reserves within its borders. The consortium had obtained a 24 percent stake in the Turkish Petroleum Company from Germany (TPC), secured as part of the payment for damages in World War I. The members were also partners with the Anglo-Persian Oil Company (BP), Royal Dutch/Shell, and a consortium of five U.S. oil companies. A turning point in its fortunes came in 1927 when oil was discovered in Iraq; this immediately catapulted CFP into the big time.

In 1929 France bought a 25 percent stake in CFP and increased this to 35 percent in 1931, mirroring Britain's move and again accentuating the European tendency to mix private industry with government. By the start of World War II, CFP had well-established refining and transporting facilities.

The German occupation of France during WWII held back CFP's expansion. And its interest in Iraq Petroleum, formerly TPC, was held by its partners. CFP continued to expand along now-familiar lines into other oil-producing areas of the world and supplied oil to Japan, South Korea, and Taiwan in the 1950s. Petrochemicals were introduced in 1956 and CFP expanded its petrochemical business in 1980 by buying Rhone-Poulenc's petrochemical business, along with Elf Aquitaine.

In 1985 CFP changed its name to Total and became listed on the New York Stock Exchange. By 1992, the French government had reduced its stake in the company to less than 1 percent.

In 1995, going against heavy U.S. pressure, Total contracted to develop two major oil fields in Iran, which in retrospect may be a significant development and a seminal point in history with respect to the California energy crisis. My point here is that the United States, due to its politics, may have given up a significant source of oil to the

French, who astutely made the deal with Iran. More important, the deal in Iran also included Russia's Gazprom and Indonesian interests. Even more astute was that France had sold its 55 percent stake in its North American operations prior to making the deal.

And perhaps the most interesting of all developments is that Ultramar Diamond Shamrock bought Total's North American operations. In May 2001, Valero Energy bought Ultramar. This is not rocket science. The Europeans play hardball and are very smart and effective in their dealings. In my opinion, the French get kudos for starting their oil industry from scratch in 1920 and remaining major global players, despite the Americans having more money and muscle in many cases. This is a pure example of guile and savvy, as they once again proved in 1999, when Total bought Belgium's Petrofina and followed the purchase with an incredibly gutsy move, as it launched a hostile bid for Elf Aquitaine 10 days after that. By 2000, Total Fina had become Total Fina Elf.

History clearly shows that the French model is one of picking their spot and moving in aggressively. They did it when they took a German oil company and turned it into a global contender in the 1920s. And they proved it again in the late 20th century when they bought two major rivals within 10 days of each other and consolidated a major portion of Europe.

The French proved that they were extremely capable by moving into Iran, which has cost the United States in the long run. This, despite media reports in early 2000 stating that Halliburton—the company for which the vice president of the United States, Dick Cheney, was once CEO—has an office in Iran, and despite the fact that Iran and the United States are slowly and quietly attempting to increase diplomatic ties as a result of the events of September 11, 2001.

Summary

This chapter has provided both a significant snapshot of what will likely be the pivotal event in the oil industry for the first 20 to 30 years of the 21st century—the September 11, 2001, attack on the World Trade Center—and a historical backbone to the all-important oil industry. By first bringing the future into focus, we find it easier to look at the past, to discover similarities. The unifying traits of the oil industry, both past and present, have been its constant motion, its drama and intrigue, and its innate and inseparable connection to world political events, especially to wars and significant changes in leadership of major geographical areas.

There are other forms of energy, but all have either come into being or their use has been diminished as a result of the petroleum industry. More important, the industry's multiple effects on the world are astounding, if we consider related industries such as chemicals, plastics, food, agriculture, and even biotechnology. In other words, if it weren't for the oil industry, we would not be concerned to such a great degree about the environment, alternative fuels, or some of the global politics that have emerged. But we also would not have some of the wonders that we so treasure, such as automobiles, hand-held computers, PCs, televisions, and other modern conveniences.

The dominant themes that emerge from our brief historical sojourn are that the petroleum industry is global and has always been global. It is prone to booms and busts and is vulnerable to huge swings in supply and demand. And it is the centerpiece of the global economy, for without it there would be significant drawbacks in generating electricity, ensuring personal hygiene, and developing agriculture and technology.

At the center of the storm remains the old Standard Oil Trust and its remaining subsidiaries, which are now part of the world's largest oil companies and which to a great degree still operate on the same philosophies defined by John D. Rockefeller, who was an aggressive and, in the eyes of some, ruthless businessman, as well as one of the most kind-hearted philanthropists in history.

This paradoxical dual personality gives the oil industry its unique character and appeal and also makes it a fascinating study of human nature and interaction. Nothing in this history does not speak of triumph, failure, suspense, and regret—four of the most basic experiences in human existence.

More important, two business models emerge: the U.S. model, which is built on the wildcatter and his freewheeling, gun-toting, cowboy way of doing business; and the European model, built on guile, opportunism, and a hint of nationalism in the form of government ownership.

Above all things, petroleum embodies a set of possibilities. Its ability to generate wealth is still present, even after 100 years of being recognized as such a vehicle. A remote village can still be turned into a boomtown if the black bubbly stuff comes out of the ground in great enough quantities for a long enough period of time. And while this is not a guarantee of riches for all the inhabitants of the village and does not come without a moral and environmental price attached, oil's staying power as a measure of wealth and potential wealth is remarkable. So while technology bubbles come and go, a petroleum find is almost a guarantee of riches to someone or to a group of individual shareholders or property owners. Petroleum itself has surpassed gold as a global currency. And those with ties to the substance can always expect excitement in their lives. I hope that I have piqued your curiosity and that you are ready to join me in discovering this amazing story and unlocking its profit potential for your portfolios.

Armed with this knowledge, we are ready to move to the agencies and entities that control, catalog, and influence the world's oil supply.

CHAPTER

3

Agencies and Organizations

By now, you should have a good idea of how the energy industry got its start and why it functions the way it does. Huge international conglomerates have properties and people everywhere. They are able to influence politics and wield a great deal of power over financial markets and just about every aspect of our daily lives. They also offer enormous profit potential to investors who know what to look for.

The most startling development I noted while researching this book was the incredible amount of information that is available. At the same time, I was amazed at the difficulty I encountered while trying to make sense of it. For example, each European country has its own energy agency, but many of them lack Web sites that I could find or make sense of in English, as the continent continues to work toward the full integration of the European Union. The European Union itself does have a Web site that provides a good deal of information in many languages and that did help me put together this chapter. And after some ingenious search engine work, I found Web sites for both the U.K. and France.

Next, I discovered that Japan's energy agency is a subsidiary of its patent office and has been restructured as a result of the government's attempt to reorganize its economy. That made finding useful information on Japan quite difficult. And even more confusing is that most Web sites and documents that I reviewed all suffered from a bad case of agenda-itis, or inflammation of the agenda, meaning that impartiality was hard to come by.

As a result, I narrowed this chapter to listing those organizations whose actions are more likely to affect investors—either through information they release or through policy initiatives. I have also included a list of Web sites that may be useful in your own search for information.

My goal in this chapter is not to point out the trivia that makes each individual situation unique. Instead, I want to provide information that can be immediately useful to someone trying to buy or sell a stock or mutual fund. As a result, the information is highly condensed and to the point. Wherever possible, I also refer to what makes this particular institution what it is and how it got to be prominent.

So, with that in mind, let's look at OPEC; the International Energy Agency; the American Petroleum Institute; and the U.K., European Union, and French energy agencies, as well as the U.S. Department of Energy. I want to reinforce and expand upon the themes already noted. I will also mention other agencies and introduce new concepts as necessary. Also, I will add key points designed to build on the previous two chapters and will set up the next step in our journey.

I will focus on two basic kinds of organizations: private and government. Although they often compete in intent, they all share similarities in design and in purpose. The name "transmission belt" fits them all quite well, whether private or government. A transmission belt, aside from being an important part of an automobile engine, is an organization whose job is to transmit information; it is often called a think tank.

These organizations form study groups, do research, have meetings in nice places, and produce reports that are read by more people than would readily admit it. The reason is that ex-government officials tend to congregate in these places between government assignments. These folks really know their business and, lucky for us, are willing to sell their expertise and experience to various organizations in exchange for a paycheck, while they wait for their parties to get back in power. Therefore, by and large, these organizations make great efforts to be objective in their reports, but often suffer from a negative public image, due to their membership or their cause.

The best known of all transmission belt organizations is the Trilateral Commission *(www.trilateral.org),* whose function and existence can be encapsulated as follows:

> Distinguished private citizens from North America, Western Europe, and Japan, including academic, business, labor, and media professionals. Encourages closer cooperation among these three democratic industrialized regions.

The organization has featured membership from high-profile dignitaries like former Federal Reserve Chairman Paul Volcker and former president George Bush, as well as the highly recognizable Japanese dignitary Kiichi Miyazawa, who has served as both prime minister and finance minister in Japan. The group meets annually to "analyze major issues confronting the trilateral area; seeks to improve public understanding of these issues," and produces and distributes information about its views.

David Rockefeller, a direct descendant of the man who founded Standard Oil, founded the Trilateral Commission in 1973. Transmission belts are often derided by the public as being clubs for rich guys and academic refugees. But the fact is, they exist. They produce information that can be useful. And they offer balance to the spin that's put out by government think tanks and agencies.

My point is not that a great conspiracy rules the world, but that influential people tend to band together, both inside and outside the conventional business world, as well as in governments. And transmission belts, whether functioning as government or private agencies, exist; act on behalf of their membership; and disseminate information, which by and large is neutral, truthful, and useful, if looked at in the proper light. This information can often help you make better investment decisions.

The International Energy Agency

Clearly, oil is an international game that involves a delicate dance between very large, influential, and well-financed organizations, in both the private and the government sectors. Later, you will see that power production is both a global and a local game, which in the face of deregulation has made life complicated in many cases for customers, government agencies, analysts, and investors alike. In these difficult times, it is important to find relatively unbiased information. And an excellent place to find it is the International Energy Agency (IEA; *www.iea.org*).

The IEA is based in France and is "linked" to the Organization for Economic Cooperation and Development (OECD), another transmission belt, whose functions are funded by the member countries, of which the United States is a charter member and its largest source of financial support. The OECD reported an annual budget of $200 million in 2001. It is no surprise that France houses the IEA, given that its entrance into the energy game, as I described in chapter 2, was nothing short of brilliant and opportunistic.

IEA is a deluxe think tank, as its function is to provide a forum for 26 countries to discuss their energy policies and to decide on common ways to deal with problems regarding prices, supplies, and potential emergencies. The IEA even has provisions for countries to share their supplies with each other in case of severe emergencies. Table 3.1 lists the countries in the IEA.

Note that several additions from the Eastern bloc have joined the IEA in the late 1990s, and that Turkey is the only country from the region bordering the Middle East.

Perhaps some of the most important work done by the IEA is in its contact with nonmember countries, where the agency's goal is to achieve greater transparency or better access to oil supply

Table 3.1: *Countries in the International Energy Agency. The year they joined is in parentheses.* (Source: www.iea.org.)

Australia (1979)	Japan (1976)
Austria (1976)	Korea (2001)
Belgium (1976)	Luxembourg (1976)
Canada (1976)	The Netherlands (1976)
Czech Republic (2001)	New Zealand (1977)
Denmark (1976)	Norway participates in the agency under a special agreement
Finland (1992)	
France (1992)	Portugal (1981)
Germany (1976)	Spain (1976)
Greece (1977)	Sweden (1976)
Hungary (1997)	Switzerland (1976)
Ireland (1976)	Turkey (1981)
Italy (1978)	United Kingdom (1976)
	United States (1976)

data. This is quite sensible, as better information allows governments and companies to make better plans for the future, with the goal of reducing market volatility.

The IEA also publishes reports, such as "China's Worldwide Quest for Energy Security." The synopsis is startling and really gave me an opportunity to look at the energy market from a different perspective. The most significant aspect of China's energy needs is that due to its rapid growth, the nation has already exceeded its own oil reserves and has become a leading importer, although exploration in its own land is very aggressive and continues to be successful. The IEA expects that by the end of the first decade of the 21st century, China's energy needs will outstrip those of most OECD countries, perhaps even the United States.

Table 3.2: *Nonmember countries of the IEA* (Source: www.iea.org).

Africa	India
Caspian Region	Latin America
Central and Eastern Europe	Middle East
Baltic Region	Republic of Korea
Ukraine	South East Asia
China	Russian Federation

The public and most investors are not really tuned in to that concept, which, even if exaggerated, is still impressive. A slumbering giant, both commercially and militarily, China is an increasingly important member of the global energy equation and must be factored into the mix. Where this becomes truly important is in China's way of doing business, which incorporates economic, ideological, and political methods. This is in contrast to Western countries, which tend not to mix the ideological with business to the same degree. China's 2001 entry into the World Trade Organization and its increased interest in creating economic ties with Taiwan, via the high-technology industry initially, is a clear signal that while Russia is getting the headlines, China will be a serious power to deal with in the energy sector and beyond, as the 21st century progresses.

It is also quite interesting, and a perfect example of China's increased influence on global affairs, that during the April 2001 U.S. spy plane incident, as the United States and China argued about the freedom of the American crew, Chinese President Jiang Zemin visited Chile, Argentina, Uruguay, Brazil, Cuba, and finally Venezuela. The latter is an important relationship to keep in mind, as there is plenty of oil in Venezuela, an OPEC member country whose politics changed dramatically in the late 20th century, taking a significant move to the left. Chinese dignitaries were also active in other areas of Central Europe, meeting with Croatian delegations and visiting Italy in early 2001, as well as increasing relationships with the oil-producing countries of the Middle East, Southeast Asia, Russia, Central Asia, and Africa.

The IEA report concluded that China's goal is to eventually participate in the management of international energy policy, an interesting concept on its own and one that will certainly get its chance to move the markets. I see the potential for serious market-moving action when China decides that it wants to get serious about modernizing its infrastructure and attempts to exert influence on the markets through mergers and acquisitions or at least strategic ownership of key oil companies. It can happen, and maybe sooner than many realize.

A friend of mine, who is a chemical engineer for a major oil company, told me that in a recent visit to Beijing, he was truly amazed at the changes he saw in that once dark and dreary city, as he described it. He noted that air quality had significantly improved, despite increased numbers of automobiles. But what truly impressed him was the suburban growth, which featured large single-family homes with all the trappings of wealth.

That is yet another major sign that China is quietly, but steadily, moving into a role as a major player in the global economy and, soon enough, into being a vocal and active participant in global energy circles.

A visit to the IEA site is extremely enlightening, even if you don't buy any of its publications, which usually cost somewhere near $100. The reports deal with all aspects of the energy equation, ranging from supplies and emergency capabilities in the fossil fuels to alternative fuels and the status of the electricity market.

The most widely read IEA publication is the "World Energy Outlook," which comes out yearly. The report is wide-ranging and offers both regional and global perspectives on energy demand, supply, effect on the environment, and potential problems and solutions. The IEA uses a mathematical model, aptly called the World Energy Model (WEM), to project the status of the global energy equation. The model begins with a set of assumptions based on gross domestic product (GDP), population, international fossil fuel prices, and technological developments.

The model plugs the assumptions into four submodels: final demand, power generation, fossil fuel supply, and emission trading. The latter is an interesting variable, because it allows utilities with high levels of pollution to continue to produce high levels of pollution, by buying credits from lesser-polluting utilities. This was one of the more creative portions of the "Clear Air Act," under the Bush "Senior" presidency. Even more interesting is that pollution credits were worked into the Kyoto treaty, according to wording on the IEA site, a treaty that George W. Bush—or George II, as the *Washington Post* and Beltway regulars sometimes call him—refused to adhere to and, for all intents and purposes, neutered.

The model analyzes global energy prospects, the environmental impact of energy use, and the effects of policy actions or technological advances. And although it is a theoretical vehicle, the model does provide a reasonable benchmark as to what the future of the energy cycle offers. As with any mathematical model, the data should be taken with assumptions, such as what variables the model did not take into account. The IEA is a serious agency, and it offers a great deal of information that is worth looking at.

Another significant theme I discovered is that the rest of the world seems to be working more aggressively toward alternative forms of energy than is the United States, where oil, natural gas, and similar fossil fuels continue to be the dominant sources of energy and are even highlighted in President Bush's energy policy released on May 17, 2001. This phenomenon might diminish as time progresses, due to new dangers posed to the U.S. energy supply if problems with Saudi Arabia come to pass.

As investors, we should keep an eye open to international developments in fossil fuels, as well as to alternative sources, especially in global financial markets, which continue to steadily progress toward round-the-clock trading.

The American Petroleum Institute

The American Petroleum Institute (API; *www.api.com*) is best known for its weekly news release "The API Report," which describes oil inventories and supplies. The statistics are released after the stock market closes on Tuesdays and often move the markets in the after-hours trading sessions, for both stocks and futures, as these statistics often fool analysts who predict what they might be ahead of time. For this reason, it is important to keep abreast of this report, which is usually featured on CNBC, *CBS Marketwatch,* and other major business news sites, as well as on the API Web site.

The API is the trade group for the entire U.S. oil industry, including drillers, explorers, retailers, and major oil companies. It is the main lobby for the industry before Congress, state legislatures, and the White House. The organization has proclaimed itself the oil industry's think tank. Its function is similar to that of the IEA, in the sense that it researches and sets standards for all areas of the oil industry. It was started in 1919; is headquartered in Washington, D.C.; has 33 regional councils; and is funded by its members. Its position is summarized quite well by this quote obtained from its Web site:

> API's members determine the petroleum industry's positions on public policy as well as the standards that govern its day-to-day operations the world over.

The bottom line is that the API handles the research, lobbying, and public opinion for the oil industry, making it an arm of the oil industry. This is not meant as a criticism, because all professions and businesses have similar organizations. But I should clearly state here that the API has as its foremost focus the interests of the oil industry. I should also note that the API "applauded" the National Energy Policy put forth by President Bush and Vice President Cheney in May 2001, which was controversial and opposed, not surprisingly, by Democrats and many environmental groups, initially, but which is likely to be implemented as time passes—again due to the new dynamics brought on by the September 11 events, and despite congressional charges that it was influenced and fashioned by Enron executives.

This energy policy, which was "applauded" by the oil industry, I believe will set the stage for the next 10 to 20 years in the oil industry, a fact that I felt was true even before the World Trade Center events. And if the market's reaction to the policy is any indication of what's to come, energy-related investments are likely to do well in the foreseeable future. The supply-and-demand equation has been tipped toward the industry, given that domestic exploration will get a big boost as America gets serious about energy independence and diversification away from OPEC.

The president formally introduced his policy on May 17, 2001, and by May 18, he was signing executive orders that would require power plant permits to be moved rapidly along regulatory lines, but not without proper legalities being conducted. Furthermore, he also signed an order that would require regulatory agencies to "consider" the ramifications of any new regulation on the flow of energy in the United States.

This—at least, at face value—tilted the balance in favor of the oil industry, whose main complaints have centered around regulatory restrictions on its ability to do business. The flip side was the response from environmental groups, as well as the huge opposition mounted by Democrats and the state of California, where Governor Gray Davis, himself a Democrat, was quite angry and extremely vocal. Environmental groups sued President Bush in December, disputing his relaxing of regulations for exploration on public lands.

This energy policy is clear in its objective, which is to increase the energy supply in the United States. The policy also included conservation measures and offered tax credits for the use of alternative energy sources. The opposition took a vigorous stand against the policy, but prior to its release, there had been little formal govern-

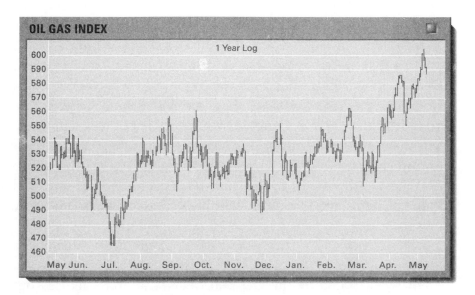

Figure 3.1: *The Amex Oil & Gas Index on May 23, 2001, courtesy of Telescan.*

ment direction in the area of energy. And as usually happens, both sides are likely to move toward a more central solution.

My job as an investor is not to make political, but rather financial, judgments, and the chart in figure 3.1 of the Amex Oil & Gas Index (XOI) clearly shows that the market liked the energy policy. I waited several days to pull this chart because I wanted to be sure that this was not a one-day move. And what it shows is several-fold.

First, we should note that the oil index rallied in April. This was in response to growing evidence that earnings would remain positive for the sector. But in early May, the California energy crisis heated up, with the bankruptcy of Pacific Gas & Electric. The index sold off in response. Yet the Bush administration began to leak bits and pieces of its energy policy soon thereafter, and the index began to rally. When the policy was formally released, the index broke to a new high.

Then, by May 23, 2001, news broke out that Senator James Jeffords, who at the time was a Republican, was about to switch parties. The initial story was that he was going to become a Democrat. As the rumor mill was replaced by inevitable leaks from more "reliable sources," the story evolved into his switch to an independent seat in Congress, which is what in fact happened. The market reacted with great disdain, as fear of a stall in the up-until-then quite efficient Bush agenda gripped traders. Most important was the switch in the short-term trend for the Amex Oil Index, which stalled in mid-breakout—a perfect example of how news-sensitive this sector is.

This is not to say that traders were pulling for Bush. Wall Street as a whole just wants stability from the incumbents. The point is illustrated by the fact that once Wall Street figured out that stability for President Clinton meant scandal, it shrugged off most things, including the impeachment scandal, by and large, and had a decade-long bull market during his terms.

Remember that the market is efficient, not random. There is rhyme and reason to the daily bump and grind of stock prices. And that means it will move based on the information that is available at the time. The market is not always right, but it will move based on that information; it will attempt to price-in all of the news that is available at the time.

I introduced the chart of the oil index in this segment because I want you to start making the connection between integrated oil stocks and this index, which is the benchmark for the sector. When things happen in energy, this is where you immediately look as an investor. The first question in your mind should be, What is XOI doing?

Next, you should make a mental note that oil stocks are very sensitive to the supply and demand for oil and to news that could change the parameters under which the sector operates. The Bush administration, which by the time this book is released will be some 18 months in office, is very much in favor of increasing oil supplies and of market forces acting as independently as possible from government control. That is a major fundamental piece of information, which should be at the top of your list as well. What does the Bush administration think of this, and what are they going to do about it? If and when this changes, either due to a change in president or to a change in policy, that should also be noted. And the American Petroleum Institute is a great place to find news about what the oil industry would like to accomplish.

The important point is that intangibles always affect the market. In this case, the change in Congress led the market to believe that there would be a difficult road in producing legislation that would favor the oil industry. Of course, the situation in politics is always fluid and may change at any time. But for the first time in many years, there is a potential for landmark developments in energy policy in Washington.

The Organization of Oil Exporting Countries (OPEC)

OPEC *(www.opec.org)* is the most successful cartel in modern history, having survived internal disagreements and external attacks since its inception. There are 11 member nations: Algeria, Indonesia, Iran, Iraq, Kuwait, Libya, Nigeria, Qatar, Saudi Arabia, the United Arab Emirates, and Venezuela. OPEC supplies 40 percent of the world's oil.

OPEC describes itself as an organization of developing countries that rely on oil revenues for most of their capital. OPEC describes its intentions benignly, saying that the members "aim to bring stability and harmony to the oil market by adjusting their oil output to help ensure a balance between supply and demand."

What OPEC fails to mention is that despite most of the cartel behaving with some semblance of reason, it is still prone to use oil as a political tool—a very important point that we, as investors, need to keep in mind.

Earlier, I provided you with a summary of the problems that, according to the Web site Stratfor.com, Saudi Arabia will have to deal with over the next several years. It is not out of place to suspect that similar scenarios are at play in most of the member countries, given the lack of Western-style democracies and the prevalence of political unrest that is commonly seen even in non-Arab members of the cartel, such as Indonesia and Venezuela. OPEC meets twice a year, with great fanfare, to decide on its output quotas. The market's view is that OPEC often cheats on its output, a notion that is likely to be more variable and difficult to predict in the future, given the cartel's experience with disaster, as a result of oil prices dropping to $10 a barrel in the late 1990s. But by the same token, the notion of OPEC unity must be questioned in the context of the new oil order, where Russia's newfound strength and political clout are likely to greatly influence the cartel's ability to move the price of oil at will.

This very interesting organization describes itself as "intergovernmental" and "permanent." It was founded in, of all places, Baghdad, Iraq, in 1960, with Iran, Iraq, Kuwait, Saudi Arabia, and Venezuela as the charter members. Qatar, Indonesia, Libya, the United Arab Emirates, Algeria, Nigeria, Ecuador, and Gabon joined subsequently. Ecuador left in 1992, having entered in 1973, and Gabon left in 1994, having entered in 1975.

OPEC, on its Web site, describes the 1960s as a formative decade, in which it began to enter the global marketplace and to make its presence known to what it describes as the "Seven Sisters," or the major oil companies at the time. By the 1970s, OPEC needed no introduction, as it had become the main player on the supply side of the equation—a situation that in my opinion will be altered for decades to come because of the World Trade Center events.

It is also important to remember that in 1973—much as in 2001, and sporadically in-between—the Arabs and the Israelis continued to wage a long-standing dispute, which is always a potential sore spot for the oil markets. This dispute reached an all-time fever pitch in December 2001, when Israel declared war on the Palestinians and renounced their recognition of Yasser Arafat as a focal point of negotiations about peace. This escalation of hostilities between the two neighbors, if it were to continue, could well become a significant irritant to the global energy markets, for Saudi Arabia had begun to hint at changing its moderate ways toward a more fundamentalist regime just as hostilities in Afghanistan reached a new level of intensity and Israel stepped up its activity against the Palestinians.

And just as in 1973, during the Nixon administration, when OPEC flexed its muscles for the first time and its embargo—which lasted from October 1973 to March 1974—triggered the first major oil crisis of the current generation, it is reasonable to consider the possibility of similar actions in the future. The effect was quite significant on Japan and other nations, while turning the page on cheap oil for the United States permanently. In 1978, the Iranian revolution also caused an oil crisis.

Therefore, the role of Russia as a swing producer in these potentially turbulent times becomes even more important. And for our purposes, we must keep this in mind and begin to think about which companies do the most business in Russia.

Interestingly, Saudi Arabia, prior to the World Trade Center problems, had signed an agreement with the major international oil companies. This elite group of companies included many of the descendants of the "Seven Sisters" and was designed to exploit Saudi Arabian natural gas properties. The agreement would be worth a potential $50 billion to Saudi Arabia over 25 years. But as the trouble began to gather steam, some very obscure reports appeared in the news about a few major oil companies being less than enthusiastic about the project, though their press releases were very upbeat.

On December 12, 2001, Schlumberger.com *(www.slb.com)*, a great Web site for energy and semiconductor sector news, reported that the deal was 90 percent done. But the missing 10 percent was crucial to concluding the deal. In fact, the deadline for signing the document was December 16, and all parties agreed that a "low-key" signing ceremony would be more likely to take place in the first quarter of 2002. This, in my opinion, was an ominous sign of potential trouble brewing.

Here is Saudi Arabia, with its economy in trouble, delaying the signing of a $25 billion deal that would bring the country what it was looking for—the potential to privatize or at least defer the risk of exploration and building up its natural gas infrastructure. The analysis here is simple: Something did not add up. And as the article went on, I became more concerned, especially when I factored in the rising trouble in the Middle East.

Among the still-not-agreed-upon 10-percent portion was a question of how much natural gas would actually be involved in the deal. One source called the amount "skimpy." And the source went on to describe the amounts of gas available as "not commercially viable." On the other hand, the article described the Saudi goal as one that would double the daily production on its fields. Another area of trouble in the negotiations was the lack of consensus on the business model that would be used for the agreement. Despite the positive spin, this kind of talk makes me nervous. And perhaps the smart money had the same idea at the time, as the stock of the leading company involved in the deal, Exxon-Mobil (which initially ballyhooed the deal), was in a very steep down trend at the time.

A cynic might say that money talks. But Middle Eastern politics are full of traditions and relationships that go back to pre-biblical times, in many cases. And in my opinion, the recent cooperation between the oil giants and OPEC will be tested as a result of the age-old conflicts in the Middle East coming to a head. The lack of agreement between Saudi Arabia and the "Seven Sisters," in December 2001, is an example of what the future could well hold.

It is unlikely, but not impossible, that the oil embargo of the 1970s will be repeated. And Russia's new role as de facto swing producer to the West is likely to alleviate, if not totally delay, such tactics by OPEC. But the evidence of history suggests and supports the notion that oil prices may not fall below those in recent memory for a long time to come. This most recent Middle East conflict also raises the question of whether OPEC has learned any financial lessons along the way. After all, politics and traditions are just fine, but money buys food, yachts, castles, beach homes in exotic places, and keeps your government in power.

Another source of trouble for OPEC is Venezuela, where in December 2001 President Hugo Chavez decreed 49 laws whose effect would hamper foreign companies in making exploration in Venezuela profitable. The largest labor group in the country actually agreed with the largest group of businessmen and held a 12-hour national strike on December 12. The upshot was one of increasing doubts about whether Chavez could finish his term, if he continued to move his country back toward the left and away from capitalist and free-market reforms. Chavez, for his own part, was quite aggressive in his condemnation of the strike, using his weekly radio program to hurl threats at the growing opposition. According to Stratfor, which again beat the mainstream media to the story, there was also growing opposition to Chavez's increasingly leftist and militant positions within his own army.

The potential for major political upheaval within the borders of two of the United States' main oil providers certainly sets the stage for a major crisis within the first decade of the new century. And the events of September 11 served as a grim reminder that the world has a whole new set of potential problems to deal with.

I'm not trying to be a cynic or a Cassandra. I want to offend no one. My purpose is to present the investor's point of view and to help you detach yourself from emotion when it comes to investing. These are the political perils of investing in the energy sector. A rise in the political fortunes of China, the threat of terrorism, former allies becoming decreasingly friendly, and even major problems with South American politics could lead to future difficulties for the United States. Events repeat themselves, and usually in a similar fashion. As an investor, you should expect them to do so. But when events don't go true to their norm, due to intangibles, that is even more important, because it means that a new paradigm has arrived. This is why the wild card that is Russia may fit the bill of both an intangible and a catalyst for a new paradigm.

In the 1980s, cheating by the individual cartel members led to softening oil prices and really set the stage for the growth of the Internet and the technology sector, fueling once again the pattern of cheap oil leading to technological development, which in turn led to increased economic activity and higher oil prices. This pattern eventually increased the disparity in wealth between the Northern Hemisphere and the Third World and since 1950 has culminated in Middle East conflicts. In 1990 this conflict took the form of Saddam Hussein invading Kuwait, another OPEC member, and oil prices climaxing, only to fall again. In 2001 the Middle East crisis took two forms. First, the World Trade Center was attacked, and the United States retaliated by bombing Afghanistan. Second and almost simultaneously, the Israeli-Palestinian conflict led to a formal declaration of war from Israel.

OPEC's view is that it averted an oil crisis in 1990 by raising production, with Saudi Arabia leading the way. But the fact is, the prelude to the invasion of Kuwait led to an oil crisis and a recession. In 2001, in the midst of an already present global recession that was exacerbated by the events at the World Trade Center, OPEC decided to try to save itself by attempting to cut back production. In 1998, OPEC's resilience was tested when the Asian crisis slowed down oil consumption and oil prices fell to $10 per barrel. But the cost was high, and OPEC was almost mortally wounded. Eventually, the cartel, with the help of non-OPEC producers, successfully drained production, and oil prices firmed. Again, in early 2001, Iraq caused trouble, by grandstanding in the United Nations and threatening to cut its portion of OPEC production from the market if the UN did not end the sanctions against it from the Gulf War. OPEC responded by increasing production and succeeded in flooding the world with oil at precisely the wrong time, when global economies were beginning to slow down.

But after September 11, things changed for the worse in the cartel, as internal politics and the survival of the governments of Saudi Arabia and Venezuela overwhelmed the cartel's willingness to work with its clients—in other words, the rest of the world, which was trying to emerge from the recession and which would benefit from cheap oil. This was a distinct departure for OPEC from its recent behavior of maintaining high levels of production and attempting to keep prices stable. So the cartel, in its haste to cover for Iraq, found itself in a no-win situation. But in the eyes of the world, OPEC, by trying to cut production during a period of economic instability, was in fact returning to its old political blackmail days of the 1970s. Right or wrong, this was a powder keg and a set of circumstances that will have long-lasting and potentially damaging consequences for the cartel.

In summary, OPEC's reign at the top of the energy heap suffered a severe setback as a result of the World Trade Center attack and of its own miscues in dealing with Iraq. The cartel—though not obsolete, by any means—now has tough competition from Russia, while facing the threat of internal political instability in two of its major producers, Saudi Arabia and Venezuela. Making the situation worse, these two countries—which had a record of reasonably warm relations with the United States—could possibly confront a hostile political environment with the world's largest and strongest economy and their number one customer. And while the effect of all this maneuvering may be to provide more stable oil prices than the world would have expected otherwise, the situation is potentially explosive, because one or two unfortunate developments could start a significant negative chain reaction. Thus, although the market and events will dictate price action, the dynamics for equilibrium in the oil market have been drastically altered.

The U.S. Department of Energy

The U.S. Department of Energy *(www.energy.gov)* is a large institution that oversees the science, research, national security, and environmental quality associated with the exploration, production, consumption, disposal, and transport of energy. The Department of Energy is a behemoth composed of multiple branches,

Table 3.3: *Functions of the Federal Energy Regulatory Commission.*

- Regulation of the transmission and sale or resale of energy in interstate commerce
- Regulation of the transmission of natural gas, electricity, and oil by pipeline in interstate commerce
- Provides licensing for and inspects private, municipal, and state hydroelectric projects
- Oversees related environmental matters
- Administers accounting and financial reporting regulations and conduct of jurisdictional companies and approves siting and abandonment of interstate pipeline facilities

departments, and field offices. We will concentrate on those that can influence the financial markets.

Federal Energy Regulatory Commission

The Federal Energy Regulatory Commission *(www.ferc.gov)* is an independent regulatory agency within the Department of Energy that has multiple functions, listed in table 3.3.

This commission was created in 1977 and was designed to be bipartisan, with no more than three of its commissioners coming from the same political party. Its Web site is rich with information and is very easy to follow. I recommend it for those who really enjoy deep background. For our purposes, note the presence and function of this commission, as well as a brief history of its origins, because the knowledge helps us frame the significance of what this agency says and does, and how its actions can affect our investments.

It is startling that until the 1973 Arab Oil Embargo, there was little more than a loosely tied and widely scattered group of agencies, offices, and commissions that each dealt with one or two specific aspects of the energy equation. The embargo led to the realization that a more uniform body was required to deal with the country's energy situations. Prior to the formation of the Department of Energy, there was no coordination of policy among these agencies. Thus, it is important to create at least an artificial distinction between the government's involvement in the U.S. energy sector before and after 1973.

When the Arab Oil Embargo struck in 1973, the government had to enforce order in what were nearly chaotic gasoline shortages. As a result, the more modern, somewhat more coordinated, Department of Energy emerged in, of all places, the White House, when President Nixon, who had been concerned about future energy problems in America for many years, assigned control of the price of oil and gasoline to the Federal Energy Office.

In fact, before 1973, the country had relied on the private sector—that is, Exxon and other companies—to make decisions about supply, demand, and various aspects of energy needs. This is clearly the origin of the conspiracy theories about big oil companies running the world. It really is no conspiracy. Those companies, in most cases, acted in a reasonably responsible manner, given the great task that the public and the government of the United States placed on them.

I am not by any means defending the environmental damage or other alleged or proven excesses that were related to or caused by some of these companies, especially in places outside of the United States. But regardless of how big or how well meaning a major corporation is, its motive is profit, whereas a government's purpose is the maintenance of order; these are totally different objectives.

It thus becomes quite clear why oil stocks rallied significantly when George Bush and Dick Cheney, both oilmen, became president and vice president. And it becomes even more clear why oil stocks began to wobble when a senator threatened to upset the balance of power in the U.S. Senate by switching parties.

The government did act regarding natural monopolies, such as gas and electricity, in order to prevent price gouging. But as the era of deregulation now begins to unfold, this is a disappearing function of the government.

Finally, in an excellent treatise found at the Office of Scientific and Technical Information *(www.osti.gov)* and penned by Terrence R. Fenner and Jack M. Holl from the history division of the U.S. Department of Energy, a January 1974 Gallup poll notes that only 7 percent of Americans at the time of the embargo blamed the Arab nations for the energy shortages; 25 percent blamed the oil companies, 23 percent blamed the federal government, 19 percent blamed Nixon personally, and 16 percent blamed American consumers for the crisis. A great deal of oil has flowed since then. And so has public opinion shifted significantly, putting much of the blame for whatever happens in the energy world on the companies themselves.

It took until 1977, under the Carter administration, for the Department of Energy, as we know it, to be created.

The Energy Efficiency and Renewable Energy Network (EREN)

The Office for Energy Efficiency and Renewable Energy *(www .eren.doe.gov)* is where I believe much attention will be focused in the next decade and where, incidentally, I believe my other favorite sector in the stock market—biotechnology—will play a significant role.

Biotech did create a bacterium that is used to mop up oil spills. And more important, bacteria break down food into methane, which is otherwise known as natural gas. It is therefore a logical assumption that biotech and energy will both walk hand-in-hand in the next decade. And you thought it was an accident that I wrote a book on biotech, followed by a book on energy?

EERE has multiple offices and works in partnership with private entities, as well as with state and local governments. The hub of the EERE is its Golden Field Office, where relationships are developed and nurtured in order to reach the agency's stated goal of obtaining the "lion's share" of the estimated $425 billion market for renewable energy. EERE concentrates on solar energy, wind power, biomass (i.e., bacteria and waste products), and hydrogen as alternate energy sources.

The science on this Web site is encouraging, with actual working models of current or recent energy research highlighted and described. In one example they use woodchips to make natural gas. And in another, molten salt is used to store solar energy. This means that if the sun isn't shining, you could still have power. EERE has partnerships with Boeing, DuPont, Pirelli, and other large companies, as well as with many other smaller companies and universities.

I found this site very encouraging and quite a contrast to the usual litany on the evening news, where politicians continue to attack each other along party lines, creating an atmosphere of crisis. Clearly, according to this site, the United States and the world will not totally be caught with their pants down when it comes to energy.

I could have spent a great deal of time on this section, but I think you get the point. Plenty of information about energy is available and in places where you normally would not think to look. More interesting is that although the domestic and international media portray the United States as gas-guzzling and backward thinking, this is only a portion of what goes on, as a review of the Department of Energy's site shows.

This is an excellent place for investors to look for information when something dramatic is shown on the evening news. Always remember that, regardless of their intentions, politicians are mostly interested in their own agendas, the media wants to get ratings, and the government wants to stay in power.

There are two ways to stay in power. First, you subjugate the masses. That usually turns out badly. The second way is to give people what they want now, but be ready to give them what they need tomorrow. And that seems to be what the Department of Energy is trying to do. Enlightening, indeed.

The View from Unified Europe

The European Union (EU; *www.europa.eu.int*) finds itself in an interesting position, as the member countries continue to slog their way into a single set of policies. As I stated earlier, Europeans have a long history of placing cultural beliefs above everything else. This is an admirable characteristic, because it shows that national pride is alive and well. But this often makes it difficult to craft long-term policy, if agreements are neither reachable nor able to be implemented.

Ideology is not a European monopoly either, as exemplified by the historic change in the United States Senate that took place in May 2001, when Senator James Jeffords, a moderate Republican from Vermont, became an independent. This event came five months into the new Bush administration and in the midst of a huge energy controversy, during which the president made it clear that no price caps would be placed on electricity for California. The defection became a non-event after the World Trade Center attacks.

As Europe prepared for a multiyear transition of policy governance, based on the peaceful transfer of power from separate countries to a central state, the United States entered a period of high levels of difficulty, brought about by supply and demand and tinged by political ideology. That period was quieted after September 11, but by December, the wrangling and the ideological rift between Democrats and Republicans were in fine form, as Congress debated the merits of tax cuts versus social welfare in order to craft an economic stimulus package to fight the recession.

This ever-increasing partisanship in Congress is both potentially explosive and a blessing. It's a powder keg because it gives foreign nations and terrorists the impression that Americans are vulnerable because they disagree loudly and on television about basic ideology. On the other hand, it's a blessing to keep such argumentative people as those who become elected officials in a place full of other argumentative people, where their influence can be well neutralized. This, I think, was the intended design of our forefathers.

A major tenet of European objectives, once the EU becomes the governing body of energy policy, is to encourage competition, with the goal of bringing down prices. And if this is not done correctly, it will turn out badly. This was the goal in California, to "deregulate" prices and encourage competition, both by deregulation and by the encouragement of alternative fuel usage. The problem in California came when subsidies were given to inefficient alternative fuel sources, at the same time that a moratorium was placed on the building of new power plants. The combination of increased demand from the technology economy and the lack of supply-generation facilities was the cause of the crisis.

The fact that the EU—at least, in principle—is keeping its eyes open to California-like folly is quite obvious and encouraging. The statement on its Web site says: "The need to take account of the distinctive nature of the energy sector (to ensure security of supply, to protect the environment and to defend consumer interests) means that this is more complex than in other sectors."

Thus, the EU proceeded in steps, creating the blueprint for a unified market in coal and petroleum, while continuing to study the natural gas and electricity markets. The first stage was to improve the transparency of gas and electricity prices. This was accomplished by rules and regulations that required producers to inform the EU about their prices and the formulas used to derive such prices. This measure was accomplished in the early 1990s. The EU also eased restrictions on exploration for oil and natural gas.

In 1996, rules and regulations for the production and transfer of electricity were adopted. This was accompanied by resolutions to develop trans-European energy networks. But as of early 2001, progress remains slow, as individual countries, according to the EU itself, "are facing administrative, financial, and environmental problems which are slowing them down."

Figure 3.2: *Comparison of price action between Total Fina Elf and Texaco, courtesy of Telescan.*

The Ademe

The French Agency for Environment and Energy Management is called the Ademe, and it has a very well-designed Web site *(www.ademe.fr)* that immediately lets you know the agency's priorities. Its first stated mission is protecting air quality. Other functions include reducing household and industrial wastes, managing energy use, promoting green products, rehabilitating polluted sites, encouraging renewable energy sources, and reducing noise.

This is a clear clash of cultures, both with the United States, where most of these functions fall within the Environmental Protection Agency's (EPA) jurisdiction, and with the EU's energy agency, which is concerned with getting Europe wired for electricity within a central network.

The site is heavy on information about alternative fuels and the use of biomass for energy, including a presentation called "In Town Without My Car," which describes the benefits of not using your automobile. Ademe touts the fact that it convinced the EU to have a Union-wide "day without my car," in the years 1999 and 2000, and has plans to make it an annual event.

What does this have to do with investing in oil and energy stocks? Everything, as it clearly shows that different countries look at the equation from different standpoints. The battle lines are clear, as was also evident in California, between environmental groups and traditional energy conglomerates in the oil industry.

What we have to do is become well versed with the major jurisdictions, understand the rules of the game as it is played regionally, and recognize how it changes over time.

A picture is worth a thousand words. The market's perception of prospects for oil profits clearly leans toward United States–based companies. But the chart of Texaco (NYSE:TX) and the chart of Total Fina Elf (NYSE:TOT) tell a better story.

In figure 3.2 we see that Elf did reasonably well during the period shown, but it was in a sideways pattern. Texaco, by comparison, was in a brisk up trend. That was partly due to the merger premium, as a result of the Chevron linkup. But although one might say that the expectations of the takeover would drive the price higher, I would add that Wall Street was also betting on the pro-oil White House during this period.

Now before anyone gets offended, let me just say that I like breathing clean air, and I love French food. This is not a knock on France, or Elf, whose praises as an astute company I sang earlier. This is a purely technical look at the markets. If given a choice, based on the information I have and based on how the market is reacting to the information, I would prefer to own Texaco rather than Elf as a stock. That is what investing is all about, the ability to distance yourself from emotion and concentrate on buying the best stock. Use Intellectual Inclusion here to encapsulate these two charts, along with the truism that the markets reflect the information available.

The message is that Wall Street was betting that Texaco had a better chance to make money than Total Fina Elf did.

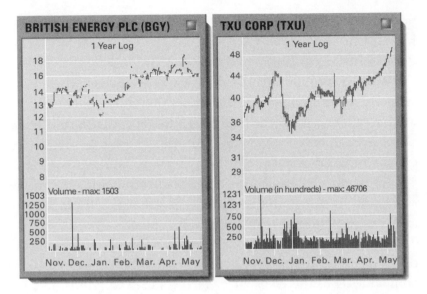

Figure 3.3: *Comparison of TXU Corp. (NYSE:TXU) and British Energy (NYSE:BGY), courtesy of Telescan.*

And the market also factored in that the United States was an oil industry–friendly place.

The U.K. Office of the Gas and Electricity Markets (OFGEM)

This government agency *(www.ofgem.gov.uk)* regulates the gas and electricity markets in Great Britain. Its stated aim is to "bring choice and value to all gas and electricity customers by promoting competition and regulating monopolies."

As in France and the EU there is little here about petroleum as used for driving trucks and automobiles, which points once again to the clear cultural differences between other countries and the United States, where—outside of major cities in the Northeast—the main form of transportation is still the automobile.

OFGEM promotes competition and regulates power production where competition is not feasible by setting price controls and assuring that customers get reasonable service.

In 1999 Great Britain became a deregulated country, with OFGEM claiming that the average customer could save 60 pounds sterling per year in natural gas and 20 to 35 pounds sterling per year in electricity, which roughly translated to $85 and $35–$50, respectively, in May 2001. This translated to $7 per month for gas and $2–$5 per month in electricity.

More important, OFGEM, which encourages switching and offers price comparison sheets on its Web site, is now targeting power generation and transportation to create more competition and lower prices.

Once again, we turn to the charts for a final answer. Figure 3.3 compares the traditional U.K. power generator British Energy and the expanding global powerhouse TXU, formerly known as Texas Utilities. This very aggressive company has done much that is right in setting itself up as a major global player and proving that things can be very big outside of Texas. TXU has expanded away from the United States by buying European and Australian power-generating companies. The charts tell an excellent story, for both companies are getting the benefit of the deregulative environment in the U.K.

Summary

This chapter was meant to provide a reasonable snapshot of different regulatory climates and political power structures in the different energy sectors of the main economies of the world. The clear difference between the United States and Europe is the degree of overt government intervention. Europe makes no bones about it; even in a deregulated country like the U.K., the government plays a key role. In the United States, there is too much inconsistency, a situation that led to the California energy crisis. And even in the wake of the World Trade Center disaster and as the government crafted an official energy policy, the country still leans heavily on the private sector, especially the oil and gas industry, to aggressively explore the world, including the United States, and to bring the energy home.

This should come as no surprise, because the United States had a very inexpensive fuel supply until the Arab Oil Embargo in 1973. The changes brought about by that single event have led the United States to where it is today.

Outside the United States, several major influences are at work. First, there is OPEC. It has the oil and is doing everything in its power to make as much money as possible for as long as possible, based on that fact. OPEC is beginning to have problems, as internal politics and rising competition from Russia are likely to reduce the cartel's influence over the next decade and perhaps beyond.

Next, we have the European take on things, which is clearly more pro-environment and more pro-electricity than it is pro-oil. This is particularly evident in France where, again due to the country having no inherent energy supply of its own, there is less direct love for the automobile for transportation.

Finally, the U.K. is way ahead of the rest of Europe and the United States, with a smooth start to the transition toward electricity deregulation.

CHAPTER
4

The Basics of the Marketplace

This chapter provides sector and subsector capsules of the energy industry and describes external and internal factors that affect stock price movements in each area discussed. The energy sector is largely influenced by fundamental factors that are highly cyclical and rarely deviate from their norm, making the sector more predictable in many ways than other investment areas. This does not mean that the energy sector can't surprise investors. But the surprise will likely be one we have seen before. Most of this chapter's emphasis will be on the oil sector and to some degree on the natural gas sector, as the power generation, nuclear energy, and alternative energy sectors will have their own chapter.

The first three chapters introduced us to the history, the influencing factors, and the supply-and-demand equation. In chapter 1, I briefly mentioned Intellectual Inclusion, a method of analysis that I developed and that has served me well as an investor and generally in the world as well. Intellectual Inclusion (I.I.) is an analytical framework that allows you to explore the world, including investments, and to catalog facts in a simple and retrievable fashion. The philosophy focuses on the innate ability of the brain to work on multiple levels simultaneously and to retrieve facts and lead to action.

The main premise is that the brain acts as a two-way filter, between the input, which comes from the environment, and the output, which is the decision that makes us take action, such as whether to buy or sell a stock. By training the filter, we find it easier to make decisions.

In chapter 2, I discussed the history of the energy sector, with a great deal of focus on the major oil companies. This is important to encapsulate because knowing how the seminal and still dominant portion of the industry came about will help us to predict the future or to note when a clear deviation from the path has occurred. In other words, oil companies will always follow a similar pattern of going about their business, and if you know that pattern, you can use it as a key determinant in making decisions as to when to buy and sell oil stocks.

For example, it is a given that political problems will affect the oil market. These often surface in the Middle East, especially in Iraq, and perhaps in the future will extend to Saudi Arabia. In the past these political developments have often affected the price of oil substantially, as in the two energy crises of the 1970s, in the Gulf War of 1990–1991, and in the aftermath of the World Trade Center attacks.

One of those surprises came in a significant departure from previous behavior, as OPEC—of which Iraq is a founding member—issued a statement at its June meeting, saying that it would study only the June 2001 situation, in which Iraq and the United Nations disagreed on terms of the food-for-oil program. OPEC announced that it would discuss the situation at a later meeting. This was a pivotal development, because it marked a major shift in OPEC's behavior. This statement was a signal that the cartel was beginning to behave as a business institution. And a serious institution, one that deserves respect, is one that carefully studies its policy decisions before jumping into flawed and costly endeavors. Unfortunately for the cartel, its only foray into customer friendliness backfired, as members used the opportunity to flood the market with oil just as the world rolled over into recession.

Separately, during the same period, both Saudi Arabia and Venezuela made statements soon after Iraq's rebellious threats that, if needed, they would unilaterally increase production in order to make up for the lack of Iraqi oil in the markets.

This was also a key development, which showed that independent members of OPEC had changed perspective from a politically dominated outlook to one in which business preceded ideology. More important, if OPEC were to reverse this newfound level-headed approach, which took the customer into account above its own politics, it would mark a change that could potentially lead to global energy-market chaos. And that, as I discussed in chapter 3, is a distinct possibility.

As in any endeavor, the energy market—which includes oil, natural gas, nuclear energy, alternative fuels, and the utility complex—contains external and internal factors that influence the marketplace and its components. In this chapter, I introduce many of these factors and develop the big picture to show how they work together.

The Basic Science and Engineering of the Oil Industry

This is not a textbook on the science of energy, but I have included at least the basics, which you can use if you want to read in more depth elsewhere. If you are a petroleum engineer, an oil analyst, a critic, a general know-it-all, or a guide on about.com, you may want to skip this section or send me your corrections privately. Don't beat up the book on Amazon.com; it hurts sales and hurts my ability to feed my family and my edge for negotiating the next book deal. This section also expands on some concepts introduced earlier, such as supply and demand and applied technology.

Oil and natural gas are fairly straightforward, from a scientific standpoint. But the image of the wild and crazy wildcatter out on the range with a shovel and a divining rod, searching for a gusher, has given way to a hybrid set of dynamics that includes input from diverse sources such as the hardware, software, and semi-conductor sectors, to go along with the more traditional hy-draulics, filters, pumps, steel pipe and tubes, and drilling sectors.

This means that energy is a very compartmentalized sector. And for investors to invest intelligently, this compartmentalization requires that they have at least a basic understanding of each step in the production of oil and natural gas. The main branches of sci-ence involved are geology, chemistry, physics, engineering, and bi-ology. Perhaps the most interesting aspect is that due to environmental concerns, biologists from many disciplines—rang-ing from microbiology to plant and animal science—are involved.

Although methods for finding oil work relatively efficiently compared to those in the past, the current technology allows oil companies to recover only one-third of the oil that they find. An interesting conversation with a friend who works in the oil indus-try revealed that the most efficient oil field in the world is in Prud-hoe Bay, Alaska, where 50 percent of the supply is extractable.

Many experts believe that most of the major finds have al-ready been made. This means that in the future, oil supplies will be more heavily influenced by the scientists' ability to improve on extraction technology than by the ability to find the reserves. Knowledge of the basic science and engineering concepts of the sector will serve those investors who know these concepts and can best apply them.

Where Petroleum and Natural Gas Come From

I realize that some people who read these lines may find them sim-plistic. Oversimplifying is not my intent. My goal is to start at the beginning and build from there. Reading a book on investing with-out learning the basics on the source of the product we invest in and its methods of processing, transportation, and distribution is like driving a car without a license. So, I will describe some rudimentary concepts. In my own experience, many of my worst investment mis-takes have come from not knowing the basics of the industry.

The organic theory of petroleum posits that oil comes from the fossilized remains of dead organisms that were processed by natural forces for millions of years. The same process that produces petroleum also produces natural gas, which is why the two substances are often found together.

Oil is found in a substance called kerogen, which is the result of the decomposition of microscopic life that fell to the bottom of the sea and was compressed by pressure into rock. As the rock was buried deeper and exposed to heat from the earth's core, the kerogen formed. The most important aspect of oil formation is the temperature at which the kerogen forms, called the "oil window." Kerogen, when heated to 212 degrees F, fragments into oil and natural gas. At temperatures above 400 degrees F, oil decomposes.

As the earth moved and shifted, much of the deeply buried oil seeped its way higher through rock layers and found its way to areas above which it could not rise, called traps. There are four kinds of traps. And in these traps, geologists go looking for oil. Geologists concentrate their search to land formations that are suggestive of these traps. Airplanes and sophisticated satellite technology are now quite commonly used to create detailed maps of potential sites prior to field studies. Geophysicists also measure the magnetic forces, the pull of gravity, and the speed with which sound moves through rock formations to identify potential drilling sites.

Each link of this chain provides potential investment opportunities, which are often missed by those who follow nothing but the big stocks and Wall Street analysts. Energy investors should take on some of the characteristics of the sector and be bold—at least in doing research and in using what they learn about one part of the sector to help them make decisions about investing in another subsector.

The key to success is understanding that energy is a very integrated, interdependent, and cyclical sector of industry. Each part has its role to fill and is part of a bigger picture, which is affected by supply and demand forces that in turn are affected by the subtle but well-defined interactions between economic and political forces.

Oil and Gas Exploration

Oil and natural gas are found together in many instances. But even after sophisticated measures for exploration have been attempted, less than 10 percent of the areas identified as potential sources actually contain oil. The odds are even worse for finding enough oil in a well to make it worth exploiting, with most estimates agreeing that only 2 percent of all potential oil-containing areas have enough oil to be commercially successful sites.

Already, we can see why the oil companies, being profit-motivated, are such influential players in world politics. It's not easy to succeed at this game. Obviously, only very large or very well-managed companies, or firms that are both large and well-managed, can succeed in the long haul.

The most common methods of drilling are either straight down or what is known as directional drilling, done at an angle. Directional drilling allows companies to get at difficult spots; for example, this technique was used for an oil well that was drilled under the state capitol of Oklahoma.

Offshore drilling is more dangerous and 10 times as expensive as on-land drilling. Weather and other logistics increase the expense. But for our purposes, offshore drilling offers great investment opportunities, as its increased prevalence has spawned a whole new support industry that includes transport, supplies, and engineering.

There are many kinds of offshore rigs. The depth of the ocean where they will be used dictates which kind of rig will be placed at that spot. A very interesting design is that of the submersible rig, which is used for depths of up to 4,000 feet and which features legs that are filled with air. When the rig is to be moved, the legs are tucked in, and the anchors that hold the rig in place are pulled up. Ships move to the next drilling site, towing the rig.

Again, this is an example of Intellectual Inclusion. While this information may seem useless for someone who just wants to buy and sell energy stocks, the astute investor should be making mental notes of interesting places along the supply, engineering, and transport chains in which to look for companies that may have been forgotten by Wall Street and might present huge profit opportunities.

Drillships are used in depths of more than 8,000 feet. These scientific and mechanical wonders must hover over the drill site and maintain precise positioning, since anchors can't be used at that depth. Another possible avenue is to look for interesting companies that make the technology and the mechanics for these marvelous vessels.

Fixed platforms are the commonly seen oil rigs on the promotional videos and television reports for oil stories. These are used only in deposits of up to 1,000 feet in depth and when the oil field has proved to be a large producer. As many as 42 wells can be drilled from a single platform.

Drilling for Oil

Oil field–testing crews want to make a quick decision about whether they have a find or a dry hole, because time is money and the odds of finding enough oil to make money are so small. So the testing process is rigorous and requires methodical and efficient analysis. Negative tests lead to the drill hole being plugged by cement and the crew moving on. Positive wells are filled with casing, which is steel tubing. As I will discuss later, the steel tube industry is extremely profitable for energy investors and also a bellwether for the oil cycle.

Wells that meet the criteria for successful production either have enough energy to bring the oil up on their own or have to have energy pumped into them to recover the oil. This means that some wells have enough pressure to cause the oil to gush into the collecting tubes, while others have to have energy pumped into them. Here again are investment opportunities with companies that produce pump equipment.

The wells that have high energy produced from water they contain tend to be some of the best producers, while the wells where the energy pressure comes from natural gas produce less. Low natural energy wells require the injection of water, natural gas, or both, from nearby wells into them. This is an area of avid research in oil technology, as more efficient means of injecting energy into low energy wells could increase their yield.

More important from an investment standpoint is that in a news release about a new oil find, information about high or low energy may be found, and investors can make decisions about the company's prospects by knowing how much money will likely be spent on developing the field. For example, if it is a vast field that has low natural energy, we now know that the yield will likely be less in the short run and that the expense of recovering the oil will likely be higher. This kind of information can be plugged into the big picture for earnings and revenues in the company's future. If the field is in deep water and is found in the Arctic Ocean, this will likely make life more difficult for the company or companies involved from a financial standpoint as well.

Oil and Gas Transport

After the petroleum is extracted, it is separated from natural gas, and the water and other impurities are separated. Oil is then stored or transported by pipeline, tanker, barge, tank truck, and railroad tank car. The most common method of transport is by pipelines, since they can be built over any terrain.

The obvious example is the Trans-Alaskan pipeline, whose existence remains controversial due to concerns over environmental effects on the caribou population and its migration habits. The high cost of pipelines is in the building stage. But since they are inexpensive to operate, the profit margin tends to get better as the pipeline matures.

Many pipeline companies operate as limited partnerships. This allows the parent company or the managing partners to shift risk away from themselves and onto the limited partners. Many limited partnerships are publicly traded, as I will discuss later.

Tankers and barges transport oil on the oceans and rivers, while trucks and railroad tank cars do the rest of the hauling. This is a tangled web of interconnected subsectors, within the larger sectors, that requires an understanding of how the system works and which companies are likely to do better than others under different circumstances.

Refining Separation and Chemical Treatment

After the oil is separated from natural gas, water, and impurities, the natural gas usually goes either to storage or directly to the consumer. The crude oil is then transported to refineries. This was an area of controversy in the spring and summer of 2001, as the Bush administration made refinery capacity and power-production plants the centerpiece of its energy policy. The Democrats countered with information that suggested that refinery capacity had been decreased purposely by the oil companies, in order to drive up the price of gasoline and other products and increase profits.

A refinery can run continuously 24 hours a day for up to five years, without being shut down for repairs. This is a remarkable feat of science and engineering, which is also a huge expense to the companies and an important piece of the cost equation to businesses and consumers.

Refineries separate petroleum into useful products like gasoline, propane, diesel fuel, and heating oil. The products are known as fractions, and the separation is performed in three steps: separation, conversion, and chemical treatment. Separation is performed by multiple methods, which all include heating the oil to different temperatures. Each fraction has a distinct temperature at which it boils and is then distilled into a separate holding tank, before going to the next step.

Gasoline accounts for 50 percent of the petroleum products used in the United States, but is only 10 percent of the initial fraction, so other steps are necessary to increase the yield. These include methods known as cracking, catalytic cracking, and hydrogenation.

At each successive step, the goal is to improve both the yield and the quality of the product. In the United States, a significant cost of refining is attributed to so-called boutique fuels, which are required by law in some cities such as Los Angeles, where air pollution is a major health hazard. These boutique fuels add more expense to the price of a gallon of gas, but also offer profit opportunities to the refiner.

Other key processes at the refinery include the removal of impurities, such as sulfur and lead, and the addition of other chemicals that make the gasoline burn more cleanly.

Distribution

Here, in the distribution networks, high profits are generated. The days of the independent gas station have largely given way to self-contained convenience stores that are usually owned by the same company whose brand name appears on the gasoline. Convenience stores are associated with fast-food chains in many cases, where companies like Exxon will feature a McDonald's, Wendy's, or Tricon Global shop next to the gas station. The trend toward making a gas station a destination will continue to expand, as wholesale warehouses like Sam's Club, Costco, and BJ's Wholesale Club also feature gas stations. Conventional food stores will likely get into the act as well, as is being seen with Kroger.

General Marketplace Factors

The energy market is more supply and demand–driven than just about any other marketplace. For now, keep in mind that the dance between supply and demand, the futures market, and the stock market is always moving in the same general direction. This dance—especially when it is affected by external factors such as economic activity, international politics, refinery explosions, oil spills, and the actions of central banks—dictates the general price trends.

Watch Out for Analysts

A perfect example of an external factor that can affect stock prices is a call from a major Wall Street analyst. Here—as was proven with the Internet stocks, which were only downgraded by analysts after many had become penny stocks—knowledge beyond that of Wall Street's recommendations is power for the individual investor. Supply and demand are the most important factors to consider in the oil market. Next in importance is the technicals and the record and actions of management.

I became bearish on the energy sector in June 2001, after having been bullish all the way through April and May, when I wrote several articles on my Web site *(www.joe-duarte.com)* that featured energy stocks. I was very lucky when Valero Energy (NYSE: VLO) bought Ultramar Diamond Shamrock, as I had a few hundred shares of Shamrock, and I sold into the takeover feeding frenzy. In fact, I wrote a piece in mid-May in which I wondered if this time was different, meaning that the oil prices had risen beyond the usually recognized fundamentals and were entering a long-term stratospheric jaunt similar to that of Internet company stocks. As it turned out, the Valero-Ultramar merger was a signal that the energy market was near a top.

I discussed Valero Energy in the piece, since the stock had actually risen after its takeover bid for Ultramar. This rise in the stock was unusual because the company doing the buying usually falls, while the company being bought usually rises in price. In the article, written on May 14, 2001 (under my daily Market's Message column at *www.joe-duarte.com*), I penned the following:

> The fact is that as the headlines get bolder, and gas prices at the pump go higher, the shares of Valero Energy (NYSE:VLO), which just became a huge refiner in the United States by buying Ultramar Diamond Shamrock (NYSE:UDS), are near a break out.

> First, this seemed wrong, given that Valero was the buyer. The stock of the buyer usually goes down, as Wall Street factors in

costs of the merger and the inevitable infighting between management types of both sides. This kind of action usually costs the acquirer money, and that usually translates into decreased profits and/or outright losses.

So why was Valero still going up? It could well be because Wall Street was missing the point. Supplies of oil could be smaller than most expect. And it could take years for refineries to build enough capacity to meet what could be growing demand, despite surveys suggesting that people are going to cut back on summer travel, and conserve.

In that article, I raised some questions, with the major theme being, Could this time really be different? But by June 19, it was obvious that this time was not different, and in that day's Market's Message column, I wrote the following:

The message? The oil sector is likely to weaken further. With gasoline stocks increasing for the summer season, oil prices dropping, and OPEC quietly exceeding its quotas according to some reports, the fundamentals of the oil market have changed.

As figure 4.1 of the Amex Oil Index shows, the oil stocks collapsed in June, with the real top coming on May 17, just three days after my "this time is different" column. In retrospect, I was part of the hype, to some degree. My saving grace was that I caught myself and turned negative before serious damage was done. And although my call could have been earlier, it was not late by any means, based on the fact that the technicals, the political, and the fundamentals coalesced simultaneously.

But even more interesting is figure 4.2, courtesy of the *Dismal Scientist,* which showed that as supplies of crude oil soared in April and May, the market was getting ready for a fall. Note also that stable oil supplies were closely correlated to stable and not very glamorous oil stock prices. When inventories began to rise, the oil stocks returned to equilibrium. Figure 4.3 shows that the number of jobs

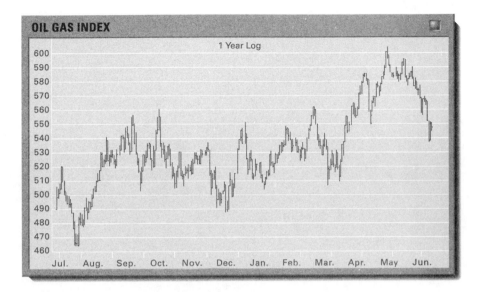

Figure 4.1: *The June 2001 Oil Collapse in the Amex Oil Index, courtesy of Telescan.*

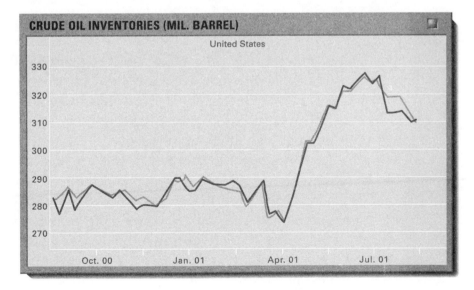

Figure 4.2: *Crude Oil Inventories October 2000–July 2001, courtesy of the* Dismal Scientist (www.dismal.com).

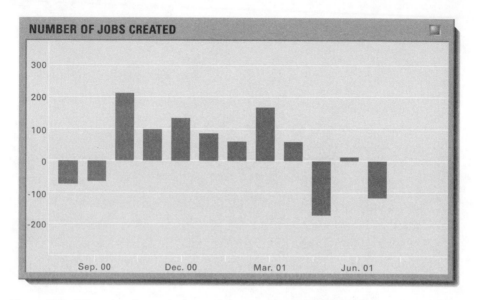

Figure 4.3: *The number of new jobs created in the United States, September 2000.*

created in the United States began to fall in September 2000, and that by June 2001 jobs were being lost as a whole. This was an obvious sign of an economic slowdown, which once again correlated with the increasing supplies of crude oil. The bottom line is that a slowing economy will lead to increased oil inventories and eventually will result in lower oil prices and lower oil stocks.

My story is not one of self-congratulation, as I've had my share of losing stock trades to go along with the winners. My point is that as the price of gasoline went up and the news got hotter out of Congress and California, analysts tended to increase their price targets on oil stocks. As analysts grew more bullish, the charts started turning more bearish. Instead of listening to hype, I suggest examining the economic statistics, such as those listed in this chapter, while simultaneously looking at the price of oil stocks. If the supply-and-demand scenario is changing at the same time the economy is changing, then it's time to start watching the oil stock charts with extreme care.

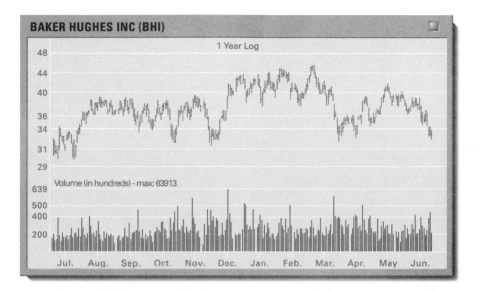

Figure 4.4: *Baker Hughes (NYSE:BHI) on July 1, after the Wall Street upgrade.*

A more interesting sign of analyst behavior came on June 29, when the oil index hit a tentative bottom that is often called a dead cat bounce in chart lingo, for the inevitable bounce in a stock or a sector after a prolonged sell-off. As the charts still said stay away for a while, analyst Arvind Sanger for Deutsche Banc Alex Brown wrote to his clients: "We believe that with the OSX [the Philadelphia Oil Sector Index] closing below 100 for the first time in seven months yesterday, this capitulation is at hand and the risk reward [ratio] has become quite compelling."

More important is that the analyst upgraded shares of Baker Hughes (NYSE:BHI) to a strong buy from a buy (see figure 4.4). Where was the sell call at the February top or the second chance to sell at the May top? And where was the mention of the huge head and shoulders top formed by the stock? To a technical analyst, this chart has ominous possibilities.

Another stock upgraded by Deutsche Banc Alex Brown was Schlumberger (NYSE:SLB), a stock that at the time was in even

Figure 4.5: *Schlumberger (NYSE:SLB) on July 1, 2001, after the analyst upgrade on June 29, courtesy of Telescan.*

worse shape and that looked as if it was ready to break down further (see figure 4.5).

I am not trying to pick on analysts, although the Internet bubble and its aftermath, including the Enron scandal, did long-term damage to their credibility. But by December 2001, as a result of many Wall Street analysts maintaining buy ratings on the already collapsed shares of Enron, Congress was considering imposing strict regulations on the community as a whole. It is a routine occurrence for Wall Street analysts to make these kinds of calls. The newscasts pick up on them and interview the analysts. These calls and the interviews often cause movement in a stock. Buying blindly on analyst recommendations without doing your own homework increases your chances of making a less than fully informed decision and sometimes losing your shirt. Instead, I suggest knowing which part of the cycle you are in and making your own decisions, based on sound principles of technical and fundamental analysis.

Interest Rates

The preceding segment provided a working capsule of how the oil market's highly complex mechanism functions in order to get energy from a remote oil field to the gas tank of John Q. Public. Major factors affecting the sector are those of supply and demand. But political and economic factors are the main influences on that supply-and-demand equation, as the California energy crisis showed us. Policy creates conditions that will eventually affect supply and demand and set up the cascade of events that leads to movement in stock prices.

All investment books should at least mention the Federal Reserve and interest rates, as these are major external influences on all stocks. The Federal Reserve has had an increasingly public role in the marketplace since Federal Reserve Chairman Greenspan has been in command. Chairman Greenspan has presided over the Fed during a watershed era in history. The period that began after the 1987 crash has been a time when major political change has resulted from an increasingly democratic and market-force driven world, leading to periodic financial market crises. The process has been accelerated by the advent of new technology, in terms of both trading and media coverage. The net effect has been that markets move much further up or down and in a shorter period of time than they used to.

For this reason—whether you like it or not—if you are going to be a trader or an investor, you need to have some basic knowledge of what the Fed does and what it means to your money. I won't go into detail here because I spent a lot of time on the Fed in *After-Hours Trading Made Easy*, but here are the basics.

The Federal Reserve

The Federal Reserve has done an excellent job under Alan Greenspan, despite having to function in a difficult environment that has spawned multiple stock and currency market crashes.

And the true benchmark of the Fed's work is that the United States has not fallen into a depression as Japan and Southeast Asia did when Japan's Central Bank raised interest rates in 1989, even after the World Trade Center attacks and their aftermath.

The slow-growth scenario and the recession in 2000–2001 were nowhere near as bad as the depression in Japan, which started in 1989 as the Bank of Japan burst the real-estate bubble. The difference, and the United States' saving grace, was that in the early 1990s the United States cleaned up its banking system—despite much pain—after the 1987 stock market crash revealed that a lot of what banks had counted as assets actually consisted of worthless junk bonds. Japan—unfortunately for that country in the short term and for the rest of the world in the long term (unless something very dramatic happens)—still had not cleaned up its banking mess as of December 2001. Instead of admitting that what they counted as assets were little more than worthless loans that could not be repaid, Japanese banks continued to lie about their balance sheets.

For this reason, Japan has continued to falter, whereas China, the now slowly awakening giant, has begun to stir. And this is a crucial thought to keep in mind, as China's rapid industrial and commercial growth is slowly but surely making the country a significant future player in global energy, as well as politics. Even more important is what could happen to the Asian economy if a repeat of the 1997 Asian meltdown occurs.

Again, I want to use Intellectual Inclusion here, as I compare Japan in 1989 to the United States in 2000. In 1989 the Japanese markets were the envy of the rest of the globe. Its companies continued to produce one blockbuster product after another, and earnings seemed to be on an ever-upward course.

If this sounds familiar, it is because in 2000 Internet companies had the same kind of paradigm attached to them: The companies would never have to make money, but instead would generate profits by just being "cool" and attaching dot-com to their names. Until, as usual, the bubble burst. In 1989 the bank of Japan raised interest rates. And in 2000 the Fed raised rates. Suddenly, the golden new paradigms were exposed for what they truly were: intricate shams.

The point is that all markets eventually fall, whether they are markets related to impressive economic growth or to a sector that truly changes the way we live. All machines that make life wonderful will eventually go the way of the toaster and the refrigerator. They are nice and useful. We can't live without them. But eventually, everybody has one, and they become commodities.

All markets rise on expectations that feed on themselves and become totally unrealistic. But something always pricks the bubble. And the most common bubble buster in the current market is the Federal Reserve or any other major global central bank. By the same token, most bull markets or meaningful intermediate-term rallies are usually related to the Federal Reserve lowering interest rates.

The Federal Reserve was established in 1913 to prevent booms and busts in the economy. Prior to the Fed, private banks were the main source of funds for a largely agricultural society that depended on the weather and the dynamics of supply and demand for farm products to survive. When the Industrial Revolution came along in the late 1800s, it added a new variable, which for a while just amplified the boom-and-bust cycle.

For a period of time in the 19th and early 20th centuries, booms and busts were dependent on the goodwill of famous bankers like J. P. Morgan. Thus, it seems ironic that only in the late 1980s did a Fed chairman emerge with the insight to navigate the incredibly murky waters of the current global economy, with a decreased effect to the U.S. economy—at least, when compared with the rest of the world.

I should also note that central banks are not immune from making mistakes. The greatest danger of central banks is that they can become politicized, as was the Bank of Japan in the 1980s and as former U.S. Feds were alleged to be prior to Paul Volcker's and Alan Greenspan's tenures. A politicized central bank loses credibility and leads to market chaos.

The two most notable central bank mistakes occurred in 1929 in the United States, when the Great Depression was brought on by too tight a money policy, and in 1989 in Japan, with the same effect. Interest rates that were too high also led to trouble in 1992 in Europe, when Germany's Bundesbank flogged a weak economy with higher rates than needed, and it triggered a global currency crisis.

Thus, the Federal Reserve is the world's leading central bank, and many consider Alan Greenspan the greatest central banker of all time, as he has perfected the art of quenching speculation, wringing out excessive inflation, and keeping the U.S. economy moving forward, despite multiple stock market crashes and recessions during his tenure. His political acumen is more revered than is his economic judgment; the latter is often questioned—in my opinion, wrongly—by pundits, rivals, and politicians. But this type of stewardship—if maintained, even by a Greenspan successor—can nurture the development of periodic bull markets in stocks and help the U.S. economy continue to move forward.

The Bond Market

Although the Fed is important, the bond market is in many ways more important, because it is the world's interest-rate policeman. The ideal environment for Treasury bond markets is a slow-growth environment and even a recession. The logic is simple. The government will always attempt to pay its debts. And if there is no inflation, then the value of the money invested in the bond maintains its worth.

Thus, a basic understanding of the bond market is important when investing in all sectors of the stock market, for all stocks are eventually interest-rate sensitive, meaning that if interest rates rise high enough, the stock market will eventually fall.

Bonds are IOUs, issued by governments and corporations. For our purposes, we will focus only on the Treasury bond market. Bond performance is measured by price and by yield. The price is what an investor pays in order to buy a bond. The yield is the interest that the bond holder receives. Rising prices mean falling yields. And rising yields mean falling prices. The worst influence on bonds is inflation. This means that when the bond market is expecting a rise in inflation, bond yields tend to rise. And when bond traders expect inflation to be tame, bond yields fall. As bond yields rise, the price of the bond drops, and vice versa.

The bond market's daily turnover is measured in trillions of dollars, or many multiples of the daily turnover in stocks.

The Relationship Between Bonds and the Oil Markets

Before the Internet, e-commerce, and the improvements in productivity brought about by the huge advances in wireless and broadband technology that we enjoy today, the relationship between bonds and the price of oil was quite predictable. Rising oil prices usually preceded a rise in bond yields. This made sense at the time because most people drove to work and depended on oil for most of their energy resources. But with improvements in technology and the increased use of natural gas, propane, and other alternatives for fuel, the price of oil and bond yields no longer have as close a relationship as they once did.

Figure 4.6 displays the 5-year period between 1998 and 2001, which is illustrative of how the bond market behaves during the new accelerated and technology-influenced business cycle. Note that bond yields bottomed in late 1998, as the Fed lowered interest rates in response to the Asian crisis and the Russian loan default. That was the right thing to do, at the time, as lower rates kept the economy from collapsing. But the Fed lowered rates too aggressively, and bond yields topped in early 1999. This was a sign that the Fed had eased enough, as bond traders began to price-in a huge boom in the economy. As it turned out, bond traders were right, and the huge injection of money from the Fed would lead to unsustainable growth and become a direct influence on the Internet bubble.

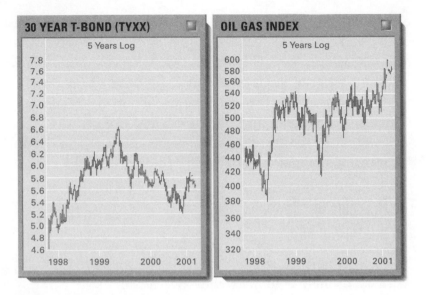

Figure 4.6: *The U.S. 30-year Treasury Bond Yield (left), compared to the price of the Amex Oil & Gas Index (XOI). A 5-year comparison, courtesy of Telescan.*

When Internet stocks began to rally, as easy money from the Federal Reserve fueled a rally in the stock market sector, this prompted cries of the "new paradigm." But the new paradigm led to higher oil prices, which, as history shows, eventually will choke off economic growth. Note also in figure 4.6 that the 1999 top in bond yields led to a significant bottom in XOI.

Supply and Demand—The Real Drivers of the Market, and Why China May Hold an Important Key

I attended a birthday party for one of my son's friends in the summer of 2001. During the afternoon, as often happens at these gatherings, the young host's father, Bill, a chemical engineer for a large oil company, and I talked about what makes the oil world move. I laid out my case, as I knew it then, based on my early research for this book. Bill listened and thought, carefully weighing the arguments I presented, as he always does before rendering judgment. Then he set me straight and pointed me in the right direction. I felt almost like Bob Woodward in a Washington, D.C., garage, talking to Deep Throat about Watergate.

As usually happens, a certain story is widely circulated in the media, and that is collectively known as the common wisdom. This story usually has enough truth in it to make it believable. As more and more people tell it and the rest of the media picks up on it, it becomes a self-fulfilling prophecy—until, of course, it falls apart.

Bill had just returned from China, which made his remarks even more interesting and timely. I still marveled at the steady, aggressive movement by the Chinese into a pivotal role in world politics and the energy markets. And he was instrumental in exciting my curiosity about China and what its presence represents for the energy market in the next quarter century, a crucial role in supply and especially demand.

To give Bill's words extra weight, I will relate here that on July 13, the International Olympic Committee granted China the 2008 Olympic games. Bill suspected that this was one top reason for what he saw during his visit, which proves that his insight has always been quite keen.

What Bill told me about China was quite astounding. First, he said that he had not been there for 10 years prior to his recent trip. When he arrived, he saw a dramatic transformation. Beijing had gone from being a smoggy, depressed city to a sprawling metropolis that in many areas boasted broadband communications and even featured suburbs with multiple-level single-family dwellings that would rival those of any self-respecting American suburb.

That kind of progress, he said, could also be seen elsewhere in China. What this means is that the increased energy demand from the world's largest population to cool and heat these new large homes and to power everyone's broadband Internet access will make California's problems look like small potatoes, if the Chinese government does not aggressively develop its own oil supply and get serious about its role in the global oil supply. And what this means for the United States is multifold, as China's need for further exploration could benefit American exploration companies, but will also lead to an expansion of China's role in the international energy arena.

The common wisdom, as espoused by OPEC and the multiple government departments of energy from most countries in the world, is that oil will run out in the next 100 years. What Bill told me is that easily obtainable oil will become increasingly harder to find and to extract, as I noted earlier. It is also important to reiterate that the technology for oil extraction is not as efficient as it could be. It is vastly improved, but at best is able to extract only one-third of the oil that is found. The supply of oil that most people refer to, however, does not commonly include the huge global reserves of oil shale and coal that, through chemical processing, could be used to produce oil-like materials. And it also does not consider that oil can still be dragged out of what many consider to be tapped-out old wells—wells that have oil left in them, but that would be too expensive to operate under the current technology and cost structure.

Anyone who has ever driven from Dallas to El Paso, a 667-mile jaunt through the state of Texas, has passed the towns of Midland and Odessa. Aside from being the hometown of President Bush, Midland is one of those places where you see small oil rigs bobbing up and down like upside-down pendulums, working away. You can also see them in parts of north Texas and remote areas of New Mexico.

You may note that these derricks are often standing still—unless the price of oil rises, when these wells suddenly become active. Sure, the yield is not what it used to be, but if the price goes high enough, these so-called dry wells are brought back into production, and eventually supply increases.

The message here is simple, but not to be taken lightly. If demand is strong enough, the oil industry will look for and produce more oil. So, here is the bottom line: Plenty of petroleum potential is out there, with huge deposits in far-out-of-the-way places, still undiscovered and untapped. And other sources of petroleum-like substances also are still untapped. This means that supply still exceeds demand at a very fundamental level. And this suggests that maybe—just maybe—we could have plenty of oil left for a lot longer than the common wisdom tells us.

But oil companies operate on a profit motive. They aren't about to go drilling expensive wells at the bottom of the sea and in the deepest malaria-infected jungles until they can make money at it. And as crass as that sounds, it makes good business sense. If you own a candy store, you only sell the popular brands. If you own a magazine store, you only stock the hot titles. And if you drill for, refine, or market oil, you only want to work the system in a way that maximizes profits.

Most interesting is that every time gasoline prices rise, Congress suggests—usually after the market has already remedied the situation—that some kind of antitrust violation and conspiracy is at work. In June 2001, when oil and gasoline prices had already begun to stabilize, Senator Ron Wyden (D-Oregon) charged oil companies with conspiring to "reduce supplies of gasoline in an effort to drive prices higher and improve profitability."

Wow, that's a shocker: An industry whose goal is profit was trying to maximize its ability to make money. The report accused oil companies of restricting refining capacity in the mid-1990s as oil prices crashed, in order to maximize profits. As I noted earlier, this news, without the allegations of fraud leveled by Congress, was already known and was one of the supporting points used by the Bush camp in drafting its controversial energy policy.

Sure, nobody likes to pay more than they have to at the gas pump. And there is always the possibility of illegal activity in an industry. But supply and demand rule in the oil market. And any time the government oversteps its duties, you have disasters like the California energy crisis. My point is that the market is eventually right, and government intervention is often too late and in most cases serves only to stir up situations that the market has already begun to address. For investors, that is the key message, as the entrance of the government into an oil crisis often signals that a change in trend is near.

We need to compartmentalize our viewpoints. We all have a responsibility to preserve our environment. And we all have responsibilities as citizens to uphold the laws and live by the rules. But as investors, we must also learn to spot opportunities and act on them in a timely and profitable fashion.

The Futures Markets

No investor in energy stocks should make a trade without understanding that the commodity futures markets are a great influence on the price of their stocks. Commodity futures prices are driven by the equilibrium between supply and demand. Anything that disrupts the balance between supply and demand will greatly and rapidly affect the price of the commodity and will transfer itself to other markets, including stocks. The most common events that affect the price of energy futures include weather; political problems; and accidents at refineries, major exploration sites, and power plants.

The perfect example of how events shape the commodity market was in the winter of 2000, when, according to the U.S. Department of Energy *(www.eia.doe.gov)*, the spot price of home heating oil at the New York Harbor went from $0.76 to $1.77 per gallon from January 14 to February 4, a 133 percent increase. The spot price for natural gas rose from $2.65 to $11.75 per million British Thermal Units (BTU), a 340 percent increase.

The difference between futures and spot prices is that futures prices are set on the exchanges and are based on the market's expectations. That means that Exxon-Mobil is speculating on the supply and demand for crude oil in December 2001 when it buys or sells short crude oil futures for delivery in December 2001.

When Exxon or some other large investor is short oil, it is doing so in order to protect itself against an expectation of lower gasoline prices at the pump. This means that it is protecting itself against decreasing profits in the future, by hedging its exposure in its current gasoline inventory, which it expects to sell for a lower price. In effect, it is betting against the future, in the hopes that if it is right, its profits will be helped by its trading savvy, since it got stuck with too much gasoline in the present.

What happened? The winter was colder than expected, and the market got caught with low supplies on hand. When supply increased by the end of February, prices fell.

The Politics

A closer-to-home example of the relationship of the energy futures markets to stocks can be seen in the six-month charts of unleaded gasoline futures and Exxon-Mobil in June 2001. Gasoline supplies, as reported by the American Petroleum Institute, expanded aggressively the week prior to the snapshot provided in the chart (see figure 4.7). Investors began to price-in a fall at the gas pump and at the same time began to sell oil stocks in expectation of either lower profits or slower profit growth. Notice the high correlation between the price of unleaded gas in the futures market and the price of Exxon-Mobil, which looks ready to topple along with unleaded gas.

Similar relationships can be seen in each market, such as the natural gas stocks and the price of natural gas futures. As John Murphy, the master intermarket technical analyst, has pointed out on many occasions, the stocks often lead the market itself. The main point of this section is to establish that the energy sector is a cyclical industry that is heavily influenced by supply and demand. This supply and demand is in turn affected by economic factors such as new technologies and their effect on consumption; political factors, such as conflicts in the Middle East and congressional pressure; other markets, such as the bond market; and, of all things, the weather, as well as consumer behavior such as the annual ritual of the driving season and its effect on companies ramping up refinery capacity in order to meet demand. As I will show

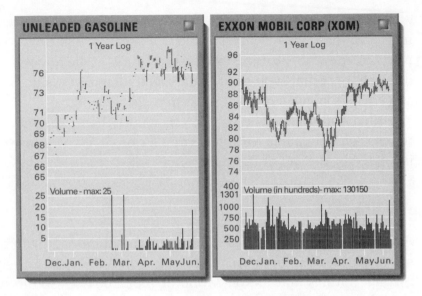

Figure 4.7: *Unleaded Gasoline Futures December 2001 (left), and Exxon-Mobil (NYSE:XOM, right), a six-month comparison, courtesy of Telescan.*

later, it is useful to keep tabs on some bellwether stocks in the energy sector that often do lead the energy markets.

The Components of the Energy Complex

Now that we understand what the main external factors are in the energy complex, we turn our attention to the component industries that make up the sector. The sector is composed of companies that explore for fuels, that provide support services to the industry, that market fuel, and that distribute, market, and trade commodities. Alternative energy sources will be treated separately later.

The energy complex is set up like a wheel, with petroleum as the hub and the rest of the subsectors as spokes. All components are interdependent on each other, with the common thread being supply and demand.

I used the petroleum industry in previous areas of the book as a benchmark and because most other subsectors of the energy complex are dependent on petroleum, either for products or for their own business. But in the next section I will look at the rest of the energy area and will relate particular connections to oil.

The main subsectors of energy are electricity, petroleum, and natural gas. Each major subsector has its own grid of smaller subsectors. My approach in this chapter is to provide a summary of each industry and then expand to companies, business strategies, and greater specifics in subsequent chapters.

Electricity

The first subsector in the energy complex is electricity. This area sustained the greatest scrutiny in the year 2001, due to the California energy crisis. From an investor's point of view, this area turned from what Wall Street used to call the sector for "widows and orphans" into a very hot, momentum-driven sector, as a result of the advent of deregulation, the Internet economy, and the California energy problems. This combination of events transformed the once-sleepy sector into one where companies that were attractive because of their dividend yields became known for their earnings momentum. This dynamic change in investor perception and behavior is a perfect example of why investors must remain both flexible in their methods of analysis and alert to what is working in the current market.

The three main areas in the electricity sector are power generation, long-distance power transmission, and local distribution. The traditional electricity industry consisted of "natural monopolies." These major utility companies would own the rights to the entire spectrum of the electricity industry for an entire area, in exchange for reliable services at a "reasonable price," which was mandated by state governments at the retail level and by the federal government at the wholesale level.

For now, remember that the electricity sector has three major components and that it is an industry in transition. It is also a must on the watch list of most investors for the 21st century.

Exploration

Companies that are involved exclusively in oil and gas exploration are the holders of key reserves. Many are holders of portions of fields, in partnerships with major oil companies. There is a great deal of overlap here, as some exploration companies are also involved in transport and support services.

Energy Service

This is a highly cyclical sector, which, as the chart of the OSX index proves, tends to exaggerate the overall trend of the energy market. It is also the subsector where the dirty work gets done. These companies drill the wells, pump the oil, set up the oil field, and build the infrastructure, such as platforms and rigs, so that it is safe and works correctly. More important, these companies offer and produce much of the key scientific equipment that is important for exploration.

These companies are heavily dependent on engineering and technology and, in many cases, have high-tech subsidiaries, such as Schlumberger (NYSE:SLB), which also designs technology solutions for its clients, including oil field monitoring and a high-speed communications network.

Integrated Oil Companies

These are major oil companies like Exxon-Mobil and Chevron-Texaco. These companies are involved in all aspects of the oil sector, including exploration, transport, refining, distribution, and retail. I will dissect these behemoths further in chapter 5.

Natural Gas

Natural gas companies are involved in exploration, transport, and trading. Natural gas continues to increase its presence on the energy scene, due to its reputation for being a cleaner-burning fuel. And although it is mostly used for home and business power generation, increased numbers of vehicles—especially those in mass transport—are switching over to natural gas as a fuel source.

Nuclear Energy

Nuclear energy is having a rebirth, as a result of the Bush administration's energy policy. Some very high peaks have occurred in this sector, as have some very low valleys, such as the Three Mile Island meltdown in the United States, and the Chernobyl accident in Russia. But this area will figure greatly in the future, and companies that can produce the technology for the reactors and the power plants are likely to benefit, as much as will companies that run the power plants.

Alternative Energy Sources

Finally, we have the alternative companies, with wind power, thermal power, hydroelectric, solar, and fuel cells as the most popular. Most of these companies suffer from the major energy companies' lack of interest, because they have low profit potential at this point. But, nevertheless, their day may come.

Summary

My goal in this chapter was to create a transition from history and basic background information to the area of investing, where we'll look at sectors and companies and how they do business, creating a road map into this complex and highly integrated industry. I delved into the main internal and external factors that affect the oil market and in later chapters will expand on this information to fit the other sectors. The most important point here is that supply and demand set the tone of the oil market. When investors remain focused on the state of the supply-and-demand equation, add smart technical and fundamental analysis, and keep a keen eye on politics, very profitable trades can be made.

5

The Integrated Oil Companies

Integrated oil companies are the highly recognized international names such as Exxon-Mobil, Texaco, and British Petroleum. As a rule, these are huge global conglomerates with many subsidiaries and tens of thousands of employees. They tend to be very steady revenue producers and usually deliver earnings and pay dividends.

Integrated means that these companies explore, refine, and market oil. They are self-contained units that are involved in most areas of the industry and often hold leadership positions in at least one of the subsectors. Their subsidiaries range in businesses from technology to alternative fuels and chemicals. Many integrated oil companies have highly respected research laboratories, which are responsible, directly or indirectly, for many of the products we take for granted and that make our lives easier.

I will use the Amex Oil Index in this chapter to provide a snapshot of the integrated oil companies, as well as a glimpse into other areas of the oil industry as featured in the index. Although the XOI index is by no means representative of the entire industry, it does give you a good overview of the well-recognized names, especially in refining and marketing. Most interesting is that some of these companies have little to do with gasoline and a great deal to do with natural gas, oil exploration, and the chemical industry.

121

Who Should Invest in These Companies?

Both traders and investors should actively follow this sector, as it can provide both long-term total returns, when dividends are included, and the potential for intermediate-term returns, as the oil cycle and economic conditions change. Very savvy investors who use options, as well as those who can sell short, can also benefit from owning these stocks.

The most important factor to remember is that while large oil companies can be controversial, they should not be ignored in lieu of more sexy sectors like technology and biotechnology. Most investors should have at least some acquaintance with these stocks, whether in a long-term buy-and-hold strategy or a timing portfolio.

Investors whose children have trusts and college plans, as well as those with 401(k) and other retirement plans—which often limit the number of times that changes to the portfolio mix can be made—should pay very close attention to these stocks, due to their income-producing and total-return characteristics.

When Is It Best to Own These Stocks?

Long-term investors should consider owning these stocks as part of a core portfolio, with perhaps a five-year or longer outlook. A 5 to 10 percent allocation is reasonable at all times, concentrating on the large dividend-paying stocks. It is better for those with larger portfolios to own the individual stocks instead of a mutual fund because of the dividend, which can be very attractive. Table 5.1 shows the dividend for selected large integrated oil stocks in July 2001.

The yields were all similar in the range of 2.5–3 percent. This is an amount that at face value seems low. But when this chart was produced in July 2001, U.S. Treasury Bills were yielding 3.63 percent, with no opportunity for capital gains. Then, as 2001 progressed, U.S. interest rates fell below 2 percent, making these dividends even more attractive. Furthermore, when taken at face

Table 5.1: *Dividend summary for selected integrated oil companies.*

Company	Dividend	Yield
Texaco	$1.80	2.69%
Chevron	$2.60	2.91%
Royal Dutch Petroleum	$1.40	2.49%

value, a sizable position in these shares, such as 1,000–2,000 shares or more, could deliver a nice income flow based on the dividend. Large oil stocks are also perfect for dividend reinvestment plans or DRIPs, in which the stocks are bought on a periodic basis from the company itself without a broker's commission. Investors can build large positions over a long period of time in this way, with low cost and mostly low stress. These large blue-chip stocks also make excellent gifts to very young children as part of their trusts or future inheritance.

Thus, to a greater degree than other areas of the market, the buy-and-hold strategy is a reasonable potential alternative for long-term investors who have an interest in large oil companies. But active investors can also do well in a period of weeks to months, if they know what to watch for. As I noted in chapters 1 and 4, the large oil stocks tend to rise when the economy is picking up steam and the signs of growth are about to emerge. By the time this stage of the economic cycle has arrived, the Federal Reserve has usually lowered interest rates more than once or perhaps several times, and there are signs not just of a bottom in an economic slowdown, but also of actual, even tentative, growth.

In prior chapters, I used the technology stocks as a sign that the stock market was beginning to factor in the possibility of economic growth. The relationship between the technology sector and oil sector is quite strong. Thus, a good rule of thumb is to watch the action in technology stocks and compare the trend there to the trend in the oil sector.

Table 5.2: *OPEC asked for 500,000 barrels per day cut from non-OPEC production and got less than it wanted.*

Proposed Non-OPEC Cuts	
Norway	150,000
Russia	150,000
Mexico	100,000
Oman	25,000
Angola	22,500
TOTAL	447,500

But perhaps the best time to start watching the oil stocks is when OPEC is beginning to feel the pinch of falling oil prices. That is when the cartel will often begin to make announcements about reductions in production quotas. The news will usually cause at least a pause in the down trend. What the investor needs to watch for is whether the change in trend occurs and if it has staying power.

In the past, just the specter of OPEC production cutbacks was the perfect excuse for traders to bid the price of crude oil higher. But, as I discussed earlier, the dynamics of the oil market changed dramatically in 2001. So instead of a certain climb in the price of crude oil, due to OPEC threats to cut production, what the markets saw was a very stout stance from Russia against OPEC's demands. What OPEC requested in late 2001 was that non-OPEC producers cut a total of 500,000 barrels per day in their production, in exchange for a 1.5 million cut per day by the cartel. By cutting production, OPEC wanted to stabilize the price of crude oil between $22–$28 per barrel. What they got was a lot less, on many levels, and at a very high cost to the cartel, financially and politically, as the figures clearly show in table 5.2, courtesy of WTRG Economics *(www.wtrg.com)*.

As table 5.2 shows, OPEC's requested cuts were not met entirely by non-OPEC producers, as Russia undercut the amount that OPEC had hoped for, by at least 200,000–300,000 barrels per day. But perhaps what hurt OPEC the most, both in financial terms and, more important, in the image department, was how Russia used the opportunity to battle the cartel in a very public forum, with high-profile press releases and press conferences, punctuated by trips to Venezuela and visits to the Kremlin from high-level OPEC officials, who during the fall of 2001 were visibly perplexed and increasingly annoyed by the tactics of confusion and double talk used by Russia. As a result, OPEC was forced to make face-saving arrangements or consider the alternative: an all-out price war.

A price war would be financial and political suicide for the cartel, as the balance of power had clearly swung away from it and to the Western-backed Russians. And in an ironic twist, AFP Energy.com reported that OPEC was considering the delay of its proposed production cutbacks: "Maybe we will wait another month, maybe the first of February" was the quote from a "high-ranking" OPEC official in Vienna.

Russia's strategy seemed to pay off, at least in the short run, as the cash-strapped and ideologically vulnerable cartel clearly could not make good on its prior threats of a "price war." The Russian strategy was brilliant right from the beginning and may in the future be considered the stuff of legend, if it pans out—as I project that it will—in setting up Russia as at least an equal to OPEC in dictating global energy policy. When OPEC began to rattle its sabers, Russia at first said it would not cut production. After a high-level OPEC official visited Moscow, Russia initially gave in, with a 30,000-barrel-per-day cutback. OPEC was offended, and Russia said it would cut an additional 20,000 barrels from its daily production. After more behind-the-scenes pleading from OPEC, Russia finally cut 150,000 barrels per day.

But oil prices did not rally on that news because Russia usually cuts back 150,000 barrels per day in production in the first quarter of the year, due to weather concerns in its drilling regions. More important, Russia's low ability to store crude is dwarfed by its ability to refine and store products such as gasoline and diesel. So, while Russia could say that it was aiding OPEC and publicly was quoted as saying that it wanted crude oil prices between $22–$25, its real strategy was quite clear to the markets: Russia would use the leverage that it gained by aiding the United States in its war against terrorism to steal market share from OPEC. And it would do so by using its high capacity to export products and flood the market, while still adhering to its promised cutback in crude production.

That strategy served two purposes and gave the markets a perfect example of how markets in the future might have to interpret and respond to strategic changes from OPEC. This is a period when, as I stated earlier, the U.S. economy was weakening, and the global economy had begun to show signs of slowing as well. Politicians on both sides of the Atlantic, as well as in Japan, were meeting in Genoa, Switzerland. The price of oil had reached the area of $25 per barrel, and OPEC had many times suggested that it wanted to keep prices near there. At the same time, the U.S. House of Representatives had just passed a bill that would allow for exploration in Alaska and would fund the study of drilling for oil in the Florida Gulf Coast.

Figure 5.1 shows that the result of the Russian maneuvering was to keep crude oil prices lower than they might have been in the past, given OPEC's former ability to move the markets without any real opposition. What it also did was to allow the global economy to attempt to recover without having to worry about the added burden of higher oil prices. And while the economic picture made the outlook for oil look bleak, the flood of oil in the markets had led to a decrease in the number of active oil drilling rigs in North America that as of December 10, 2001, was down 34 percent on a year-over-year basis, while international oil rig activity was flat. What this set of data did was to suggest that to a

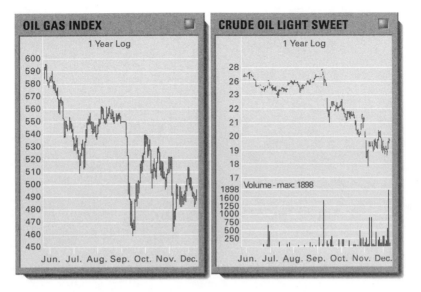

Figure 5.1: *Amex Oil Index (XOI; left) and March 2002 Crude Oil Futures (CLH@; right), courtesy of Telescan.*

great degree the market had already begun to adjust, in order to create the classic scenario of a decrease in future supply, which would already be in place when an economic recovery took place. This dynamic was market-based and already well under way even before OPEC began to clamor for supply cuts late in 2001.

Figure 5.2 shows the market's response to the news of the day, as shares of Chevron-Texaco, whose involvement in Russian oil pipelines was more intense than that of Exxon-Mobil's, was in the progress of making a complex bottom. More to Exxon-Mobil's detriment was that it was the largest participant, with an investment of $5 billion, in a Saudi Arabia natural gas venture that had run into trouble. The weekend press on December 15 had reported that the signing date for the deal had been moved to March 2002, amidst increasing concern from the oil companies and the Saudis' inability to come to terms in key areas of the contracts.

Figure 5.2: *Chevron-Texaco (NYSE:CVX; left) and Exxon-Mobil (NYSE:XOM; right) on December 17, 2001, showing distinct responses to the news of the day that suggested that Russia had won the battle of the production cutbacks.*

What Are the Factors That Best Tell an Investor What Stocks to Buy and Sell?

The classic company in the integrated oil sector is Exxon-Mobil (NYSE:XOM), whose March 2001 earnings of $4.6 billion made business news headlines for several days. But just because the company is the best known and the largest, that doesn't mean it is the best investment, as figure 5.2 shows and as the changing dynamics of the oil game for the future clearly suggest. The key for Exxon's ability to grow is, in my opinion, the degree to which it can decrease its exposure to Saudi Arabia and diversify into other OPEC countries, such as the increasingly interesting Libya and, in the future, Iran, as well as a defused Iraq, which is a plausible, but still longer-term, project. Exxon will also have to move aggressively into Russia and consider joint ventures with China, as Chevron-Texaco is a company that is building a full head of steam.

Because oil investing is an old-fashioned game, it requires old-fashioned scrutiny of balance sheets and earnings reports, along with a thorough evaluation of management's ability to deliver, and close attention to stock charts, which I have already alluded to, but will discuss in greater detail in the chapter on technical and fundamental analysis. As it is an established cyclical sector, the more common notions of growth investment, such as double digit and sequential earnings growth, are less applicable. Instead, special attention has to be paid to curmudgeonly factors like book value, price/earnings ratio, return on equity, and the amount of cash on the balance sheet, which I will also discuss in greater detail in the technical and fundamental analysis.

The Amex Oil and Gas Index (XOI)

The most widely followed benchmark for the oil sector is the Amex Oil Index (XOI), and it will serve as a centerpiece of this chapter because the tendencies, successes, and failures of these companies will help us build a winning business model that we can then use as a benchmark. XOI is easy to follow, as it is widely quoted on the major online news outlets like *CBS.Marketwatch (www.cbsmarketwatch.com)* and Barron's *(www.barrons.com)*. The XOI is updated in real time on the CNBC ticker during trading hours. Table 5.3 summarizes the stocks in the index. The commentary will be divided into subsections, based on geography and the subsector of the industry.

A quick glance at table 5.3 reveals that these are all highly recognizable names, such as Chevron-Texaco and Exxon-Mobil. But lesser known names are included that are equally important, like Repsol YPF, an Argentinean-Spanish conglomerate with a significant presence in South America, and Unocal Corporation, a former well-known refiner and marketer that turned to exploration as its

---

Table 5.3: *The Amex Oil Index (XOI), courtesy of* www.amex.com.

Amerada Hess Corporation (AHC)

Repsol, YPF, S.A. (REP)

BP Amoco PLC (BP)

Royal Dutch Petroleum Co. (RD)

Chevron-Texaco (CVX)

Sunoco Inc. (SUN)

Conoco Inc. (COC)*

Exxon-Mobil Corporation (XOM)

Total Fina Elf S.A. (TOT)

Kerr-McGee Corporation (KMG)

Unocal Corporation (UCL)

Occidental Petroleum Corporation (OXY)

USX-Marathon Group (MRO)

Phillips Petroleum Corporation (P)*

---

* As of December 17, 2001, Phillips and Conoco had agreed to merge, but the transaction had not been completed.

major business. The index is clearly international and offers a well-diversified capsule of the business, including that of chemical companies such as Occidental Petroleum, a leader in the chlorinated chemical business. This section provides capsules of each company, emphasizing their potential strengths and weaknesses, their business plans, and their ability to execute and communicate.

Exxon-Mobil (NYSE:XOM)

This is the world's largest oil company and came from the merger of Exxon and Mobil, two of the original Standard Oil companies. This behemoth is involved in every phase of the oil business and has a market capitalization of nearly $300 billion. It has over 21 billion barrels of oil equivalents in reserves; has 40,000 gas stations around the world, with 16,000 in the United States; and can refine 6 million barrels of oil per day. In the year 2000 it produced nearly $233 billion in revenue. And in the first quarter of 2001 alone, it showed profits of $4.6 billion. In comparison, IBM's market capitalization in July 2001 was $188 billion, and its year 2000 revenues were $88 billion.

This is a company that grows by mergers and acquisitions, but does not like to keep fat around. When it merged with Mobil, the combined entity would eventually shed 14,000 jobs by the end of 2002. Exxon does not like to rest on its laurels, thus has continued aggressive exploration in Africa and, most important, Russia, where the vast and still relatively untapped reserves are waiting to be harvested.

Exxon is also big on natural gas and is really the traditional benchmark for the sector—not just because of its size, but because it is the largest survivor of the Standard Oil Trust and thus has encapsulated the business model of the original giant company in the sector. Exxon knows how to do business in the whole world and has survived major problems in the past, such as the Exxon *Valdez* environmental disaster in Alaska. The company has excellent public relations and funds a program to preserve the tiger from extinction, which it uses as its mascot and emblem.

While this may seem insignificant, it is actually a brilliant strategy for both erasing the *Valdez* memory and building a brand, especially when one takes into account that the *Valdez* incident faded from the news, despite the environmental damage possibly leaving permanent reminders of the hazards of the energy industry. But when a child goes to a zoo and a huge exhibit with wonderful beasts is being paid for by Exxon, that logo, which is strategically placed in that park, tends to etch itself in the mind of the consumer, with very positive implications. Exxon continued its campaign to clean up its image after its 1998 gaffe when CEO Lee Raymond upset environmentalists by publicly questioning the global warming theory, which in the mild winter of 2001 is becoming harder to refute. In 2001 Exxon joined the California Fuel Cell Partnership, a group looking for alternatives and additives to the internal combustion engine.

Exxon is also very active globally, with long-term ties to Saudi Arabia, which may be an emerging weakness in the changing marketplace and which may make Exxon a less influential player than it once was. Its fate, however, could be like OPEC's—still the leader, but certainly a diminished one that for once truly has to notice what the competition is doing. Nevertheless, the company has huge resources and knows how to make them work efficiently.

Exxon is the benchmark because it is the biggest oil company in the world. Regardless of what the market throws at it, either in the field of public relations or after major problems like the 11-million-barrel Alaskan oil spill, the company delivers. And whether you personally like what the company does or not, as an investor you must admit that it does all that is possible to deliver the goods and to enhance shareholder value.

A Glance at Revenues and Earnings

The revenues and net earnings numbers clearly support the notion that Exxon-Mobil delivers. Table 5.4 shows the financial performance of the company over the 13 quarters that began in March 1998 and ran until March 2001. Note that in a bad year like 1998, Exxon-Mobil still made money, even in a declining revenue and earnings environment. Also note the acceleration in earnings from the December 1998 lows at 39 cents per share, as the company put on a nine-quarter burst of sequentially rising earnings. More important, the company delivered rising earnings even as its revenues were slightly flat in some of the quarters. That is the sign of a well-run, efficient company and is a distinctive characteristic of the big oil companies in comparison to technology companies, which are often judged on their top line or

Table 5.4: *Three years and one quarter of Exxon-Mobil revenues and earnings, courtesy of* Market Guide.

Revenues (Millions of U.S. Dollars)

Quarters	1998	1999	2000	2001
March	43,594	38,682	54,081	57,300
June	42,598	43,277	55,956	
September	41,982	48,986	58,568	
December	41,468	54,582	64,143	
TOTAL	169,642	185,527	232,748	

Earnings Per Share

Quarters	1998	1999	2000	2001
March	0.730	0.420	0.860	1.420
June	0.630	0.560	1.130	
September	0.540	0.620	1.158	
December	0.391	0.650	1.400	
TOTAL	2.291	2.250	4.548	

revenue growth. If Exxon-Mobil can deliver both sequential revenue and earnings growth, then it is a bonus. But long-term investors need to focus more on the earnings, since that is where the dividends come from.

Intermediate-term investors should focus on both the charts and the top- and bottom-line numbers, looking for sequential growth in both. In the chapter on technical and fundamental analysis we will go into how to make even more discerning comparisons about company fundamentals, based on performance relative to the industry, as well as to the market.

Where Does Exxon Do Business, and How Much of It Comes from What Branches of Its Empire?

It is important to use Exxon-Mobil's business distribution, both in its business mix and its geographical sense, to cull potential benchmarks from which to develop our successful business model.

Exxon-Mobil has operations in over 200 countries. The company has oil and gas assets in Angola, Australia, Argentina, Azerbaijan, Cameroon, Canada, Chad, Equatorial Guinea, France, Germany, Indonesia, Italy, Japan, Kazakhstan, Malaysia, the Netherlands, Nigeria, Norway, Papua New Guinea, Qatar, Thailand, the U.K., the United States (including the Gulf of Mexico), Venezuela, and Yemen. Over 30 percent of its business comes from the United States, with the second largest portion, over 40 percent, being spread around the world. Japan, the United Kingdom, and Canada bring up the rear.

The fact that the United States makes up one-third of Exxon's business is positive, because the U.S. economy, as measured by GDP, continues to show long-term growth potential, guaranteeing some kind of baseline sales action for Exxon, even in a significant economic slowdown. This was quite apparent when the company reported earnings for its June quarter and missed earnings estimates by 2 cents, in July 2001. The total earnings for the quarter were still $4.46 billion. Most interesting is that Exxon stated that the miss was due to merger-related charges, not to a weak economy. This is a clear sign of a well-managed company with a well-established business model and management team. Another favorable aspect of the business mix is apparent when Canada, the U.K., and Japan are added. This means that nearly 60 percent of Exxon's business is located in developed countries, whose automobile consumption and general energy needs are likely to remain relatively steady due to their high degree of economic activity.

The company's main area of activity is downstream, which refers to marketing operations such as gas stations and convenience stores. This 80 percent of sales nearly dwarfs its upstream revenues from exploration, drilling, transport, and refining operations. It is obvious from these figures that selling oil and gas products is much more profitable than looking for oil or gas and refining it. And the rationale is sensible. The supply-and-demand scenario for the marketing side is less volatile than for the upstream side of the equation, where market forces are more likely to dominate matters. Consumers and businesses are always going to need fuel for their vehicles, as well as for machinery, technology, and climate control. Economic slowdowns usually lead to stockpiling of inventory, which can sometimes take several months to work off. But the downstream companies will still have business, especially when they have convenience stores at their gas stations and offer other services at truck stops such as banking, hygiene, and temporary lodging.

BP (NYSE:BP)

British Petroleum is the number-three integrated oil company in the world. But its profile and, to some degree, its results are quite different from Exxon-Mobil's, making it a great company to know. The British government was a partial owner of BP until 1996. Just like Exxon, BP—as it is now—is the result of a merger with another Standard Oil subsidiary of old, Amoco, which was Standard Oil of Indiana. BP expanded further, with a later purchase of Atlantic Richfield; this brought the popular ARCO brand into BP's empire. BP did the right things, as Amoco had rich international reserves of oil and gas, while ARCO's fleet of retail stations improved the potential for downstream income.

BP has proven reserves of about 15 billion barrels of oil equivalent, compared to Exxon's 21 billion barrels. BP's total includes large Alaskan holdings that have helped make it the number one U.S. oil and gas producer. BP also has significant production activities in Canada, the Gulf of Mexico, the North Sea, and Trinidad. BP owns 29,000 service stations worldwide, including more than

17,100 in the United States. Also a top refiner (2.9 million barrels of oil per day capacity) and manufacturer of petrochemicals and specialty chemicals, BP has expanded with the acquisition of motor oil–maker Burma Castrol.

The comparison between BP and Exxon-Mobil is quite clear. Exxon has more reserves, more gas stations, and a greater refinery capacity. Exxon has fewer gas stations in the United States, but its U.S. sales in 2000 were almost identical to BP's. This suggests that either its gas stations are in better locations or it has a better ability to increase sales by better promotions, higher prices, or the ability to piggyback gasoline purchases onto soft drinks and other convenience store products.

Where Exxon clearly becomes number one is in its global coverage of gas stations. It receives 27 percent of its sales from Japan, Canada, and the U.K., which means that its share of sales from developed countries with a larger automobile-driving population is higher. And since most of the profits and sales come from gasoline, this is Exxon's edge.

BP derived 21 percent of its year 2000 sales from a combination of power production and natural gas and oil exploration and production—a more cyclical, more expensive, and less profitable business than that of retailing and marketing of gasoline. Exxon's upstream operations are only 9 percent of its sales, as it concentrates on areas that make the most money.

BP has an interesting and distinguishing characteristic, however, as it has tended over its history to diversify its holdings with investments that are at least on the surface totally unrelated to the energy game—such as when it bought a Purina animal feed unit in the 1970s. BP did exit the nutrition business in the early 1990s. In 2000, BP's involvement with power generation was significant. But in 2001, BP sold much of its power generation to a German utility company and expanded its gasoline station network in Germany. This may be a good step in the long run, given the Enron-related difficulties in the power-generation sector.

BP's diverse investment portfolio in 2001 also included a biotech company called Vysis (Nasdaq:VYSI), which was finally purchased by Abbott Labs. Vysis makes products that test for cancer and birth defects. This investment makes more sense for a company like Abbott than for a large oil company, in the eyes of Wall Street. Sure, there is always the potential to put biotechnology together with oil; after all, in the early days of biotech, Exxon's development of oil-eating bacteria to clean up oil spills greatly contributed to the credibility of the biotech sector. But at a time when energy consumption continues to steadily increase and OPEC is finding rivals, Wall Street is focusing on oil companies that act like oil companies, not like diversified mutual funds. And in all fairness, Vysis came along with the Amoco deal.

But on July 4, 2001—true to form—BP bought a huge solar cell production plant from Agere Systems. Agere Systems is a spin-off from Lucent Technologies and makes chip systems and other electronics. This made BP's lead in solar power even bigger, with the company accounting for 20 percent of the solar cell market. This could prove to be a very decisive step in the company's future, but not one that impressed Wall Street much in the present.

BP's stock is not usually among the most vibrant in the energy sector, which implies that Wall Street is not that comfortable with the way BP runs its business, in comparison to a company like Chevron-Texaco. This is not to say that BP is not an excellent company or that solar energy is a loser. It is an illustration of the mindset that an investor has to develop. Wall Street wants oil companies to be oil companies and, to a certain degree, chemical companies— not semiconductor companies, not solar power companies, and most definitely not food companies. BP continues to stray from the fold, although it is more focused now on its core businesses than in past decades. And only time will tell whether BP was right in making a big move to solar power. As an investor, I am willing to watch BP for signs of improvement, as I own Texaco and consider Exxon-Mobil and Chevron interesting stocks. When BP begins to deliver on solar power, the stock could well begin to show it. If BP stock begins to act right, it then becomes worth investing in. For now, Wall Street seems to regard BP as a large oil company that is not particularly well focused.

It is important for investors to deduce what Wall Street thinks about a company. Stocks move because big money either buys or sells them. The rest of us can do little more than learn to discern the signs of big money moving in or out of stocks. When big money streams in, we want to follow. And when it shows signs of trying to sneak out the back door, we should be early rather than late in leaving the party. This means that whether we like it or not, we have to be in tune with what Wall Street thinks. It doesn't mean that we can't be independent thinkers, but we have to learn to predict what Wall Street will do when faced with a particular set of circumstances. In the chapter on technical analysis, I will expand further on this area.

Royal Dutch Petroleum (NYSE:RD) and Total Fina Elf (NYSE:TOT)

Royal Dutch/Shell is a truly international player and operates in more than 135 countries. It has major oil and gas interests in Argentina, Australia, Bangladesh, Brunei, Canada, China, Colombia, Denmark, Egypt, Gabon, Germany, Kazakhstan, Malaysia, the Netherlands, New Zealand, Nigeria, Norway, Oman, Pakistan, Peru, the Philippines, Russia, Syria, United Arab Emirates, the United Kingdom, the United States, and Venezuela.

Shell is a visible player in the United States, even though only 17 percent of its year 2000 sales came from there. In contrast, nearly 46 percent of sales came from Europe and 69 percent of all sales come from the Eastern Hemisphere. But its sales as a whole were almost identical to those of BP in the amount of money generated—nearly $150 billion in the year 2000. Again, note that the largest portion of sales comes from oil-related products, while the

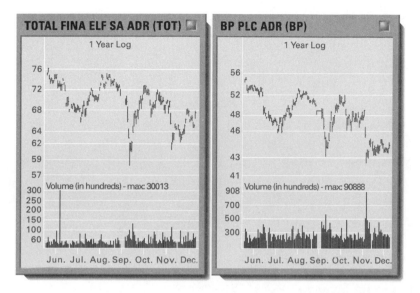

Figure 5.3: *Total Fina Elf (NYSE:TOT; left) and BP (NYSE:BP; right), courtesy of Telescan.*

remainder is divided along the traditional subsectors like chemicals, power generation, and exploration.

The knock on Shell, as a company, is that due to its far-flung corporate structure, it has a great deal of difficulty being nimble when it comes to making deals. This was quite clear when it botched the takeover of Barrett Resources, finally losing out to Williams Companies in a process that was not run smoothly by Shell, which clearly should have had the upper hand, given its size and resources.

Total Fina Elf has operations in more than 100 countries, and this is where we begin to note the difference between the very large multinational companies and those that are not so large. Its sales, compared in 2000, were roughly 70 percent of those reported by BP and Royal Dutch/Shell, at roughly $108 billion. Its North American presence was even more subdued, due to the sale of its U.S. gas stations and refining operations to Ultramar Diamond

Shamrock, which eventually sold its assets to Valero Energy. Instead, Elf made its move into Iran, Russia, and more geographically strategic locations with high levels of reserves. This kind of strategy is sensible for a company whose size makes it an unlikely player in the very large stakes game between Exxon-Mobil, Royal Dutch, Chevron-Texaco, and, to a certain degree, BP.

Figure 5.3 provides another interesting glimpse into the mind of Wall Street. Both BP and Total have a strong presence in Russia. But Total is a more focused oil company, while Wall Street views BP as less than focused. As a result, on December 17, 2001, when OPEC began to leak its intentions to back out of the production-cut deal, Total got a much healthier bounce than BP did.

Chevron-Texaco (NYSE:CVX)

Texaco and Chevron were the number-two and number-three oil companies in the United States in 2001 prior to their merger, which cemented their position as number two in the United States, with just under $100 billion of combined sales in the year 2000. After their merger, they would become the number-four integrated oil company in the world, behind Exxon-Mobil, Royal Dutch, and BP. The combination brought together a potential 47,000 gas stations around the world, as well as nearly 10 billion barrels of oil in reserves, huge refining potential, and 9.5 trillion feet of natural gas that would be courtesy of Chevron—which, when combined with Texaco's 25 percent stake in the beleaguered energy trader and power-producer Dynegy, had the makings of being a serious player in natural gas.

Chevron had a well-developed U.S. presence, while Texaco had a significant position in the U.K.—an interesting observation, given the company's humble beginnings in Texas, where a wildcatter and a financier developed an incredibly successful symbiotic partnership with an incredible amount of synergy. There is something of a legacy from that initial relationship when we look at the merger and why it made sense, as it brought together the more traditional Chevron and the more progressive Texaco.

This merger also made sense from a business model stand-point for Texaco, whose gas stations and refineries in the United States were all part of joint ventures with Royal Dutch and Saudi Aramco. Once again, note the international and furtive nature of the oil industry, where anyone can join hands with anyone else, regardless of politics or geography, if the deal makes sense. Further research also revealed that Texaco and Chevron own a 50-50 refining and marketing venture called Caltex, with operations in Africa, Asia, and the Middle East.

Chevron has integrated oil operations in the United States and more than 100 other countries and territories. It has major exploration and development operations in Angola, Argentina, Australia, Azerbaijan, Canada, China, Colombia, Congo, Indonesia, Kazakhstan, the Netherlands, Nigeria, Norway, Papua New Guinea, Qatar, Thailand, and Venezuela, as well as in the U.K.'s North Sea and the Persian Gulf. In the United States it has holdings in the Gulf of Mexico, the Rocky Mountains, California, and Texas. Texaco's holdings are also quite broad, and its goal is to increase its drilling and exploration activities as a result of the merger.

A look at the sales breakdown for both companies suggests that Chevron derives less of its sales from refined products and more from the sale of crude oil. This is the opposite of Texaco, which earns 70 percent of its money from downstream work, especially from its huge gas station and convenience store network. Texaco also gets 30 percent of its sales from power- and exploration-related areas. With Chevron's huge natural gas reserves and Texaco's power infrastructure, the merger could create a natural gas powerhouse on top of a major oil company.

Repsol YPF (NYSE:REP)

Repsol is the largest oil company in Spain, and it expanded to South America by buying Argentina's YPF. But severe and potentially long-lasting financial problems for Argentina could be very costly to this company—a fact that did not escape investors in

2001, as the stock was steadily sold. Repsol has proven reserves of 4.8 billion barrels of oil equivalent, mostly in Latin America, the Middle East, and North Africa, as well as over 7,000 gas stations. Here again, the company shows that it has more geographical risk, as it owns reserves in both Latin America and the Middle East, with little elsewhere. Over half the gas stations are in Spain, with the remainder in South America. Its main target area for growth is Latin America. Eighty-five percent of Repsol's sales come from Spain and Argentina, with 67 percent of all sales coming from refining and marketing.

Amerada Hess (NYSE:AHC)

Amerada Hess thinks of itself as a "super independent." The company bought Triton Energy in July 2001 in order to expand its upstream operations, especially its exploration operations, which were expected to be able to deliver an increase from 435,000 barrels of oil per day to 600,000 per day by 2003. At first blush, it would seem as if the breakdown of this company's operations is similar to that of its larger competitors, since refining and marketing in the United States are worth 75 percent of sales, while Europe is worth 25 percent of sales. But what is most remarkable is that a full 25 percent of its $12 billion in sales for 2000 came from exploration. More important is that nearly one-third of sales came from natural gas, while 18 percent came from crude oil sales themselves and 45 percent came from petroleum products, including gasoline. Amerada Hess has over 900 gas stations, mostly in the Eastern United States, with a significant number of them providing the added convenience store revenues.

Amerada Hess is an interesting company to keep track of, since it has aggressively expanded into natural gas and oil exploration. The key here is the expansion into natural gas, which is an increasingly popular fuel. This suggests that a rise in the price of natural gas would likely be a positive factor for these shares. The move into Triton says that management has carefully studied the market and sees that Exxon-Mobil and the larger companies really have a stranglehold on the profitable downstream side of the business. Management also recognized that consolidation is inevitable and that by expanding into the exploration niche, it could delay or totally avoid being taken over in the near future, while at the same time recognizing that once its consolidation with Triton is finalized, it would then become a much more attractive company for a major to buy or merge with. That could set up either a profitable spin-off or a profitable asset sale, even if the whole company were not put up for sale.

Conoco (NYSE:COC)

On November 18, 2001, Conoco and Phillips announced their intention to join forces in a $35 billion merger of equals. The union would create the third-largest integrated oil company in the United States and the sixth largest in the world. The new company would carry the name ConocoPhillips and would boast a wide range of properties in a broad geographical area, including Alaska, Canada, the lower 48 states, the North Sea, Venezuela, China, the Timor Sea, Indonesia, Vietnam, the Middle East, Russia, and the Caspian area. The three incredibly strong points are the potentially huge growth areas of Alaska, Russia, and the Caspian Sea; the latter is a large target of the Russian oil industry, where a great deal of pipeline capacity was being aimed and positioned in the early 21st century.

ConocoPhillips will operate or have equity interests in 19 refineries in the United States, the U.K., Ireland, Germany, the Czech Republic, and Malaysia, with a refining capacity of 2.6 million barrels a day. It will also have a strong marketing presence in the United States. Conoco, on its own, operated more than 7,000 gas stations in the United States, Europe, and Thailand, while Phillips, after its previous merger with Tosco, had 11,000 gas stations and convenience stores. This number will likely be reduced, due to overlap in certain markets and regulatory and antitrust concerns. But the bottom line is that this merger created a significant competitor in the downstream marketing segment to Exxon-Mobil and Chevron-Texaco.

Conoco was a unit of chemical giant DuPont and had proven reserves of about 3.7 billion barrels of oil equivalent in Europe, Southeast Asia, and the Americas, prior to the merger announcement. The company added to its stockpile of reserves by more than 1 billion barrels of oil equivalent in 2001, by buying Gulf Canada Resources. Conoco also stood out from the pack because it runs about 6,000 miles of U.S. pipeline, a major contributor of diversification to the merger with Phillips. Conoco also had power plant–building and power-trading operations, which are likely to be enhanced because ConocoPhillips will continue Phillips's equity participation in the natural gas gathering and processing joint venture Duke Energy Field Service and in the chemicals and plastics joint venture Chevron Phillips Chemicals.

Prior to the merger, Conoco aggressively entered the power-generation game. A weak point of the merger is that Conoco owned 30 percent of the Saudi Arabia natural gas development that was opened to foreign companies in 2001, a potential problem area for the companies involved.

Phillips Petroleum (NYSE:P)

Phillips Petroleum is another highly recognized American brand that, prior to the merger with Conoco, was already on its way to changing its business and diversifying away from a pure dependence on exploration and marketing, as well as cementing its position in the lucrative retail market through acquisitions. This aggressive expansion was more of a necessity than anything else, as the company had little choice, given that the larger companies in the sector were all merging and creating an almost insurmountable competitive environment in the lucrative gasoline retail market. Philips explores for, produces, refines, transports, and markets oil and natural gas in 20 countries.

Phillips doubled its proven reserves to 5 billion barrels of oil equivalent by acquiring ARCO's Alaska properties, which had to be sold when BP acquired ARCO. More aggressive and perhaps timely, given the events in California, Phillips merged its gas-gathering and processing business with that of Duke Energy, and it combined its chemicals division with that of Chevron. Phillips expanded its refining and marketing operations by buying Tosco. This kind of joint venture and partnership formation tends to spread the risk, as well as expand the customer and relationship base for the company, which are both excellent long-term benefits of joint ventures and partnerships. This kind of long-term thinking is a superb characteristic of management and made the merger with Conoco a sensible undertaking.

Phillips showed that its management is on the ball when it did the right things at the right time in response to the emerging trends in energy. The company immediately grasped the need for both mergers and acquisitions, undertaking a final huge deal in which it lost a good deal of autonomy, while eventually realizing survival and a potential increase in profits from refining, a larger retail base, and power generation.

Unocal (NYSE:UCL)

Unocal was a fixture in the California landscape when I grew up in Los Angeles. Its sponsorship of televised Los Angeles Dodgers games and its colorful orange and blue logos with the slogan "The Spirit of 76" to accompany them on its gas stations made the company seem like an entity with a long future. But trouble started in the 1980s when takeover artist T. Boone Pickens tried to take over the company, which defended itself by buying stock back with $5.5 billion of borrowed money. Saddled with debt, the company struggled and in 1994 pleaded no contest to accusations of having contaminated groundwater in California. By 1997, as the case settled, Unocal began to divest itself of its refining and marketing operations and became a pure exploration company.

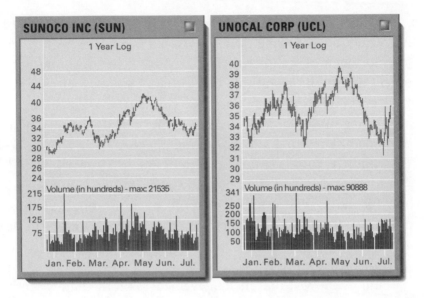

Figure 5.4: *Comparison of Sunoco (NYSE:SUN; left) to Unocal (NYSE: UCL; right). Courtesy of Telescan.*

As a result, it is now one of the largest U.S.-based independent oil and gas exploration and production companies, with crude oil and natural gas properties in the Gulf of Mexico, Asia, Africa, and Latin America and proven reserves of 6.5 trillion cubic feet of natural gas and 632 million barrels of crude oil and condensate. Seventy-one percent of its reserves are in Asia and the lower 48 United States. The company produces geothermal energy in Indonesia and the Philippines and manufactures petroleum coke and specialty minerals. Unocal's Global Trade unit also trades oil and natural gas commodities. Sixty-five percent of its sales come from petroleum, while a significant 28 percent come from natural gas.

Sunoco (NYSE:SUN)

Sunoco is a large independent integrated oil company, with a largely regional U.S. base of operations. SUN operates 5 refineries and 10,000 miles of oil pipelines, with 17 terminals, and 4,100 gas stations and convenience stores. SUN is going against the grain by increasing its participation in the chemical sector, from which only 5 percent of its $12 billion in 2000 sales came.

The company spent much of the 1990s restructuring, having exited its oil exploration and production activities to focus on refining, marketing, and chemicals. The stock tends to lag behind the rest of the sector in rising markets, due to its regional tendency and its apparent focus on increasing its dependence on the very cyclical and relatively low-profit-margin chemical business. Sixty-five percent of its sales come from refining and marketing in the Northeastern United States, while 17 percent come from its Midwestern operations.

Kerr-McGee (NYSE:KMG)

Kerr-McGee is a nearly pure play on exploration and chemicals, with a much smaller sales total of nearly $4 billion—less than even the smaller integrated oil companies like Phillips before its merger. The nonintegrated oil and gas company has proven reserves of 1.1 billion barrels of oil equivalent and conducts nearly 90 percent of its business in the United States and U.K. Kerr-McGee explores for and produces oil and gas mainly in the Gulf of Mexico and the U.K.'s North Sea, as well as in Africa, Asia, Europe, and Latin America. The company's main focus of expansion is in chemicals, where it is a major producer of titanium dioxide (a white pigment used in paint, plastics, and paper). KMG sold off its noncore assets to concentrate on chemicals, where it competes with DuPont.

Kerr suffers from two weaknesses, in the eyes of Wall Street. First, it is a smaller company than the ever-growing majors. And second, it is increasingly dependent on the cyclical chemical business, although it has become very aggressive in its movement in deep-water exploration and the natural gas business. But because the market likes oil companies with large retail operations and gas stations, KMG is rarely a stock market leader. KMG is looked upon as a chemical company that uses petroleum as its material source. Its products are more directly dependent upon businesses, rather than on individual motorists who have to drive cars to get places and so must spend money, and thus its revenue and earnings streams are much more cyclical than the majors.

Occidental Petroleum (NYSE:OXY)

Occidental Petroleum is almost a pure play in oil and gas exploration, with 72 percent of its sales coming from exploration and production, while 28 percent of its revenues come from basic chemicals, plastics, and petrochemicals. It has proven reserves of 2.2 billion barrels of oil equivalent in the United States, the Middle East, and Latin America. Key subsidiaries include Occidental Chemical (OxyChem), which produces acids and chlorine, along with specialty products (chlorinated aromatics). Just like others in the field, OXY continues to expand its infrastructure and owns oil- and gas-producer Altura Energy, a former partnership of BP and Shell Oil, as well as 76 percent of Oxy Vinyls, the number-one producer of polyvinyl chloride (PVC) resin in North America. Occidental also owns 30 percent of Equistar Chemicals, a producer of ethylene, propylene, and ethylene oxide.

Occidental is a highly focused company that sold off many nonstrategic assets, including a pipeline, in order to buy oil and gas reserves from the U.S. government. But OXY is a well-disciplined company with a very well-managed revenues and earnings stream, putting it in the top tier of nonretail-market-oriented oil companies.

USX-Marathon Group (NYSE:MRO)

USX-Marathon Group is a subsidiary of USX Corporation. USX-U.S. Steel is the other subsidiary. MRO is worth 80 percent of the business to the mother company, while the steel side makes up the rest. Marathon explores for, develops, and produces oil and gas in 11 countries. It has net proven reserves of 1.2 billion barrels of oil equivalent, with 57 percent of reserves in the United States, giving this company a great advantage. MRO owns 62 percent of Marathon Ashland Petroleum (MAP), a joint venture with Ashland that has a network of gas stations that I described earlier. In the United States, MAP operates pipelines, terminals, seven refineries, and more than 5,900 retail outlets under such brands as SuperAmerica and Speedway. Marathon is also an investor in power-generation projects.

Marathon is like a souped-up version of the majors, as it tends to exaggerate the major underlying trend of the sector. This means that the stock is well suited for more aggressive intermediate- and short-term trading.

China's Big Players

Aside from the Amex Oil Index, I also want to summarize other large companies around the world because they are often involved in joint ventures and partnerships with the large U.S. and European multinationals. Among the more interesting companies are China's two largest and publicly traded oil companies, whose growing influence is not totally noted in the relatively low trading volume of their American Depository Receipts (ADRs). But their presence in world markets gives investors a truly international opportunity to invest in the energy markets.

China National Petroleum Corporation (CNPC) subsidiary PetroChina, whose ADRs trade on the NYSE under the symbol PTR, is the largest of the two. PetroChina produces two-thirds of China's oil and gas and has proven reserves of 11 billion barrels of oil and 33 trillion cubic feet of natural gas. It engages in domestic exploration; owns nearly 7,000 miles of pipeline in China; and operates 29 refineries, 17 chemical plants, and 4,700 gas stations. It also markets through another 6,600 jointly owned or franchise stations. PetroChina (NYSE:PTR) was created in 2000 as a separate company to manage domestic operations of parent CNPC, which handles international activities.

China Petroleum and Chemical formed Sinopec Corp., spun off bits and pieces of the government-owned integrated oil company, and sold them to the public. One of them is Sinopec Beijing Yanhua Petrochemical Company Ltd., whose ADRs trade on the New York Stock Exchange under the symbol BYH.

BYH ADRs tend to exaggerate the oil sector's trends, both on the up and to the down side. For aggressive investors, this could be the stock to trade, while at the same time it paid a 5-percent dividend. PTR is a more sedate stock, as the company delivered $6.7 billion worth of earnings in the year 2000 on $29.7 billion worth of revenues. Those are impressive numbers, even by U.S. standards.

Sinopec Corp. produces oil and gas from six fields in China; it has reserves of more than 3 billion barrels of oil equivalent. The company sells its refined products under the Sinopec brand at more than 13,700 company-owned gas stations throughout East and South China. Sinopec Corp.'s petrochemical products include synthetic resins, monomers and polymers, and intermediate products.

Where these companies and their subsidiaries become important is that they are China's gateway to the global oil and capital markets, as their stocks become currency and leverage with which to raise money and eventually to craft joint ventures and partnerships like the rest of the international stocks in the sector. Earlier, I noted that the Chinese are a potential force to reckon with in the international oil markets, and this is the centerpiece of that strategy: two very large and well-run companies. In June 2001 Sinopec's petrochemical company bought National Star, a refinery operation, from the Chinese government for $770 million, in order to diversify its earnings channels.

Sinopec Group posted profits of $16.1 billion in the year 2000, and its half-year profits for 2001 were $967 million. The company became listed in China in July of 2001. The Chinese IPO proceeds were to be used to fund the National Star acquisition and to build a pipeline.

This is a steadily moving but very interesting set of developments, as it shows that the Chinese are getting a great deal of business advice from Hong Kong, where Western-style markets and, to a great degree, British culture are still ingrained. I look for Chinese influence to increase in the oil markets as time passes. The lure for Western oil companies to have access to the huge potential gasoline market in China is attractive, while at the same time China's own desire to export its culture and to bring back hard global currency to fuel its own economy complements the equation and sets up the energy market for a very interesting set of dynamics.

Summary

This chapter provides a clear window into how the major oil stocks operate. There are three basic kinds of integrated oil companies: those with a great deal of emphasis on refining and marketing, those with emphasis on exploration and chemicals, and those that tend to do a little of each. The market seems to reward companies that are large, have a significant presence in refining and marketing, and have a major presence in the United States and the U.K.

The oil index is a basket of large companies and provides a snapshot of the sector, but it is not complete. For example, it excludes some companies that operate in Latin America, Japan, and China, which are areas of huge potential growth.

One of the most interesting findings in this chapter is BP's interest in solar energy and the market's apparent disinterest in the alternative energy source. This is manifested in the relatively flat performance of the stock, compared to rivals like Texaco and Exxon-Mobil, whose reliance on the refining and marketing of gasoline makes them very profitable.

Both long-term investors and traders can find what they are looking for in the integrated oil sector. This chapter provided hints for both disciplines and what to look for in these companies' stocks.

Finally, note that Russia and China continue to make inroads into the global oil market. China joined the World Trade Organization in 2001 and trades its oil stocks on major exchanges around the world. It is ahead of Russia in its degree of international sophistication in many ways that relate to this sector.

Russia used guile and opportunity in December 2001 to place itself as a serious rival to OPEC. Its actions were quite well received by the West and should pay off handsomely for Russia in the form of increased interest by Western oil companies in developing a more modern infrastructure for the Russian oil industry.

It is important for investors to keep these two former communist countries in mind as they invest in this sector. For the times have truly changed.

CHAPTER

6

The Oil Service Sector

In chapter 5 we examined the integrated oil stocks, representing companies whose main business lines were quite diversified and were geared toward the delivery of products to businesses and consumers. The prototype integrated oil company is Exxon-Mobil, whose huge network of gas stations and convenience stores has made it an internationally recognized juggernaut. Other interesting integrated oils include Occidental Petroleum, whose main area of business is petrochemicals.

In this chapter I examine the oil service sector, which is composed of companies that do the fieldwork, usually under contract to the integrated oil companies. This group includes the oil drillers, as well as those companies that build the infrastructure required for exploring, extracting, processing, and transporting oil and natural gas. Oil service consists of a highly interesting group of companies, whose focus has as much to do with technical, logistical, and engineering matters as it does with geology. This is a huge sector and in no way could it be covered completely in a single chapter if I provided in-depth profiles of each company. But thanks to indexing, we can get a clear glimpse into the sector.

The Philadelphia Oil Service Index (OSX) represents this group well, but is by no means all there is to the sector. Some companies are in similar businesses or in synergistic portions of the business. As I analyze these companies, I will identify their particular niche, as well as their potential to be predictors of the overall trend in the sector and perhaps, to some degree, in the economy. Table 6.1 lists the companies in the oil service index.

The Science of Oil Wells

Once the location for a well has been identified, the work truly begins. As in chapter 5, my goal here is to summarize the basics of oil drilling; this background will help you make better sense of what companies in the sector do. This is a bare-bones basic primer and is not meant to be a graduate-level course on geology, engineering, or physics.

Well drilling integrates physics, engineering, software, hardware, and a great deal of knowledge about rock formations. An oil well is in fact the only connection or conduit between the oil reservoir and the surface. The two most important factors that face drillers and designers are that the well must be built sturdy enough to last at least fifty years and be flexible enough to adapt to new technologies.

More important, drilling must be gentle enough on the rock formation not to collapse the well, must assure the maximum productive capacity of the well, and should not cause any external damage to the environment. This means that drilling problems must be anticipated prior to drilling, and any subsequent problems during the actual process must then be diagnosed, based on the pressure data that is transmitted from the bottom of the well to sensors located on the rig floor. The worst thing that could happen to an oil well, from an economic standpoint, is that the work has to be stopped after money has been spent. That is the reason for the development of advanced drilling technologies.

After the well has been drilled, it is lined with pipe, and the connection with the surface must be optimized. Completion requires fitting it with the right tubing or casing and then cementing it in place. Other steps include the installment of equipment to

Table 6.1: *The Philadelphia Oil Service Index*

Company	Symbol
Schlumberger Ltd.	NYSE:SLB
Smith International	NYSE:SII
Cooper Cameron	NYSE:CAM
Weatherford International	NYSE:WFT
Halliburton	NYSE:HAL
Baker Hughes	NYSE:BHI
Tidewater	NYSE:TDW
Transocean Sedco Forex	NYSE:RIG
Noble Drilling	NYSE:NE
Nabors Industries	NYSE:NBR
BJ Services Company	NYSE:BJS
Rowan Companies	NYSE:RDC
Global Santa Fe	NYSE:GSF
Varco International	NYSE:VRC
Global Industries Ltd.	Nasdaq:GLBL

"stimulate" the well, the process by which air or water is pumped into the well so that the oil moves into the casing and is forced to the surface.

The most advanced drilling techniques available in 2001 were developed in conjunction with the U.S. Department of Energy (DOE) and involve specialized drills that transmit location information to the surface by way of pressure pulses. In this fashion, the engineers and the drillers have a better idea about where they are and what adjustments, if any, have to be made. The DOE has contributed other developments since 1992, including advanced techniques of well stimulation.

Future goals include the ability to drill deeper, faster, and cheaper, with zero environmental damage.

What Are the Variables That Move the Energy Service Sector?

As with the integrated oil stocks, supply and demand rule. The slight difference is that the integrated oils have a bit of an easier time making money because most of them have gas stations and, to a lesser degree, chemical operations. The integrated oil companies with gas stations have a better cash flow and tend to weather the bad times less painfully than do companies in the oil service sector, because the latter are utterly dependent on economic conditions and oil demand for their business.

Figure 6.1, courtesy of James Williams and energyeconomist .com, shows a great relationship over 25 years between the price of oil and the number of active rigs. This information is released on a weekly basis by the U.S. Department of Energy and is fully charted and interpreted by Williams, whose subscription service is superb. The chart clearly shows that when the price of oil rises, the number of active rigs also rises, as demand increases. As with every market, there comes a turning point. When the rig count is high enough that oil is plentiful, the price of crude falls.

Figure 6.2 looks at the five-year period between 1996 and 2001 and shows the effects of the oil glut in 1997 and 1998, as the price of oil collapsed while the number of active rigs continued to rise. Eventually, the rig count bottomed and began to rise once again when the price of oil rose. Note how the change in the price of oil leads a change in the rig count.

Figure 6.3, when compared to figure 6.2, clearly shows the close correlation between the price of oil, the rig count, and the oil service industry. The OSX seemed to anticipate a change in the rig count in 1997, where it topped prior to the rig count, and in 2000, where it bottomed prior to the rig count. In 2001, the index

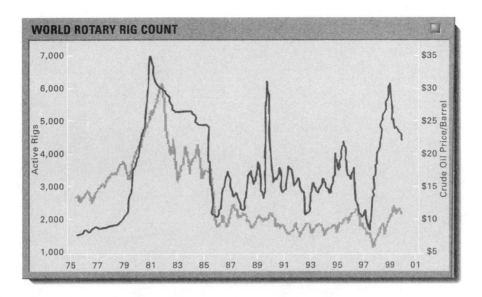

Figure 6.1: *World Rotary Rig Count, courtesy of www.energyeconomist .com.*

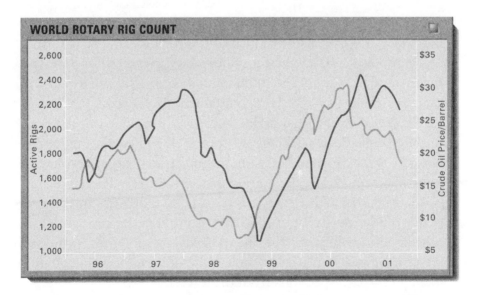

Figure 6.2: *World Rig Count 1996–2001, courtesy of www.energyeconomist .com.*

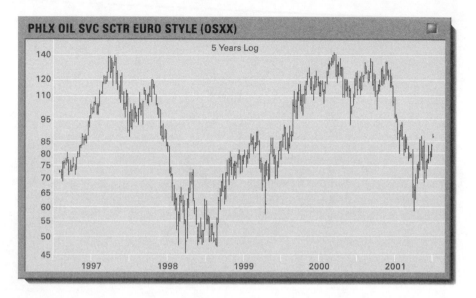

Figure 6.3: *The Philadelphia Oil Service Index (OSX) 1996–2001. Courtesy of Telescan.*

still predicted that rig counts were to fall, as indeed they continued to do, as OPEC cut production targets a total of four times.

In August 2001, a perfect opportunity presented itself to truly understand and apply the fundamentals of the oil market and the market's reactions to those fundamentals. In fact, this was a smaller version of the so-called Perfect Storm. Due to the politics of the Middle East, which at the time included escalating tensions between Israel and the Palestinians and Iraq's downing of a U.S. unmanned spy plane, the market was very jittery. There were also problems in the refinery sector, as CITGO had a fire in one of its major refineries that shut it down for months. Exxon-Mobil had scheduled maintenance for one of their key refineries in the midwestern United States at the same time, due to upcoming environmental impact inspections from the government.

As a result of all these factors, which came together simultaneously, the weekly API reports began to show a downward trend in gasoline inventory. This happened even as the driving season was

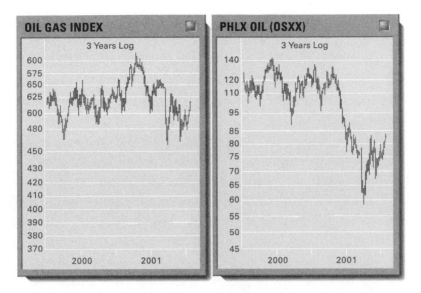

Figure 6.4: *Comparison of the Amex Oil Index (XOI; left) and the Philadelphia Oil Service Index (OSX; right) in December 2001.*

expected to wind down, which in fact it didn't to the degree that analysts had expected. And to add more fuel to the fire, August is also the time when oil investors begin to think about winter supplies of heating oil, which, of course, require full refinery capacity.

Investors began to buy the refiners and the integrated oil stocks, but ignored the oil service stocks, due to the continued economic slump in the United States and Japan, which had begun to spread to Europe. Figure 6.4 clearly shows that even as the XOI was beginning to creep toward new highs, the OSX was still struggling to find a bottom. The key here was that there was a bottleneck in the system, but not one that would likely spur the need for increased rig capacity. As a result, the refiners and marketers got the bounce, while the drillers and oil service remained in their slump.

But, as the chart clearly shows, the events of September 11 changed everything and created a whole new set of dynamics for the oil service sector. As a result of the war in Afghanistan, two things happened. Russia's role in global oil supplies became increasingly important, and the United States and Europe slowly but surely began to look to diversify their oil and natural gas supplies away from OPEC. Russia's vast oil and natural gas supplies and generally poor infrastructure, the market reasoned, would be a boom for the oil service industry, as demand for its products and services would increase. At the same time, the United States began to aggressively open its government-protected natural reserves in the Gulf of Mexico and the Rocky Mountains to exploration, doubly boosting the positive prospects for the sector. The net result was a significant improvement in the fundamentals for oil exploration, drilling, and service companies. Thus, the OSX bottomed in late September, along with the rest of the stock market, and mounted an impressive rally that was further fueled in December 2001 as economic statistics in the United States began to improve, and the allies won the war in Afghanistan.

The points to remember are:

1. Oil service stocks are more sensitive to the supply and demand of the economy than are integrated companies.

2. Changes in the trend of the oil service index are very sensitive to the number of active rigs and often precede changes in the trend of the rig count.

3. You should examine all the indexes, and only buy the one that shows strength.

4. The long-term fundamentals for the oil service index were improved by the rising tensions in the Middle East and Russia's increasingly important role in the global oil-and-natural-gas equation.

Who Should Own the Energy Service Sector?

The most important point to remember about this subsector of energy is that it is not an ideal buy-and-hold sector, because it is

Table 6.2: *Dividend yields in selected oil service stocks in August 2001.*

Company	Dividend Yield
Halliburton	1.57%
Smith International	None
Schlumberger	1.44%

extremely volatile and tends to exaggerate the major trend of the energy market. These companies don't have the luxury of running a fleet of convenience stores, where the price of a gallon of gas and its related profits are usually padded by the purchase of snacks, drinks, lottery tickets, and so on. The great thing about this sector, as figure 6.3 shows, is that it is influenced mainly by the supply and demand for oil, and when it trends, it tends to stay in the same trend for several weeks to months, and it conforms well to technical and fundamental analysis, as I will describe. This is an ideal sector for intermediate-term market timing, meaning for those investors who like to hold a position for several weeks to months.

In chapter 5, I noted that the integrated oil companies were more suited to the buy-and-hold method of investing, due to their dividend yields. Table 6.2 clearly shows that this is not the case with oil service, as Smith International, one of the better-known companies in the sector, doesn't even pay a dividend. This reinforces the notion that these are stocks to be owned in the timing portion of a diversified portfolio.

The general rules in timing the energy service sector are:

1. Examine the fundamentals of supply and demand in the oil sector.

2. Routinely scan the earnings and revenue trends of the companies on your list, which can start with those in the index, but should be expanded.

3. Pinpoint entry points by knowing which companies are in the best shape fundamentally, as a guide. But let the technicals guide where you make your buys. The stocks that come out of the gate best are likely to be the winners in the early going.

4. Be ready to sell, either into strength or as the market shows early signs of weakening.

How Much of a Portfolio Should Be Designated to Energy Service Stocks?

As a general rule, no more than 10 or 15 percent should be allotted to any sector, including energy, in a well-diversified portfolio that finds itself in a neutral market. However, energy service is a perfect component of the aggressive portion of any portfolio, and for very experienced investors it could at times be overweighted by more, if the sector is working well and the investor is nimble enough to know when to back out and do some selling.

One of the biggest lessons of how *not* to diversify a portfolio was learned by investors in the year 2000 bear market, as a common version of diversification was to be 100 percent invested in technology stocks, with Cisco, EBay, America Online, Texas Instruments, and other names making up the bulk of the portfolio. That is not diversification. That is what anyone with any sense would call a big mistake, which caused severe damage not just to morale, but to many people's retirement funds.

A good rule of thumb may be to make energy a maximum of 20 percent of the portfolio and to allocate one-third each to integrated oils, energy service, and natural gas, at a time when they are all working. At times when only one subsector is working or one is working better than the others, a slight overweighting can take place. More important for stock pickers is to pick the best stocks in the sector, a process that I will describe as we go along and in the chapter on technical and fundamental analysis.

Halliburton—The Bellwether

One of my favorite parts of writing this book was digging into a company's history. This was an excellent exercise, because it helped me put a human face on the business model and see why these companies act the way they do. What I found is that, in most cases, the personality of the founder is the main influence on how the company does business. And Halliburton, the biggest oil service company in the world, also sports one of the best stories of them all.

In 1919 Halliburton was formed from humble beginnings. Halliburton Oil Well Cementing Company was the backbone of the empire. A few years earlier Halliburton had figured out that by lining oil wells with cement, there was less seepage of oil into the water table and less chance of losing oil unnecessarily. The idea did not immediately catch on, but Halliburton patented it, and when it did catch on, he collected royalties. By 1924, he had convinced seven large oil companies to invest in the company and then took it public. Halliburton and his wife, Vida, were so committed to their business that they once pawned her wedding ring to keep the company going. She got her ring back, and the rest is history. The important lesson here is that Halliburton is about applied technology and engineering, which is the basis for the oil energy industry.

Halliburton has operations in 120 countries, had $11.9 billion in sales in the year 2000, and operates in two distinct units: the energy services unit, which accounted for 66 percent of sales, and the engineering and construction services unit. The company was best known in the late 1990s and early 2000 because Vice President Dick Cheney was the CEO, beginning in 1995. But the company also had a colorful beginning, as its founder Earle Halliburton proved that tenacity and a little vision could go a long way.

The energy services unit provides an entire spectrum of services, beginning with oil drilling and well cementing, to well completion. But the most interesting branch of Halliburton is Landmark Graphics, its high-technology subsidiary. Landmark makes software that allows for the integration of the energy exploration process with management of the reservoir. What this means is that the software pinpoints the best areas to explore, and once it helps scientists choose where to drill, it also decides whether the reservoir is worth drilling. As I discussed earlier, finding oil is not as important as being able to get it out of the ground and process it profitably.

Landmark's software can be networked so that more than one team can access the data simultaneously. Landmark's software continues to be enhanced and also offers the ability to produce models into which economic projections can be programmed. This means that the oil industry now goes into a find with a higher degree of certainty than ever, including whether the chances of profitability are high enough to spend resources on a potential field.

Halliburton's Fundamentals

As the largest company in its field, Halliburton's fundamentals are important and will serve as a benchmark for the rest of the sector. Table 6.3 illustrates the earnings and revenues for the company over 14 quarters.

The first thing to do is look at the overall trend of revenues and earnings, which for Halliburton during the period listed was negative. That raises some questions about the health of the company. The truth is that when we see a company like Halliburton, which has trouble in its earnings momentum, we should always ask, Is it the market or is it the company?

With Halliburton, it was a bit of both, and this is an important lesson to learn for both investors and companies. We know that 1999 and 2000 were good years for the energy sector. And as figure 6.5 shows, with the Oil Service Index and Halliburton side by side, the Oil Service Index got the better of the two. In fact, on December 9, 2001, Halliburton shares collapsed, as the company was on the losing side of a $30 million asbestos-related judgment that it had inherited when it bought Dresser Industries in 1998.

Table 6.3: *Halliburton's revenues and earnings from 1998 to June 2001.*

Revenues (Thousands of U.S. Dollars)

Quarters	1998	1999	2000	2001
March	4,255,000	3,261,000	2,859,000	3,144,000
June	4,585,000	3,053,000	2,868,000	3,339,000
September	4,224,000	2,973,000	3,024,000	
December	4,289,000	3,026,000	3,193,000	
TOTAL	17,353,000	12,313,000	11,944,000	

Earnings per Share

Quarters	1998	1999	2000	2001
March	0.460	0.120	0.060	0.200
June	0.550	0.120	0.120	0.330
September	−1.200	0.090	0.290	
December	0.150	0.060	−0.050	
TOTAL	−0.040	0.390	0.420	

This event had wide implications. First, it happened soon after the Enron debacle. And to Wall Street, it was too close a call to ask questions first and decide later. Here was another prominent Texas energy company with a huge problem, at first glance—and at second and third glance as well. And the market sold, and sold, and sold some more. The company assured investors that its insurance would cover the claims, but in the wake of the Enron story, no one listened, and the stock took a huge beating. The major ratings agencies immediately cut down the ratings on Halliburton's debt, and I began to look for reasons not to buy the stock.

I couldn't find any, as I went to the company's financials, so I bought after the dust settled near $13. I made the decision fully aware that other nasty surprises could pop up, and they did, as rumors circulated on the Internet about a possible bankruptcy.

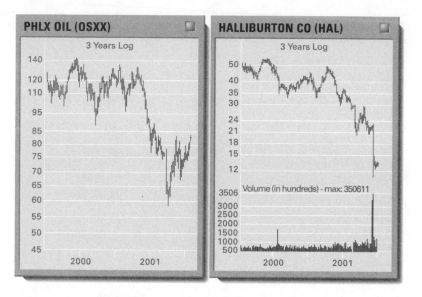

Figure 6.5: *The Philadelphia Oil Service Index (OSX; left) and Halliburton (NYSE:HAL; right), 2000–2001. Courtesy of Telescan.*

Plus, the stock dropped below 10 at one point, which tripped my sell stop and I was gone—bruised, but not bankrupt.

Why did I buy the stock in the middle of such a bad news streak? Because when I am in a trading frame of mind, I am looking for a large profit in a short amount of time. And in the past, as I showed in the chapter on the utility sector with the shares of PCG, when a leading company's shares are battered by news, especially after a very bad period of falling prices, it often marks a good trading opportunity. Sometimes you are right, and sometimes you are wrong. With Halliburton, this time, I was wrong. I admitted it, took my losses, and moved on. That is the kind of thinking that goes into trading, but not investing.

A look at HAL's balance sheet—assuming that the company was not lying, as Enron did—showed me that HAL was in the best shape it had been in for quite a few quarters, as it had pared down its short-term debt to $217 million in its September quarter, from $724 million in its prior quarter and $777 million a year earlier. I noted that total liabilities were $6 billion, while the total assets were $10 billion—which included $227 million in cash, easily enough to cover the lawsuit and several others whose costs at the time were estimated at $150 million. That meant that the company could write a check out of its reserves and settle the suits, even if the insurance companies would not cover the payments. And most important, the company had $4 billion in receivables, meaning that its potential cash flow was just fine.

So, while it was obvious that the company had some problems and that there were still questions to be answered, from my viewpoint most of the worst had been factored in. In fact, a news search for August 2000, when Halliburton initially topped out, shows that Dick Cheney had resigned from the company to become a vice presidential candidate. The announcement was made on August 12 and was reported in the *New York Times,* but the decision had been made in late July. Cheney received a $20 million package. Yet prior to that, on August 3, 2000, Halliburton had sunk $55 million into high-technology investments, especially geared at e-commerce for oil and natural gas. This was clearly bad timing, as the Internet bubble was continuing its implosion. On August 8, 2001, Landmark Graphics, a Halliburton subsidiary, awarded $31.5 million in university grants.

The point is that a great deal of uncertainty and trouble had been brewing at HAL for a long time, because Dick Cheney was leaving the company and there was no real evidence of a plan for a successor. At the same time, the company continued to branch out into technology, a sector that was clearly out of favor at the time. Especially troublesome for the market was the fact that Halliburton was a leader in the formation of the business-to-business exchange for the energy industry, which I noted earlier. This announcement was clearly a very late-in-the-cycle development, which would likely be more costly and negative for the company, at least in the short term, than the smart money wanted to stick around for. Then came the election and a great deal of bad press about the oil industry and the environment.

The bottom line is that Halliburton got hit from all sides over a 16-month period. Its leader left. It was spending too much money on the wrong things at the wrong time. And it was part of an industry that was ripe for political scapegoating. But in my opinion, the asbestos ruling, the debt downgrades, and the huge hit to the stock were signs that the worst was over for the company. When I bought the stock, I also noted that I could be wrong, so I set a mental stop at $12. If the stock fell below that point, I would sell.

So, while investors were selling into what was not good news, I looked at the company's balance sheet and noted that even as the asbestos problems could linger, the fundamentals for the oil service industry were improving. I looked at the company itself, especially the fact that over the 16 months when the stock fell, the company was improving its position and announcing that new business was coming online. On December 19, HAL was awarded a significant portion of a $1 billion natural gas plant project in Egypt. And on December 20, Landmark Graphics received a huge contract for data management from Shell. These are not the same signs that we saw when Enron collapsed. And the comparison is an important one to remember. When in doubt, look at the chart, and see if the fundamentals jibe. If they don't and you assume that you are still at risk and set your loss limits early, this kind of a news event–triggered disaster can well be an excellent long-term buying opportunity. My initial foray into the stock was clearly not profitable. But the decision on how much I was going to lose if I was wrong and the method of analysis were both correct.

When we look at charts, especially of an industry leader, we should notice whether it is leading or lagging its sector. And we should always be aware of the news background. By combining the technical and the fundamentals, we can make better decisions.

Schlumberger (NYSE:SLB)

The number-two player in oil service is Schlumberger. This is a very interesting company, which is truly a major player in high technology, as well as in oil service. From its humble beginnings, SLB's emphasis was on the science of the oil market, as its founder Conrad Schlumberger was a physicist who developed oil-prospecting technology by filling his bathtub with sand and applying electric currents.

Schlumberger had $9.6 billion in sales in 2000. Seventy-three percent of its business is in oil service. But the company is a leader in smart cards, such as ATMs and toll road tags. Most interesting is that Schlumberger also makes the meters used to keep tabs on natural gas consumption for homes and businesses. Twenty-six percent of its business is in high technology, which is impressive. Once again, this reliance on technology made the stock a double-edged sword in the year 2000, as the inherent cyclicality of the oil market, combined with the downturn in high technology, drilled the stock lower.

Schlumberger's businesses are similar to Halliburton's, as it evaluates oil finds to see if there is profit potential and then finishes and manages the well. The company sold its oil-drilling unit to Trans Sedco Forex and merged its seismic operations unit with that of Baker Hughes. This move out of drilling by both of the bellwethers underscores what I outlined in the introductory section of this chapter. Drilling is the riskiest part of the oil service game, as any interruption in the process can lead to huge expenses. By the same token, the market did not really reward either company for the move.

Schlumberger's aggressive move into high tech began in 1999, as it bought several companies, adding to the various other ventures it already owned, which included a cable company. The high-tech move was not applauded by the markets in 2000, but it may be a huge strategic bonus in years to come. The purchase of Sema, an information technology company whose emphasis is in metering systems and information management, allows Schlumberger to become a provider of strategic technical solutions to the utility industry, and its other telecommunications properties provide a huge infrastructure grid that gives the company a chance to connect the energy sector. The strategy makes sense. Get rid of high-risk, high-cost businesses and move into more predictable, cash flow–generating businesses. The only problem is that, as the high-tech bear market of 2000–2001 showed, high technology is a very cyclical business. What the market really did not like about the Sema purchase was the price paid: $5 billion.

Again, as in Halliburton's case, the market is very focused on the decisions made by management. And with SLB, the market's displeasure at the Sema purchase was displayed in the usual form: by selling, in August 2000, along with the rest of the sector. But a look at SLB's balance sheet showed a $1.4 billion cash horde and $4.5 billion in receivables, to go along with $24 billion in total assets and $6.5 billion in debt, of which $1.2 billion was short term. So, here was a company with decent numbers, running its business reasonably well in a tough market. If the company could do this well in a tough market, imagine what it could do when the fundamentals improved.

And that is what happened. While Halliburton slid down a slippery slope, money found a better home in Schlumberger, where shares got a nice bounce late in 2001 when both the high-tech and oil service stocks began to recover, as shown in figure 6.5; SLB stayed near its all-time high during the correction in the oil service sector during 2001. This is a sign of long-term money being patient and an excellent vote of confidence for those with a very long-term time horizon.

Smith International (NYSE:SII)

While the two largest companies in the oil service sector were trying to become high-tech juggernauts, there are still many of the blue chips in the sector that focus solely on the oil service market. Among them is Smith International, a pure play on drilling equipment and drilling activity. Smith makes drills, drilling fluids, and all related pipes, tubes, fittings, and accessories. It also owns mining sites, which produce the raw materials needed for the drilling fluids.

Table 6.4: *Revenues and earnings for Smith International, courtesy of Telescan.*

Revenues (Thousands of U.S. Dollars)

Quarters	1998	1999	2000	2001
March	578,933	397,022	625,432	865,311
June	557,749	389,695	657,229	872,389
September	520,209	481,541	718,470	
December	461,824	537,895	759,883	
TOTAL	2,118,715	1,806,153	2,761,014	

Earnings per Share

Quarters	1998	1999	2000	2001
March	0.700	0.140	0.230	0.680
June	–0.160	–0.060	0.300	0.750
September	0.500	0.950	0.410	
December	–0.330	0.130	0.520	

Table 6.4 confirms that Smith's focus on its core business also paid off. Beginning in the second quarter of 1999, the company's revenues began to increase sequentially, meaning that not only was business good, but that the company had a significant amount of market share. And beginning in the fourth quarter of 1998, earnings also began to increase sequentially. Note as well the consistent doubling of earnings in the comparisons of the March and June quarters in 2000 and 2001. In contrast, Halliburton's revenues grew, but in a less predictable fashion, despite its earnings growth. A company that is growing its earnings, but not its revenues, is usually one whose growth prospects are not as healthy.

The market prefers Smith International's more focused approach to the business. This is shown by Smith clearly outpacing Schlumberger in the 20-year-plus period (see figure 6.6). The chart shows that Smith fell much less and recovered better in December 2001.

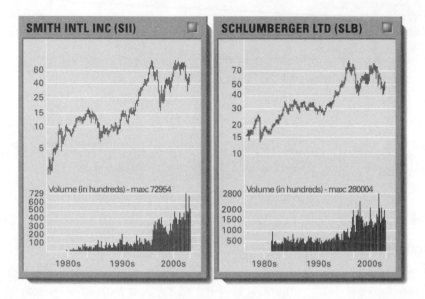

Figure 6.6: *Long-term comparison of Smith International (NYSE:SII; left) and Schlumberger (NYSE:SLB; right), courtesy of Telescan.*

But the right side of the chart also demonstrates that the fundamentals of the market rule the action in both stocks, which very much trended along with the rest of the sector. This is a reminder for investors of how important it is to keep abreast of the fundamentals of a company, while at the same time watching the charts. As of the June 2001 quarter, Smith had reported nine straight quarters of rising revenues, with a 32 percent year-over-year increase in the June quarter. More important, the company had reported seven straight quarters of rising earnings and had improved its June earnings by 150 percent over the prior year.

In his book *Being Right or Making Money,* Ned Davis, of Davis Research, made the point that this example clearly illustrates. Smith International was in top form in 2001, and the stock was getting clobbered. So, a pure fundamentalist would have been in heaven, looking at the growth rates and the sequential revenues, while a pure technician would have been short the stock. A rational investor, as described by John Bollinger in *Bollinger on*

Bollinger Bands, would have avoided the stock in the short term, but noted that when the market turned up, Smith would be a good company to keep a close eye on because its fundamentals showed that it could execute on its business plan. And that is the type of company that attracts money in a good market.

Cooper Cameron (NYSE:CAM)

Before we get to some companies that actually drill for oil, we should look at Cooper Cameron, which makes all of the pressure-sensitive equipment used in the process. In fact, Cooper is a well-diversified provider of parts and key equipment to the entire energy sector, including the power-generating sector. As a result, we can use its stock price and its prospects as sort of a bellwether of things to come.

The OSX index topped in the summer and eventually rolled over in late 2000. But a look at Cooper Cameron's earnings and revenues for 2000, in table 6.5, shows that demand for its products, as reflected in flat revenues and falling earnings, clearly predicted the slowdown in the sector, which then spread to the rest of the sector. More important, the weakness in revenues and earnings for Cooper Cameron began to pick up in June 2001, which suggested that at some point in the next few months a rise in activity could develop. And in fact, by the September quarter, revenues and earnings had already improved, as companies began to step up their exploration and production efforts in non–Middle Eastern countries, because growing trouble there, even before September 11, suggested that other sources of fossil fuels might be increasingly important in the near future.

As investors, we should get into the habit of looking beyond the stocks we own and trying to understand the industry. One of my favorite exercises is to look at companies that make the parts used by the well-known sector participants. In other words, Cooper Cameron is part of the supply chain that makes companies like Halliburton go. When Halliburton sees no demand for its

Table 6.5: *Earnings and revenues for Cooper Cameron, courtesy of Market Guide.*

Revenues (Thousands of U.S. Dollars)

Quarters	1998	1999	2000	2001
March	426,900	385,776	338,302	334,900
June	502,700	387,990	349,993	404,600
September	477,200	376,860	349,978	417,200
December	475,311	324,435	348,436	
TOTAL	1,882,111	1,475,061	1,386,709	

Earnings per Share

Quarters	1998	1999	2000	2001
March	0.600	0.200	0.240	0.260
June	0.810	0.170	0.290	0.350
September	0.580	0.290	0.150	0.600
December	0.490	0.130	−0.180	
TOTAL	2.480	0.790	0.500	

business, it in turn doesn't order from Cooper Cameron. Cooper Cameron is a smaller company, with a less-diversified set of businesses. This means that it is more vulnerable than the larger companies. This then translates into its stock and its earnings and revenue numbers changing much earlier than the rest of the sector, which offers us an early warning system for both upturns and downturns in the sector.

Varco International (NYSE:VRC)

Although Cooper Cameron is a key provider of equipment to the oil drilling industry, so is Varco International, the leader in steel pipes, tubes, and related materials and services. Steel pipes and

Figure 6.7: *Varco International (NYSE:VRC; left) and Cooper Cameron (NYSE:CAM; right), courtesy of Telescan.*

tubes are key components in well design, operation, and maintenance. Varco is the result of the merger of Tuboscope and the old Varco. Tuboscope then assumed the name. Of Varco's $867 million in year 2000 sales, 29 percent came from tubular products, while 32 and 29 percent came from drilling services and drilling equipment, respectively. This diversification of products and significant involvement with drilling led Varco's earnings and revenues to have good growth in 2000–2001, compared to the problems faced by Cooper Cameron, whose reliance on one segment of the industry led to a troublesome earnings pattern.

Tuboscope developed plastic coating for the inside of steel pipes used in drilling for oil. The process coated the pipes and protected them from corrosion, especially in very harsh environments. The company is quite aggressive and has expanded by acquisitions.

Since Varco and Cooper Cameron are bellwethers, I like to look at them together, to confirm the market's expectations for the oil service sector. Varco's earnings and revenues bottomed in the first quarter of 2000 and began to improve significantly in the first quarter of 2001. By the third quarter of 2001, revenues were the best they had been in 15 quarters, while earnings had more than doubled, both sequentially and on a year-over-year basis, as the company cut its merger-related expenses and once again noted in its quarterly report that sales growth had improved on all business segments. This is hardly the picture of a company in tatters.

Figure 6.7 clearly shows that the stocks bottomed, as the market began to factor in the improvement in the businesses of both companies after September 2001, when the market made its bottom. Note the lag in time from the earnings recovery until the stock finally took off. It took five quarters for the market to finally recognize that the oil service sector had plenty of life in it. Finally, as the charts point out, after retesting the lows in November 2001, following the September bottom, the stocks took off, predicting that times were improving and confirming the strength in the overall sector.

This is a clear pattern that, in my opinion, is a textbook example of how the oil service sector works. By looking for both the top and the trough in the earnings of the bellwethers, you can then begin to look for confirmation from the charts. I prefer to let the charts confirm the fundamentals when I'm interested in an intermediate-term trend of weeks to months or even a longer-term investment. And this example once again shows the importance of combining chart analysis with fundamental analysis, by preventing us from buying too early. When it comes to the market, I'd rather make money than be right.

BJ Services (NYSE:BJS)

BJ Services is a leader in pressure-pumping devices, along with Schlumberger and Halliburton. The company's activities are responsible for making sure that the oil and gas can be pumped out of the reservoir. BJ had $1.55 billion in sales in the year 2000, with 50 percent coming from the United States and 80 percent re-

Table 6.6: *Earnings and revenues for BJ Services, courtesy of* Market Guide.

Revenues (Thousands of U.S. Dollars)

Quarters	1998	1999	2000	2001
December	415,360	294,435	354,820	489,678
March	395,602	269,601	390,755	549,661
June	365,343	253,093	371,294	579,839
September	351,163	314,205	438,520	

Earnings per Share

Quarters	1998	1999	2000	2001
December	0.260	–0.050	0.125	0.380
March	0.235	–0.080	0.175	0.480
June	0.205	–0.115	0.155	0.630
September	0.010	0.032	0.250	

sulting from oil-field pumping services. The company provides the whole spectrum of drilling support services, including the provision of specialty chemicals, well cementing, and the placement of steel pipes and tubes into wells.

Table 6.6 shows that BJ Services had a great time in 2000–2001, delivering seven quarters of sequentially rising earnings, as well as rising revenues for eight out of nine quarters going back as far as 1999. And yet the stock chart told a different story, as the stock fell along with the rest of the sector until the bottom in September. When I see a company that is firing on all cylinders, as the earnings and revenue figures show, with a horrible looking chart such as that of BJ Services, this stock usually makes it to the top of my watch list.

The reason is that either the market is wrong or the company is lying about its prospects. More than likely, barring a hoax like Enron, Wall Street is just out of touch, and the stock will rise, as

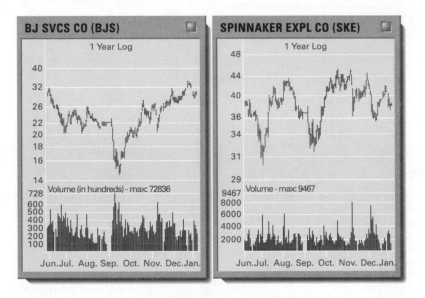

Figure 6.8: *BJ Services (NYSE:BJS; left) and Spinnaker Exploration (NYSE:SKE; right), courtesy of Telescan.*

money managers figure out that they've missed the boat badly. The chart shows that BJS failed to fall to a new low, beyond 22, on its last tag of the area near the July lows. Also note that in August, volume was falling on days in which the stock fell, while it rose on up days for the stock. Finally, when the September bottom was made, it was accompanied by a huge surge in volume, which was repeated every time the stock dipped. That is evidence that smart money has started to recognize value in this company and is buying on the dips. For that reason, it would be a stock to place very high on a shopping list, with a buy being triggered if things improve. I'll give more details in the technical and fundamental analysis chapter. The key point is that BJ Services in 2001 was a company firing on all cylinders, fundamentally, and the market clearly did not recognize it, until the buyers finally overwhelmed the sellers.

Confirmation of this argument was in *Barron's* in the September 3, 2001, issue, when value money manager Susan Byrne, who is a frequent co-host of CNBC's *Squawk Box* program, listed many stocks in the energy sector whose characteristics were similar to BJ Services. Among Byrne's picks in the interview was Spinnaker Exploration (NYSE:SKE), pictured in figure 6.8, alongside BJS.

Byrne liked Spinnaker, which meant that at the time, there were likely other big institutional investors that liked it and the sector as well. Most institutions, like Byrne's Westwood funds, like to buy stocks over long periods of time, even during periods of weakness, as they can amass very large positions and then wait for the market's momentum to catch up. This is the main reason that the stock had held up much better than BJ Services during the summer months of 2001: institutional nibbling. September 11 was the equalizer for most stocks, and Byrne's plans may have gone awry, given the stock's performance into January 2002, as money clearly flowed into BJS more aggressively. Spinnaker is not a member of the OSX index, which also means that it is less likely to be involved in sector fund trading, because most energy sector funds, which I will describe later, are trying to outperform the energy sector indexes. This means that Spinnaker is not as wide a swinger in many cases as a stock like BJ Services. More important—and perhaps the fine point here—is that Spinnaker is primarily in gas exploration, and the natural gas sector was lagging the oil service sector during this period, once again bringing up the strong link between the fundamentals and the technicals in the energy sector.

Baker Hughes (NYSE:BHI)

Baker Hughes is an interesting story in the oil service sector. The company was formed in 1909, when Howard Hughes, Sr., developed the first drill bit for oil wells and formed Sharp & Hughes, which became Hughes Tools when his partner Walter Sharp died. In 1913 drilling contractor Carl Baker formed a company, which was to become Baker Oil Tools. Both companies grew and merged in 1987, as a result of the slowdown in drilling activity. Baker Hughes continued to spin off pieces, with the most notable being

BJ Services (NYSE:BJS), another member of the OSX index. In 1997, BHI bought Petrolite and Western Atlas in order to shore up its seismic business.

Baker Hughes is involved in oil and gas exploration, as well as in providing drill bits, fluid, and other materials to drill and maintain wells, and chemicals for the refining industry. The company also offers submersible pumps that deliver oil to the surface for deep ocean drilling. Of the $5.6 billion of sales for the year 2000, 51 percent came from the United States, Canada, and the U.K. This "domestic" and non–Middle Eastern focus makes the company's stock attractive and one to keep an eye on and trade when the cycle reaches a positive tone.

Nabors Industries (NYSE:NBR)

Nabors Industries is a pure play on oil drilling, as 88 percent of its $1.323 billion in sales for the year 2000 came from contract drilling operations, on both land and sea, in the United States (68 percent) as well as most of the world (32 percent). The company's predecessor, Anglo Industries, went bankrupt in 1984 and emerged from its restructuring as Nabors. Nabors used the weakness in the mid-1980s to diversify its operations internationally, a move that paid off well, given its doubling of sales from 1999 to 2000. This kind of action by management is noteworthy, as it gives us an idea about how to judge the action of companies when times get hard. Those companies that make the best decisions during bad times will usually have the best payoff when good times return.

The company has over 1,200 land rigs and is a leader in the Alaska oil-drilling region. Nabors also has a fleet of 30 offshore vessels and operates over 40 offshore drilling rigs. This is a well-diversified oil-drilling company, whose management learned a few lessons after its bankruptcy, as it continues to shed portions of the business that aren't working.

Noble Drilling (NYSE:NE)

Noble Drilling is another pure drilling play, with 86 percent of its activity being offshore. Noble had $882 million in global sales for the year 2000, 67 percent of this coming from the United States and Brazil. The company, which is a specialist in harsh environment drilling, has the entire gamut of offshore rigs available, including submersibles, semisubmersibles, and even dynamically positioned ships, whose mechanisms allow them to remain stationary over the well as they drill.

Noble is a well-run but cyclical company that has placed itself in a nearly indispensable position, meaning that because it goes where others don't want to drill for oil, it is likely to get jobs during difficult times. This does not mean that the stock will always go up. But it does mean that it has a slight advantage in some circumstances, such as when the economy starts showing signs of picking up and the market begins to factor in an increase in drilling.

Weatherford International (NYSE:WFT)

Weatherford International is a key player in drilling, drilling services, and well completion. The company spun off two divisions, one in gas compression and the other in steel pipe and tubes, while expanding further into flow control, completion services, drilling equipment, and control systems. More important, the company diversified its expansion geographically, by buying companies in Canada, the U.K., and Scotland.

This is a stock whose price goes right along with the rest of the sector. It is an excellent trading vehicle that follows the market's expectations for the supply-and-demand scenario.

What I do like about these highly cyclical companies, such as Weatherford and Noble Drilling, is that regardless of their stock price, they all continue to position themselves more and more into their core businesses. That is what Wall Street likes, and that is why these companies will do well when the cycle turns up, and Wall Street recognizes the leanest and meanest, as well as the most focused, companies in the sector.

Weatherford had $1.8 billion in sales in 2000, and 76 percent of its business came from the United States, Canada, and Latin America. Forty-nine percent of the business came from drilling services, while 24 percent came from artificial lift systems, which actually draw the oil out from the well. This heavy dependence on the actual extraction of oil makes Weatherford a big winner in the up cycle and a big decliner when the cycle turns down.

The poor performance of stocks in the oil-drilling sector during 2000 was a direct result of Wall Street predicting a significant down draft in oil prices and, by default, in economic activity. Weatherford's stock price peaked in May 2001, but just as the energy service sector was struggling to bottom, hints were arising that the economy had started to grope for its own bottom. This came in late August, as the government report on U.S. factory orders and the Chicago Purchasing Manager's Index stopped falling and showed signs of a slight upturn. The economic recovery was, of course, delayed by September 11. And these were very early indications of a potential recovery indeed, but at the same time that the oil service stocks were groping for a bottom and the economic statistics showed slight improvement, the press had begun to beat the drum loudly about recession, job losses, and the end of life as we once knew it. At that time, it was best to concentrate on those companies in the oil service sector whose revenues and earnings were strong and whose charts flirted with a bottom. It wasn't time to rush out and buy, but it was time to start getting ready to, early in the cycle, when the market turned in September.

Global Santa Fe (NYSE:GSF)

Global Marine provides offshore drilling services and runs its own exploration activities in the Gulf of Mexico. On September 4, 2001, Global Marine merged with Santa Fe International, form-

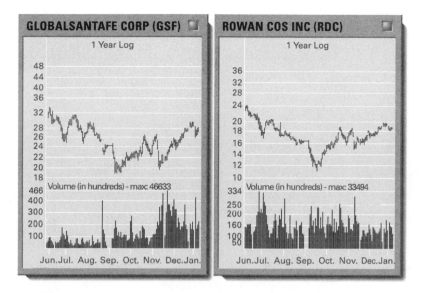

Figure 6.9: *Global Santa Fe (NYSE:GSF; left) and Rowan Companies (NYSE:RDC; right), courtesy of Telescan.*

ing Global Santa Fe (NYSE:GSF). The merger expanded the Global Marine drilling fleet and brought the Kuwaiti government–owned oil industry a larger foothold in global drilling, because it had owned 36 percent of Santa Fe before the merger was announced. This merger was significant in many ways. First, it proved the point that I made earlier. The energy industry continues to be extremely dynamic, as the quest for dominance among the players makes mergers and acquisitions the primary method of growth in the sector. And the second, and perhaps more global, point was that just a week later, the September 11 disaster occurred. That severe decline was responsible for the drop in the stock in September and set up the nice bottom and rally into January 2002.

Global Marine was spun off in 1956 from a partnership between Conoco, Unocal, and Shell that had been formed in 1946. Prior to the spin-off, the company had participated in the conversion of a Navy surplus ship and a land-based rig to create the first

Table 6.7: *Earnings and revenues for Global Marine, courtesy of Telescan.*

Revenues (Thousands of U.S. Dollars)

Quarters	1998	1999	2000	2001
March	275,100	228,000	204,100	274,800
June	356,000	195,700	231,300	376,400
September	272,200	168,600	272,000	
December	258,900	198,700	332,400	
TOTAL	1,162,200	791,000	1,039,800	

Earnings per Share

Quarters	1998	1999	2000	2001
March	0.390	0.210	0.070	0.230
June	0.420	0.160	0.160	0.460
September	0.270	0.080	0.180	
December	0.200	0.060	0.230	
TOTAL	1.280	0.510	0.640	

offshore drilling rig. The company went public in 1964 and was the first to use an offshore drilling rig in the North Sea.

The company's sales in 2000 were just over $1 billion and were 80 percent dependent on the United States and the U.K., with the latter accounting for 10 percent. Contract drilling was 56 percent of the sales, while 42 percent was for drilling management services.

Table 6.7 shows that Global Marine's revenues and earnings were quite good in the 2000–2001 period, prior to the merger. But Wall Street ignored the good performance of the company, once again preoccupied with the larger picture of economic malaise, bloated supply, and decreased demand for oil.

Rowan Companies (NYSE:RDC)

Rowan Companies is a well-diversified oil service company that operates offshore and on land with its fleet of rigs; it features the heavy-duty Gorilla-class rigs. Rowan also operates a steel mill that builds off-road trucks, cranes, and lumber loading and transportation equipment. But perhaps its most important sideline is its fleet of airplanes and helicopters, which are used for sightseeing, as well as in commercial and charter applications that include transporting personnel to and from offshore drilling sites.

Of Rowan's $646 million in sales for the year 2000, 65 percent came from oil drilling, with 19 percent and 16 percent coming, respectively, from the transportation and steel-related businesses. Its well-diversified businesses led to strong and very steady revenue and earnings growth in the 1999–2001 period. But as the chart in figure 6.9 shows, the market was as unforgiving to Rowan as it was to the rest of the stocks in the index.

Rowan does provide an interesting variation to the rest of the sector, as its diversification remains within the oil sector. In other words, the company has placed itself in a position to survive down trends, because it provides services such as air travel that can be converted and targeted to other areas beyond energy. Its logging and heavy equipment construction divisions are directly related to the mining and, more important, the paper and construction industries. Figure 6.9 shows that Rowan formed what should now be a familiar chart pattern for the period of time described in this chapter, as an illustration of a realistic and classic period for the oil service sector.

But more important, Rowan serves as a bridge to smaller companies in the sector, which are often beyond the radar of large analysts and brokerage firms and can be profitable when their time comes. These niche companies are important to investors because they often trade at lower prices than the larger blue chips and can move impressively, if conditions are right.

Tetra Technologies (NYSE:TTI)

A very interesting small stock in the energy sector is Tetra Technologies. The company specializes in closing down and cleaning up abandoned and idled gas and oil wells. Tetra is a counter-trend play, as its business tends to rise when higher numbers of wells are being shut down, either for low production or when the cycle is turning down. This is a stock to watch as the rig count drops and wells are taken off line, increasing Tetra's shut-down and clean-up activity. This was quite evident when the company's revenues and earnings rose for four straight quarters, beginning in September 2000. But as the oil service sector recovered, the stock began to flatten out.

Offshore Logistics (NASDAQ:OLOG)

Offshore Logistics is another small niche company in the sector that is worth noting. The company provides helicopter services for oil and gas companies. Offshore's fleet of more than 370 aircraft is mostly made up of helicopters, which operate mainly in the Gulf of Mexico and the North Sea. Offshore also serves the Alyeska Pipeline area in Alaska and provides emergency medical transportation, general aviation, and support services to the agriculture and forestry industries. Subsidiary Grasso Production Management provides personnel and production management on more than 200 oil rigs in the Gulf of Mexico. Offshore had $416 million in sales in 2000, with 64 percent coming from the United States and the U.K.

Petroleum Helicopters, Inc. (NASDAQ:PHEL)

Petroleum Helicopters has a fleet of more than 280 aircraft, mainly helicopters, and provides contract transport services to the oil industry, mostly in the Gulf of Mexico. The company had $232 million in year 2000 sales, with 91 percent coming from

Table 6.8: *Comparison of earnings between Petroleum Helicopters and Offshore Logistics, courtesy of Telescan/*Market Guide.

Petroleum Helicopters Earnings

Quarters	2000	2001
March	−0.280	0.010
June	−0.060	0.530
September	−0.200	
December	−1.840	

Offshore Logistics Earnings

Quarters	2000	2001
June	0.190	0.470
September	0.400	
December	0.370	
March	0.350	

the United States and 64 percent from the oil and energy side of the business. Twenty percent of sales came from the medical transport side of the business, while the rest came from its aircraft repair business.

Both Offshore Logistics and Petroleum Helicopters are companies that tend to trend with the fortunes of the OSX. During 2000–2001, the market preferred shares of the smaller of the two, PHEL. This was a turnaround play at the time, as its earnings and revenues were beginning to pick up steam after several quarters of losses. The sequential growth in the first two quarters of 2001 were impressive, compared to the more static numbers presented by OLOG, which included a shortfall in the December quarter. Wall Street likes to see large leaps in growth and likes to see the momentum sustained. Table 6.8 compares the earnings and revenues for the two companies.

Transocean Sedco Forex (NYSE:RIG)

This is a deepwater drilling specialist that was formed in 1999, when Schlumberger spin-off Sedco Forex merged with Transocean Offshore and then bought R&B Falcon. RIG has the usual rack of jack-up rigs and submersibles to go along with a fleet of 13 drill ships, which is most useful in hard-to-get-at wells in deep waters. The company had $1.2 billion in sales for the year 2000, with 22 percent in the United States and 20 percent in Norway. A total of 26 percent of sales were in the U.K. and Brazil, respectively. This is a very large company with a global scope, which makes money in the good times and tends to not make as much money when times are really hard, once again underscoring the cyclicality of the business.

But, in the future, as the world continues the drive to diversify its oil sources, this company is likely to benefit, as increasing amounts of petroleum will likely come from very difficult places, especially in the deep ocean.

Tidewater Inc. (NYSE:TDW)

Tidewater is the world's largest offshore supply ship provider. Its fleet carries supplies and personnel and tows oil rigs to offshore drilling sites. It owns a shipyard and also lays down transoceanic cable. I saved this capsule for last, given the company's crucial positioning in the industry as the largest transporter of supplies for the sector. What makes this company most interesting is that in the year 2000, it only had $100 million in sales. This underscores that it is way down in the scheme of things and is totally dependent on the state of the marketplace for its business.

Again, as more oil comes from the farthest reaches of the earth, Tidewater's role as a key transporter of supplies will likely improve the company's standing and translate into higher sales.

Summary

This chapter provided a glimpse into the oil service sector and a brief look at business practices that make the larger companies in the sector profitable. This is a highly cyclical sector and is not suited for the buy-and-hold approach. Wall Street also likes to treat the sector as a basket of stocks, rather than as individual companies. This is a key point, because when one of these companies falls, it means that the rest of them are likely to follow. This point is not as prominent on the up side, where Wall Street is very picky and likes to take some of these companies higher, at a faster rate than others in the sector. The market prefers to give the best rallies to those companies that are very focused on their area of expertise and tends to applaud a company when it sells a division that either underperforms or does not work within the company's main focus.

I found, in writing this chapter, a handful of companies that serve not only as useful investments, but also as bellwethers and signal providers in the sector, given their placement in the scheme of things and their increased sensitivity to supply and demand.

The companies that tend to do best when the sector turns up are those that are focused on their own core businesses. This means that Wall Street wants drillers to drill, explorers to explore, and so on. Wall Street does not like the oil business to be an aside in a much larger business mix. It particularly turns thumbs down on the mixture of high technology and energy service, as witnessed in the largest two oil service stocks, Halliburton and Schlumberger.

The combination of technical analysis and fundamental analysis, when taken together in this context, works better than either one separately. This was well illustrated in many instances where we looked at charts of companies that were mired in down trends, while their earnings and revenues were actually positive.

Finally, this chapter should dispel the myth that all oil companies are the same. I found that although similarities exist among these companies, their vast differences and slight nuances make each individual company behave uniquely in its relationship to the overall sector and the market.

CHAPTER
7

The Electricity Sector

The electricity, or power, sector is where the entire energy complex converges. It is a hybrid, in which natural gas, crude oil, and other forms of energy (including nuclear, hydroelectric, and alternative fuels) all combine within the common area of electricity and power production. This chapter is divided into several sections and contains a brief, but inclusive, history and an exploration of the regulatory environment, especially in the United States, where the California energy crisis was and is likely to remain a focal point for many years.

I am a strong advocate of the markets. But in my opinion, on a perfect day, in a perfect world, with lots of luck, deregulation barely works. It is the dream of a torturer, whose goal is to think of unpleasant things to unleash on the free people of the world. The road is littered with industries that have been deregulated into the ground, such as the airlines and the telecom sectors. The mere mention of the word *deregulation* sends shivers down my spine, as I reach for my pocketbook, which I know will be ably picked by countless numbers of people whose intended role in life, according to the proponents of the practice, is to help me save money. But the truth is, due to its cumbersome process, deregulation usually ends up costing me money and endless hours of aggravation.

In *A Shock to the System,* Timothy J. Brennan and his co-authors at the Resources for the Future think tank *(www.rff.org)* produced a forward-looking book that not only organizes the electric utility industry, but also clearly foretold the potential difficulties that deregulation would bring. The book was published in 1996 and provided an excellent skeleton for the introductory portion of this chapter, because many things have not changed since the book was written.

Among the key introductory remarks of Brennan's book is a reference—which I also made in an earlier chapter—to the dangers of deregulation. The government's desire to have its cake and eat it, too—in other words, having the private sector do the heavy lifting, while taking away the profit motive—has often led to disaster, as the marketplace has run amok and created, in many cases, a worse bubble than would have otherwise occurred.

The problem with deregulation is that the government continues to regulate it. On the one hand is the implied marketplace benefit of deregulation that would come from lower electricity prices, if there were unleashed competition. But at the same time, the government's real goal is to get private industry to build overcapacity in order to prepare for a potential emergency. The trouble is that for the government, the lower prices brought on by deregulation—if and when the market finally settles down—can lead to a true survival of the fittest, a situation that threatens the government. Just look at the Microsoft trial. Sure, Microsoft bullied its competition. How else can you be top dog in the business world? Global governments don't tolerate insurrection from fringe elements, but they feel threatened when corporations, especially in key services like communications, power generation, and media, start to expand toward a monopoly situation. From my standpoint, I used to get better telephone service before the Bell system was broken up. The operators could read and write and could actually help me find the right numbers when I called information. Call me a curmudgeon, but from this vantage point, deregulation, as it has been implemented in any industry in the United States, is a disaster that is likely to be repeated over and over again.

What governments don't seem to understand is that businesses interpret deregulation as an invitation to build out their infrastructure in order to steal market share and crush the competition. So from a business standpoint, this is nothing more than an opportunity to form another monopoly. In other words, when the huge behemoth utilities expand their operations all over the world and build power plants in all the counties of a single state, they are trying to squelch, not encourage, competition. This in turn leads the government to put restrictions on where and how businesses can deregulate. This inconsistency, in both focus and intention from all parties involved, led to the problems in California.

And they all should have known better. Nowhere were these dangers more clearly illustrated than with the deregulation of the telecom industry, where supply—especially in high-speed telephone access—clearly exceeded demand, while at the same time the legislation in place banned a true laissez-faire approach by industries. Sure, at the beginning of the process, any venture capitalist with a good business plan and a couple of high-profile board members could secure enough money to start a company. After the company lands a couple of good contracts, it attracts more financing and the cycle repeats. All of the money goes into building factories, hiring employees, and going out to implement the contracts. Eventually, the company goes public and the stock soars, as revenues begin to build. But at some point, revenues have to turn to earnings. And when that fails to happen, credit lines get cut off and the stock plummets. Bankruptcies ensue and the bubble bursts.

If this sounds familiar, it's because that's what happened when the United States deregulated the telecom industry and the CLECs (Competitive Local Exchange Carriers) flooded the stock market with promise-powered equity and dug holes all over metropolitan areas in the United States to create the Information Superhighway and give us all high-speed Internet access.

What really happened is that thousands of miles of dead fiber-optic bands now lie under our less smoothly paved streets. And instead of having a lower phone bill, in many cases consumers like myself had to change phone companies several times in two years in order to have high-speed Internet access. Finally, after the company that installed wireless broadband in my home went bankrupt, I settled on DSL. But because of how the laws are written, the government won't allow the large and very dominant phone company to act like the monopoly that it is in reality, and I have to wait two extra weeks to install the DSL myself, while I pay someone at the phone company an installation fee for something I will do myself after I receive the mail-ordered installation kit. I don't see how I saved money. What I see is a flawed process that failed miserably in telecom, as it led to a huge unwinding of the excess, a huge bear market in stocks, and a recession, which we lived through in the early part of the 21st century. And what I see, as I watched Enron implode and begin to drag down the rest of the so-called power generators, is that it happened once again in electricity.

Not only did deregulation nearly kill the telecom industry, it severely hampered the electricity industry and led to a similar set of dynamics. We all witnessed this with the demise of Enron and the very unpleasant aftermath, in which companies like Dynegy and Calpine also got hurt because of Wall Street's guilt-by-association way of doing business.

Perhaps the most important fact to note before we move into a discussion of the electricity sector comes from the U.S. government itself on the Energy Information Agency's Web site *(www .eia.doe.gov)*. Here, in its summary of the supply and demand of electricity for the United States, the U.S. government states that the electric power industry really does not know how much over-capacity to build in order to have excess generation capacity, or "capacity margin," that could handle power-generation emergencies. The same statement also makes it clear that the government hopes that deregulation will open up competition. The implication is that companies would try to compete in a deregulated environment and would overbuild, to take market share away from competitors. In this indirect manner, the government would shift the burden of power generation to the private sector and let consumers foot the bill.

So, what we have in effect is a government that is trying to change a century-old system with a flawed premise and an industry that is in transition and doesn't really know where it's heading. Despite all of my fire and brimstone, I am not knocking the industry or the government. I only highlight what was obvious in the aftermath of the California energy crisis. The electricity and power industry is suffering from a lack of direction and perhaps a lack of patience and foresight on the part of everyone involved.

The problem in California thus came about because the mandate to increase capacity was pressed on the private sector, at the same time that the government buckled down under pressure from environmental groups. This situation allowed an industry to deregulate, but did not allow the market to act to balance the equation by building new power plants, in order to accommodate the increasing demands of the economy. Ironically, deregulation in California proceeded without heeding the basic tenet that the federal government hoped would result from the deregulation: an overbuilding of generating capacity that would be available at times of extreme need, such as the power needs of the information technology economy during a very hot spring and summer.

The combination of these two factors—a lack of new power plants, just as demand peaked due to the rise of the Internet economy, and laws restricting rate hikes by utilities—led to the crisis. As a result of incomplete deregulation and its inherent problems, the utility sector as an investment had a new dimension added to it: volatility. Where stocks in the sector were once considered high dividend–paying plays for "widows and orphans," investors suddenly had a new-growth sector, the power generators, whose inherent volatility and growth potential were supposed to lead investors to the Promised Land and do so safely. After all, these were the widow and orphan stocks owned by Grandma and Grandpa.

Although the prior discussion may seem out of place in an investment book, it is impossible to make profitable judgments in this sector without clearly understanding the misguided logic of deregulation, in the form that it was proposed in the early 21st century in the United States. Preventing a repeat of the Enron collapse, in which billions of dollars in retirement funds were wiped out, is the perfect reason to spend time dissecting how and why these disasters happen. In my opinion, it is just as important a part of investing in the energy sector as more traditional aspects, such as interest rates and individual stock analysis.

In this chapter, I frame the discussion in terms of situational analysis, based on the companies in the Dow Jones Utilities Index, with two notable exceptions—Nisource and Williams Companies—which are primarily natural gas companies that are covered in the natural gas chapter. I chose the situational analysis model because it provides us with insight into what makes a company successful and what makes others fail. For example, those companies that recognized what the upcoming deregulation would do to them and acted in the most reasonable and timely manner were most able to survive the bear market of 2000–2001. By framing your thought patterns along these lines and using this type of analysis as a benchmark, you will be able to make better choices in investing.

History

In the prior section I introduced the situation faced by investors in the utility sector in the summer and early winter of 2001. As I wrote this chapter, the unfortunate events of the World Trade Center terrorist attack and its aftermath occurred. These events accelerated a process of unwinding that was already underway. They are likely to have a great, long-lasting, and significant influence on all of the subsectors of the energy complex, with the electricity sector not likely to be spared.

This section is not an all-inclusive historical snapshot of the electricity sector. In fact, it is narrow by design and is meant to give you a bare-bones, hands-on introduction to the focal point of the utility industry. This section focuses on key aspects of the history of regulation and deregulation, which is an extra layer of fundamental criteria that separates the power generation and utility industry from the oil industry. The spectrum of regulation and deregulation is the catalyst for the future of prices in the sector and is the primary variable that will increase the volatility of the sector, as time passes.

In 1907, states began to regulate the rates that utilities could charge their retail customers. The regulation created "natural monopolies," and the prices charged were designed to provide investors with a "fair rate of return." The justification for the natural monopolies was purely logistical and was largely determined by technological limitations of that era, as the cost in both time and capital required to build power-generation plants and other portions of infrastructure was correctly diagnosed by government to be best handled by a single company in each location. The result was the creation of optimum service for the population in that area.

In 1935, the U.S. federal government passed the Public Utilities Holding Company Act, which set up the regulated environment and is still in place, to a great degree, in the United States. In 1976, the Federal Power Commission was recommissioned to become the Federal Energy Regulatory Commission (FERC), whose job is to enforce the regulatory environment. But as technology advanced, it became possible for smaller portable generators to be used and to produce electricity at equally economical rates as those produced by larger plants.

By the same token, the characteristics that in 1907 created the natural monopolies had now led to a situation in which efficiency was not the most important part of the system. This became painfully obvious during the energy crises of the 1970s and those that followed. As a result of the convergence of inefficient power generators and technological improvement, the call for competition and deregulation arose.

In 1992, Congress passed the Energy Policy Act, which empowered the FERC to force power transmission–owning utilities to sell power to wholesalers and other utilities at nondiscriminatory prices. By 1996, the FERC had crafted Orders 888 and 889 to implement this requirement. The stated intent of the orders was to "remove impediments to competition in wholesale trade and to bring more efficient, lower cost power to the nation's electricity customers."

In 1995, 29 states and the District of Columbia formally considered deregulation plans. Interestingly, it was California that in December 1995 formally announced a plan to deregulate its utility industry by January 2003. The plan was very ambitious, as its goal was to allow even residential customers to purchase their power from electricity suppliers by direct contract. But, as I have repeatedly noted, deregulation's most aggressive experiment got off to a rocky start in the year 2000.

A Brief Summary of Deregulation in the Electricity Industry

Before looking at the nuts and bolts of deregulation, we should get our bearings and understand what is actually being deregulated. There are three basic parts to the process of providing electricity to a home or business: generation, transmission, and distribution. Generation is the process of using fuel to power a turbine that produces the electricity. Transmission is the actual movement of the electricity along power lines. Transmission is done at very high voltages. And distribution is the conversion of high voltage electricity to a lower voltage, which can be used in a home or business.

The object of deregulation is the power generation and wholesale segment. This means that individuals could choose which company's electricity was delivered to their homes or businesses,

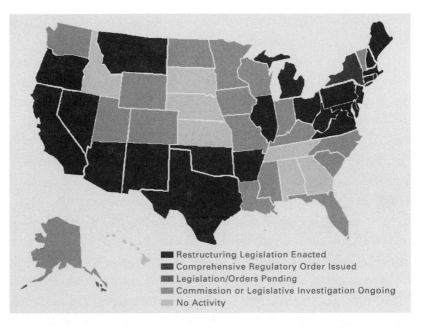

Legend:
- Restructuring Legislation Enacted
- Comprehensive Regulatory Order Issued
- Legislation/Orders Pending
- Commission or Legislative Investigation Ongoing
- No Activity

Figure 7.1: *Summary of the status of deregulation in the United States of America, as of August 2001. Map patterned after figure appearing on the Energy Information Administration Web site,* www.eia.doe.gov.

via the already existing grid of transmission and distribution. The producers are in effect renting the power lines from a different company. By 2001, 90 million Americans had the right to choose their electricity-generating company. And as figure 7.1 shows, only seven states in the union had no involvement with any type of deregulation. The deregulation problems in California were foreshadowed by problems in Arkansas, New York, Delaware, and Illinois in 1999, where power shortages were quite common, despite no moratoriums on the building of new power plants being in place. So even where the industry had the freedom to build as many plants as it could, the switch was not smooth, especially in states with high consumption such as New York and Illinois, which are highly industrial and densely populated.

The model for successful deregulation in the United States is the state of Pennsylvania, which won the year 2000 Retail Energy

Deregulation "Red Carpet Award" for the smoothest transition from the natural monopoly system to the new deregulated process. A pilot program that used 230,000 customers to test the "Electric Choice" system paved the road to success in Pennsylvania and should actually be used as a benchmark for investors. Conversely, California is the default for a failed model. On one side is a state that took its time and used a small sample population to work the kinks out of its system, while on the other is a state that rushed headlong into deregulation, but left half of the equation on the cutting-room floor.

Yet deregulation is more than a U.S. initiative. The United States is actually a late arrival at the nuptials. Internationally, Chile and the U.K. are cited as successful models, which began in 1978 and 1983, respectively. This means that it took at least two decades to get the systems to actually function. That is a crucial concept, as far as time frame goes. Both successful systems were implemented in a stepwise fashion, where each subsequent step was taken based on the successful completion of the step that preceded it. The key in both cases was restructuring the state-owned industry, followed by its privatization. A great deal of the emphasis on privatization was influenced by huge debts incurred by emerging market utilities in the 1980s, but in the case of the U.K., it was more of a return to a market economy after the failure of socialism in that nation.

Investors should be wary of how a particular state undertakes deregulation. Remember that the problem in California (which may be repeated elsewhere) was caused by a faulty assumption by governments and regulators—the belief that forced, government-regulated competition, instead of a true market-driven solution, will always lead to lower costs. The success of the government-intrusive form of deregulation is more likely to occur at a time of ample power supply and slack, or not unusually high, demand. This means that unless the market is allowed to act in a full and independent fashion, the success is usually a temporary phenomenon. The increasing demands of the booming Internet economy, which was at its height during the crisis, proved to the world that supply and demand still rule. When political excess—from either the industry or its opponents—is introduced, the only possible outcome is disaster.

In fact, international studies cited by Michael G. Pollit (in his review of the global electricity industry entitled "The Impact of Liberalization on the Performance of the Electricity Supply Industry: An International Survey" and published in the *Journal of Energy Literature* in 1997) show that results for deregulation are mixed. On the positive side are potential gains in productivity for the utility, as well as potential huge gains for shareholders. These, however, can be countered by greater costs of restructuring and privatizing, as well as by possible negative environmental impact, because deregulated, cleaner-burning, more efficient utilities may find themselves competing head to head with state-supported, dirtier, and less-efficient monopolies in nonderegulated states.

Pollit also cites a 1995 study by the World Bank, in which the political aspects of deregulation are highlighted. In other words, governments cannot simultaneously force companies to buy power at market prices and sell it at a discount. If there is going to be deregulation and competition, governments will have to let the markets work or else devise a set of ground rules that prohibit price gouging. The bottom line is that efficient markets work best when the trading rules are conducive to an orderly market. This means that in the same way that stocks and bonds have bear markets, regulators have to become accustomed to the idea that deregulation of utilities may lead to periods of severely depressed, as well as exuberant, price swings, based on the status of supply and demand.

A Basic Primer on Electricity

Although this chapter deals with the investment aspects of electricity—namely, individual companies and how to analyze their stocks—it is important to recognize that electricity is a ubiquitous force in the universe. It holds atomic particles together and, as such, is indispensable in the structure of just about everything and everyone. And other than powering our homes and businesses, electricity functions in nerve conduction, the generation of our heartbeats, skeletal muscle action, and our senses of sight, smell, touch, hearing, and taste. Electrical energy makes our world function, greatly influencing the way we live, communicate, and store information. When many electrical charges travel together, they form an electrical current that travels along the transmission wires and into our homes and businesses. Electrical energy is converted into light and heat, powering our appliances and other electronics.

Again, I am merely providing information that will help us focus on the investment aspects of the electrical industry, not trying to make us into electrical engineers. Readers are invited to further pursue their thirst for knowledge about electricity, magnetism, quantum theory, and string theory in many fine texts that are available.

Electricity to power devices can come from batteries, which produce electricity from a chemical reaction, or from generators, which convert mechanical energy into electrical energy. Batteries and power cells are covered in the chapter on alternative energy sources. This section focuses on the basics of power generation from nonbattery sources.

Generally, to produce electricity to power homes and businesses, some form of energy—such as coal, petroleum, natural gas, solar energy, wind, water, nuclear reaction, and even biomass—is burned or harnessed to drive a turbine, which in turn runs a generator, which then produces the electric current that makes its way to end users. Most of the energy produced in the United States comes from steam turbines, in which fuels such as oil or natural gas are used to heat water and produce steam. The most common electricity-generating fuel in the United States is coal, with 52 percent of 1998's electric power coming from it. In 1998, natural gas was used to produce 15 percent of the United States' electrical power, while petroleum was used for only 3 percent. Natural gas is the fuel of choice to produce power during periods of high demand. Nuclear power accounts for 19 percent of the United States' electrical production, and hydropower is good for 9 percent. Geothermal, solar, wind, and biomass account for 1 percent each of the power produced.

Kinds of Electric Companies

There are more than 3,100 traditional electric utilities in the United States, whose job is to ensure adequate power supplies to their customers at a reasonable price. Many are investor owned or publicly owned, while others are federally owned or cooperatives. Power marketers and producers are also considered utilities. The former are just as involved as the latter in buying and selling power in the open markets, but power marketers don't own any kind of generation or transmission facilities. Local, state, and federal authorities regulate utilities.

State Public Service Commissions oversee the vertically integrated, investor-owned electric utilities that still control most of the power-generation and transmission capacity of the United States, where 239 of these companies reside. Although these large conglomerates, which operate as regional monopolies, own 75 percent of the power and transmission, the rest is provided by over 2,000 publicly owned firms, 912 consumer-owned rural electric cooperatives, and 10 federal electric utilities.

Interstate activities are under federal regulation, while intrastate activities of the utility companies are under state supervision. More important for investors is that wholesale rates—the rates at which electricity is purchased by and sold among electric utilities—is regulated by the federal government.

The main thrust in the rest of this chapter is on investor-owned utilities, and we'll start with a basic overview. These are privately owned companies that represent 8 percent of the total number of electric utilities and produce most of the electric utility generating capability, generation, sales, and revenue in the United States. Investor-owned electric companies are in business to provide returns for their investors, as either dividends or capital gains.

The traditional system, as I described earlier, gave investor-owned electric utilities service monopolies in certain geographic areas, in exchange for the near guarantee of the best possible service to all who could pay for it. These legal monopolies are regulated and required to charge reasonable prices, to charge comparable prices to similar classifications of consumers, and to give consumers access to services under similar conditions. The majority of investor-owned electric utilities are operating companies that provide basic services for the generation, transmission, and distribution of electricity. These are referred to as vertically integrated utilities, as they perform all three functions. Investor-owned utilities operate in all states except Nebraska, where electric utilities consist primarily of municipal systems and public power districts.

The Texas Giant That Went Global

A perfect example of an investor-owned utility company for the future is the one that powers my PC: TXU (NYSE:TXU). TXU is a member of the Dow Jones and the Philadelphia Utility Indexes—the two commonly cited stock index benchmarks for the sector—and is a well-diversified company. In January 2002 TXU became a former monopoly, whose business hub is in Dallas, Texas. As the map in figure 7.1 shows, Texas is one U.S. state that is en route to deregulation. The TXU holding company owns subsidiaries in Australia, Europe, Bermuda, Mexico, China, and Texas and has interests in natural gas, pipelines, mining, power generation, transmission, wholesale energy trading, marketing, and telecommunications, where it owns a 50 percent stake in Pinnacle One, a local telephone company. In Texas, TXU has 4 million customers, while globally it has another 7 million, bringing the total to 11 million customers served. TXU also has 23 power generation plants in the state of Texas, including one that uses nuclear power, as well as the 7,200-mile Lone Star Pipeline.

TXU had $22 billion in sales in the year 2000, with 51 percent of the total coming from electricity, 25 percent coming from U.S. energy marketing, and 15 percent from European wholesale energy operations. Only 7 percent came from its TXU Gas Company, while the pipeline produced only 1 percent. Perhaps the most interesting statistic is that of the power that TXU sold in the United States, 33 percent was generated by natural gas and oil, while 37 percent came from coal, and 16 percent came from nuclear power. The last figure is impressive, given that the average person may not be aware of such a significant amount of power coming from this nonfossil fuel.

What I see as a major coup in business planning is TXU's aggressive overseas penetration in deregulated markets, which the company accomplished through acquisition. Its purchase of Norweb Energi in the U.K. made the company the largest power generator in the deregulated U.K., where it has 10 power plants, as well as a marketer of energy throughout Europe. This says several things, not the least of which is that the company will be ready to compete in 2002 when Texas becomes deregulated. In fact, on its own Web site *(www.txu.com)*, the company makes clear that it was a serious lobbying force to bring deregulation to Texas.

This kind of thinking is classic for the success of an evolving business. The company's first move into the international deregulated arena came in 1996, when it moved into Australia and at the same time bought the largest natural gas company in Texas. In 1999, TXU expanded its Australian operations with another purchase. And in between, it moved into the U.K. and Europe. The line of thought and action exhibited here is quite sensible and is a great benchmark for how a utility company should behave. First, TXU understood that the world was moving toward deregulation. This move began in the 1970s, as I mentioned earlier by using Chile and the U.K. as examples. Second, the company did not

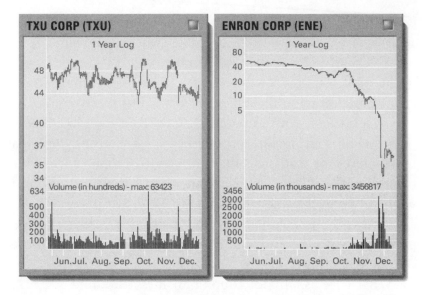

Figure 7.2: *TXU (NYSE:TXU; left) compared to Enron (NYSE:ENE) during the 2000–2001 bear market, courtesy of Telescan.*

rush headlong into the process, but instead waited for the bugs to be worked out of the system. Third, once it had become comfortable with its foreign deregulated properties, TXU aggressively prepared to implement its global strategy at home. By learning its lessons overseas, this company came back to its home ground and energetically lobbied for the change on its own turf, where it could enjoy the home-field advantage and combine this with its global experience.

Figure 7.2 is a picture of relative strength, as the shares of TXU held their value quite well, while Enron imploded. Note that in mid-September, as a result of the terrorist attack on the World Trade Center in New York City, both stocks suffered, but while Enron continued its downward path, TXU remained in a well-defined consolidation pattern. This figure also highlights the power of technical analysis when making buy-or-sell decisions. A pure fundamental or emotional trader might have sold his TXU when the market sank. But an investor familiar with technical analysis was more likely to keep the stock during the period, saving himself commission costs and heartache.

Two Examples of Why Being Trendy Can Cost You in the Utility Sector

Figure 7.3 is a picture of two companies in trouble. One, Montana Power, strayed from its well-protected and profitable near-monopoly in energy production, as well as in other diversified businesses, to become the next big-time telephone company. The other is Calpine, one of the first true pioneers in pure power production. But the chart clearly shows that trendy investing is not the same thing as trend investing—at least, not in my book. The former is investing in companies that are doing trendy things, like entering a business they've never been in before and neglecting their old steady business model and practices. This can be a recipe for disaster. The latter means buying stocks when they are going up and meeting certain technical and fundamental criteria, such as accelerating earnings growth and beating expectations, or shorting stocks that are breaking down. Trendy companies are best avoided, while those whose stocks are in an up trend should be bought or held, just as bad stocks should be shorted, depending on other parameters that I discuss in the technical analysis chapter.

As in the energy sector, the market likes to see that utility companies don't stray too far from their core business. A perfect example of trendy investing gone sour is Montana Power (NYSE:MTP), pictured in figure 7.3. Here is a company that had a well-diversified, profitable monopoly in the utilities business, but began to transform itself into a telephone company, providing local, long distance, and Internet access to its customers. The company began to aggressively move away from the utility business; as the chart shows, as long as the technology and telecom sector did well, the stock also did well. But when the tech sector rolled over, it became obvious that MTP had become a telecom company—at least insofar as building a cross-country fiber-optic network and incurring a great deal of debt

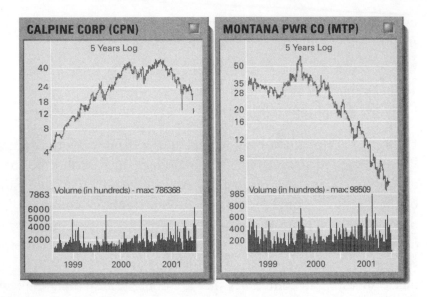

Figure 7.3: *Calpine (NYSE:CPN; left) and Montana Power (NYSE:MTP; right), courtesy of Telescan.*

along the way. When you compare figure 7.3 to figure 7.2 of TXU, the charts speak for themselves. When you buy utilities, it is best to choose those that are in the business of electricity.

Next, I will discuss another form of trendy investing: buying stock in clean companies—in other words, those that use natural gas and other forms of power instead of coal and oil for the generation of electricity. Calpine is the perfect barometer of the effects of the aftermath of Enron's collapse and of the confluence of factors in the power industry. It is also a great example of why investors should be careful to separate their political causes from their investments. I do not advocate investing in companies that pollute the environment. I merely note that if your only reason for buying a utility is that it burns clean fuels, then you should brush up on your technical and fundamental analysis before you click that mouse on your online trading account.

Calpine is a pure power producer, an aggressive company that landed a 10-year multibillion-dollar guaranteed contract from the state of California, as a result of that state's energy crisis. With its future seemingly so assured and with an apparently booming business, why did the stock fall? Because when Enron's problems began, Wall Street made a leap of faith and decided that Calpine was likely the next power producer to go down, based on its high level of debt and the public's complete loss of faith in the sector, when it became clear that Enron executives had lied and cheated their employees and their shareholders.

The charts clearly show that Calpine topped out at nearly the same time that Enron did in the spring of 2001. And the initial reason was the obvious slowing in the U.S. economy and the complete collapse of the Internet economy, which in turn had been the leading reason for the increase in demand for power. But by the end of the year and as more information became available, serious questions were raised about the company, including the company's alleged "cute" responses to SEC queries about its accounting practices. Moody's Investor Services downgraded Calpine's debt to junk on December 14, just one day after announcing that the company was under review. Moody's cited the reasons for the downgrade as concerns for Calpine's "near-term cash flow, liquidity sources, and financial flexibility."

And while the stock got beaten, the company maintained its innocence—pleas that, thanks to Enron, fell mostly on Wall Street's deaf and ruthless ears. What makes Calpine unique is that it is the leader in geothermal energy, which is energy derived from naturally occurring hot water springs. Calpine also has a significant involvement in natural gas–powered gas-generation plants, as well as sizable natural gas reserves. Thus, Calpine is, for lack of a better term, a "green" utility, meaning that it generates electricity by using cleaner-burning fuels than coal or crude oil and as a result had a significant portion of its business selling power to California utilities.

But the problem with the company was clearly shown on its balance sheet, which listed $158 billion in assets and $15 billion in liabilities as of September 2001. Of the liabilities, the balance sheet listed $9 billion as long-term debt and $1 billion in short-term debt. The company listed $1 billion in receivables and only $476 million in cash. The short version is that Calpine had $1.5 billion in liquid assets and $15 billion in liabilities and the potential for legal problems in the future, if its own accounting came under the same scrutiny as Enron's—a very tough spot to be in. Sure, Calpine had 18 power plants, but in a recession and in the midst of a credit crunch and an uncertain war, it would likely be difficult to sell assets at a reasonable price. The point is that in good economic times, Wall Street will give rapidly growing companies the benefit of the doubt. But when times get ugly, things get merciless in a hurry.

Perhaps the most interesting aspect of the stock's action is that during the time that the stock really skidded in late 2001, Calpine had just reported a nearly fourfold increase in revenues for its most recent quarter and had nearly doubled its earnings. But the debt load in a bad time seemed to carry the day.

Who Should Own Utility Stocks?

The Enron and Calpine examples certainly make this an excellent question to tackle. In days gone past, utility stocks were known as the perfect investment vehicles for "widows and orphans." These companies comprised one of the safest and the most dependable of all industry sectors. The combination of their protected monopolies and their dividend yields made them ideal for long-term income-seeking investors.

More important was that the sector was considered to be "interest rate–sensitive." In other words, the utilities were also a market barometer for future actions by the Federal Reserve. The logic was that because utilities functioned on borrowed money, when money became difficult to borrow, these were the first companies to feel the pinch. Smart investors would begin to sell these shares at key turning points in the business cycle, and the market would get a signal that a change in interest rates was coming. This relationship is not as valid now as it used to be, given the newly in-

Figure 7.4: *Comparison of the Philadelphia Utility Index (UTY; left) and the U.S. 10-Year Treasury Note Yield (TNX; right), courtesy of Telescan.*

fused growth potential into the power sector as a result of deregulation, but it can still be useful, as the charts of the Philadelphia Utility Index and the U.S. 10-Year Note Yield show in figure 7.4.

Note that the 10-Year Note Yield topped in late 1999 and began to fall, as the bond market predicted that the U.S. economy had started to weaken. And the utility stocks began to rise. But as the note yields rose in 2001, so did the utilities crumble. Also, the last down leg in note yields was not enough to revive the utility index. The message is clear: Even lower interest rates can't revive the utility sector, if the economy, and thus the demand for power, begins to fall, as it did during the recession of 2001. This means that as a utility investor, you have to be able to time the sweet spot, which is when the economy is still rising as a result of interest rates falling.

Note that this inverse relationship held up quite well in 2000, but as 2001 neared and as trouble for the sector became more evident, the relationship between bond yields and utility stocks was not as pronounced. This is a key relationship for investors to follow, because if this traditional intermarket relationship breaks down, it will mark a significant turning point in technical analysis of the financial markets and will mean that utility investors will have one less reliable indicator to use in their search for profits in the sector.

The main reason to invest in utilities in decades past had been in search of dividend yield. We have already seen that the integrated oil companies can provide a fairly good yield to investors, whereas the oil service stocks usually do not. Table 7.1 provides a comparison in dividend yield of the Dow Jones Industrials, the Dow Jones Transports, and the Dow Jones Utility averages on September 21, 2001. Table 7.2 provides a glimpse at the yield offered by the Dow Jones Utility Average's components.

The two tables clearly show that utility stocks can have excellent yields. And just to be complete, I ran a stock screen for high-yielding utility stocks at *www.hoovers.com,* using just its default criteria. The screen gave me one pick—Puget Energy (NYSE:PSD), a Washington State utility, with a nice 8 percent dividend yield. But a look at the chart in figure 7.5 shows that the stock wasn't that attractive to investors, despite its nice dividend yield. The bottom line is that stocks should not be picked based on dividend yields alone. That's a nice first step. But looking at a chart and examining balance sheets and other fundamentals are essential.

The first thing to consider when a high-yielding stock falls in price is that something could be wrong, and that's why the stock is paying such a high dividend, especially when compared to the benchmark provided by the Dow Utilities Index.

A news search for PSD revealed that nothing was really wrong, but that the company was running an experimental program in which its customers were being charged variable rates for using electricity at different times of the day. The object of the program was conservation. Although I liked the green aspects of the plan, from looking at the stock's chart, I couldn't help but think that this company could have trouble with its future earn-

Table 7.1: *Comparison of dividend yields in the Dow Jones Averages on September 21, 2001.*

Market Index	Dividend Yield
Dow Jones Utility	3.96%
Dow Jones Industrials	2.96%
Dow Jones Transports	1.81%

Table 7.2: *Dividend yield of the Dow Jones Utilities on September 21, 2001.*

Symbol	Stock	Yield
AEP	American Electric Power Co. Inc.	5.3%
AES	AES Corporation	0%
D	Dominion Resources	4.4%
DUK	Duke Power Co.	3.0%
ED	Consolidated Edison Co. of New York	5.4%
EIX	Edison International Inc.	0%
ENE	Enron Corporation	1.8%
EXC	Exelon Corporation	3.3%
NI	Nisource Inc.	5.0%
PCG	PG&E Corporation	0%
PEG	Public Service Enterprise Group Inc.	5.0%
REI	Houston Industries	5.01%
SO	Southern Co.	5.2%
TXU	TXU Corporation	5.2%
WMB	Williams Companies Inc.	2.8%

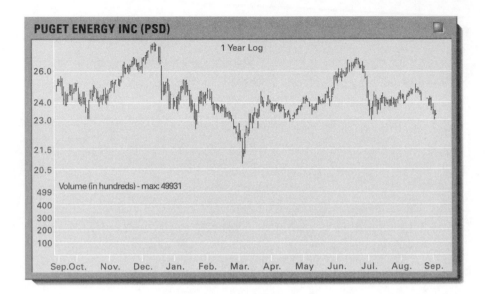

Figure 7.5: *Puget Sound Utilities (NYSE:PSD), courtesy of Telescan.*

ings, due to this encouragement of conservation without any apparent offsetting of its generating costs. This was a red flag that also suggested that, at some point, the dividend could get cut.

Perhaps the best way to get yield from a utility is to use the preferred stock series. Preferred stocks are stocks that pay a higher dividend than do common stocks. The main difference is that common stock holders are allowed to vote in company matters, such as in the election of board members, whereas preferred stock holders do not vote, but receive a higher yield in exchange.

The best place to look for preferred stocks is in a leading utility company, such as TXU's Preferred Class A stock, which in October 2001 paid a 7.5 percent yield, compared to U.S. Treasury bills, whose yields had fallen to 2.61 percent, due to the Fed's easing of monetary policy in response to the World Trade Center collapse and the economic worries that followed. It is important to make sure that the preferred stock moves along with the underlying common stock. And in this case, TXU's "Class A" preferred stock was moving in a similar pattern to the TXU common stock in figure 7.2. If the preferred is not moving higher, then you at least want to see it moving sideways, meaning that people are not selling or bailing out. If they are, it is an indication that trouble is brewing and that conservative yield-seeking investors are looking to put their money elsewhere. The message is clear: If you are looking for yield, the utility sector can provide it. But if you want more yield than you would find in common stocks, preferred stocks can give you a bonus in exchange for taking away your right to vote on company issues. For most of us, it is a nice right to give up in exchange for extra yield.

The most important thing to do when buying preferred stock is to look for the date that the stock expires—that is, think of these stocks as bonds, which in effect many of them are. The yield you get is not guaranteed forever. Just to be thorough, I placed a call to TXU, as I wrote this chapter, and found that the TXU Preferred Class A stock was issued with a callable date of December 2003, even though the series was scheduled to be available until December 2029. What this meant is that investors who had planned to hold the preferred stock until 2029 might have it bought back from them as early as 2003. This, of course, rises in probability as interest rates fall, because companies want to retire the higher-yielding debt and issue lower-yielding debt.

When Should You Invest in Utilities?

As I've shown, and despite the new factors and increased volatility introduced into the sector, utility stocks are actually still worthy of consideration for long-term diversified portfolios, as long as careful analysis of the company's fundamentals and technicals are performed. The allocation of the portfolio into this sector should be dictated by the investor's affinity, first, for income and, second, for growth. The classic play on utilities is to own them as interest rates begin to fall, as during this time the best total return can be achieved. But because of the increased risk of utilities due to deregulation and the dark cloud over the sector that emerged in late 2001 when Enron Corp. collapsed, the axiom "low interest rate equals higher utility stock prices" is no longer nearly automatic. Traditionally, though, it is when interest rates are falling that the dividend yield of these companies becomes attractive and can provide an added boost to the stocks. And note that due to the increased pressures on management to deliver a higher stock price, many utilities have stopped paying or have greatly reduced their dividends, in order to plow the money back into growth. Finally, yield-seeking investors should realize that it might be best to look at the preferred shares of utility companies whose charts are holding up best.

Utility stocks can also be part of growth-oriented portfolios, as long as investors are well versed in the use of technical and fundamental analysis. I cannot stress enough that utility stocks can fall as hard and as fast as any other sector, due to individual factors such as earnings shortfalls or management miscues.

The Companies in the Dow Jones Utility Average

The Dow Jones Utility average is the most widely recognized benchmark in the utility industry. It is not complete, by any means, but it does provide a nice illustrative snapshot of the industry. As in the prior chapters, the goal here is to show how each company differs from others in the field and why certain management teams are successful where others aren't.

Southern Company (NYSE:SO)

I have already used TXU as a benchmark, given its global reach. But a similar well-run vertically integrated utility company is Southern Company, which operates Alabama Power, Georgia Power, Gulf Power, Mississippi Power, and Savannah Electric—companies that together service 3.9 million customers. As with TXU, Southern Company also operates a telecom unit, but, interestingly, has spun off its power-trading business, the former

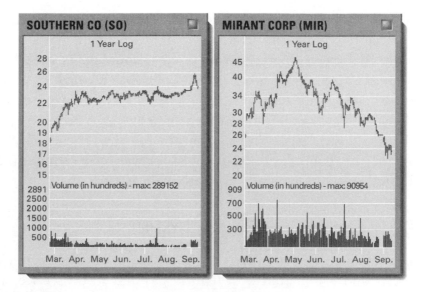

Figure 7.6: *Southern Company (NYSE:SO; left) and Mirant Corp. (NYSE:MIR; right), courtesy of Telescan.*

Southern Energy, to its shareholders, calling the new company Mirant (NYSE:MIR).

And here is a classic example of an excellent business decision, as the parent company sold off its power-trading company. Mirant's business is similar to Enron's, which, of course, proved to be a dismal set of circumstances for all involved, especially for the company's employees. Figure 7.6 clearly illustrates that investors approved of the spin-off, as shares of Mirant plummeted while the parent company shares remained in an up trend during a period that marked a disastrous bear market. The lesson here is quite simple: A well-run firm like Southern Company is likely to make the right moves at the right time, such as limiting its risks from energy trading, which, like any other form of trading, will have its ups and downs.

The Southern Company also operates three nuclear plants through its subsidiary Southern Nuclear, which produce over 20 percent of the energy used in Alabama and Georgia. With over

$10 billion in sales in the year 2000, this is a significant utility company, which still produces over 76 percent of its power from coal and 16 percent from nuclear sources. As with TXU, Southern Company has a European presence through its power-transmission unit in the U.K., having sold its power-generation division. This again is an excellent management decision, given that there were larger rivals in Europe for power generation. Instead, the company expanded its power generation in the United States by moving into the Northeast.

Consolidated Edison of New York (NYSE:ED)

Consolidated Edison powers much of New York City with electricity and Manhattan with natural gas and steam service. The company is also diversified along the lines of the other large players in the industry, through telecommunications, power marketing, and trading operations.

While TXU and Southern Company had a relatively good go at things in the late 1990s and early 21st century, Con Ed had its share of problems, beginning with a failed merger with Boston's Northeast Utilities and including the shutting down of a nuclear plant that leaked radioactive steam. Table 7.3 shows Con Ed's revenues and earnings from 1998 to 2001. The overall trend is encouraging for revenues, which, at least on a year-to-year basis from 1998 to 2000, showed an upward trend. But a look at the earnings during the period shows that they began to fall in the year 2000. This is a sign of trouble because the year 2000 provided opportunities for stable earnings in the utility sector, especially for those with energy-trading operations.

Table 7.4 provides us with an opportunity to compare the performance of Con Ed to that of TXU, which represents the benchmark for the new kind of emerging utility company. Note that during the period, TXU's revenues and earnings were more predictable and showed a greater rate of growth on a year-over-year basis. Also note the significant decrease in earnings in the year

Table 7.3: *Revenues and earnings for Consolidated Edison, courtesy of Market Guide.*

Revenues (Thousands of U.S. Dollars)

Quarters	1998	1999	2000	2001
March	1,853,047	1,776,586	2,318,591	2,886,264
June	1,561,041	1,479,081	2,041,894	2,112,215
September	2,061,622	2,346,241	2,820,779	
December	1,617,338	1,889,415	2,250,127	
TOTAL	7,093,048	7,491,323	9,431,391	

Earnings per Share

Quarters	1998	1999	2000	2001
March	0.730	0.760	0.880	0.840
June	0.260	0.295	0.325	0.478
September	1.490	1.520	1.320	
December	0.570	0.560	0.220	
TOTAL	3.050	3.135	2.745	

2000 for Con Ed, while TXU nearly equaled its prior year's earnings. This is a sign that Con Ed was having trouble managing its operations and that expenses ran higher than expected. Also note the nice streak of rising sequential revenue gains for TXU that began in June of 1999 and lasted until March 2001. This is the mark of a company whose markets are expanding.

Edison International (NYSE:EIX)

Across the United States—in California—is Edison International, a company that grew from a regional utility company to global player. And it is this global capacity that saved the company from the fate of its intrastate rival, Pacific Gas & Electric's PG&E unit,

Table 7.4: *Revenues and earnings for TXU, courtesy of* Market Guide.

Revenues (Millions of U.S. Dollars)

Quarters	1998	1999	2000	2001
March	2,499	4,468	4,776	8,375
June	3,236	3,729	4,592	6,127
September	4,380	4,435	5,834	
December	4,620	4,486	6,807	
TOTAL	14,735	17,118	22,009	

Earnings per Share

Quarters	1998	1999	2000	2001
March	0.520	0.650	0.710	0.760
June	0.330	0.350	0.865	0.780
September	1.040	1.310	1.250	
December	0.840	1.240	0.610	
TOTAL	2.730	3.550	3.435	

which declared bankruptcy as a result of the California energy crisis. Edison International's best-known unit is Southern California Edison, which has 4.3 million customers in the state.

But the trouble caused by the crisis did not evade Edison International completely, as the company had to agree to sell its transmission grid to the state of California to keep from going into bankruptcy. As the deregulation juggernaut begins to gather steam in the United States, it is increasingly important to become discriminating about which utility companies to invest in. Those that are vertically integrated, such as TXU and Southern Company, proved to be more resilient during the tough testing period of the year 2000, where the key dynamic was the ability to capitalize on power-trading profits from the sale to California in the spot market, in order to offset the losses from decreasing power consumption

Table 7.5: *Revenues and earnings for Edison International, courtesy of* Market Guide.

Revenues (Thousands of U.S. Dollars)

Quarters	1998	1999	2000	2001
March	1,909,560	2,095,900	2,723,320	2,462,000
June	1,939,035	2,120,899	2,749,164	2,627,000
September	2,753,648	2,962,797	3,653,203	
December	2,257,757	2,516,404	2,591,313	
TOTAL	8,860,000	9,696,000	11,717,000	

Earnings per Share

Quarters	1998	1999	2000	2001
March	0.384	0.410	0.320	−1.890
June	0.400	0.370	0.410	−0.310
September	0.600	0.730	1.110	
December	0.440	0.280	−7.830	
TOTAL	1.824	1.790	−5.990	

caused by a slowing economy. Edison International had a global portfolio and assets to sell, such as its transmission grid, which gave it an advantage in a tough market during a tough period.

Edison Mission Energy is the global subsidiary of Edison International and has power plants in Asia, Europe, and North America. Other subsidiaries include telecommunications operations, as well as natural gas utilities and power plant designing and building operations. Ninety-three percent of the $9.4 billion in sales for the entire company in the year 2000 came from electricity and natural gas.

The information in table 7.5 provides an excellent example of how a company can set itself up for trouble, as it shows that Edison International had a great deal of trouble in the years 2000 and early 2001. These massive losses were a direct result of the California energy crisis. But the company's vulnerability really began in 1999, when it aggressively bought several power plants in the midwestern United States for $5 billion, as well as two more power plants in the U.K. These moves came late in the game and cost the company dearly. As I showed earlier, TXU was buying utilities abroad as early as 1997, showing that its management team was acting in a timelier manner. More important, TXU concentrated its efforts in the U.K. and Europe, while EIX spread its expansion to many places on the globe simultaneously, showing in retrospect that the company was in some sense panicking. This proved true when Edison Mission Energy CEO Edward Muller abruptly resigned in mid-2000. Management changes in the midst of an aggressive expansion, coinciding with a rising energy crisis or any other difficult period, are always a tip-off that all is not right with a company. A sudden management change was also a noticeable feature of Enron's problems in late 2001.

The red lights were going off here, as this company was very aggressive in its expansion at a time when the U.S. economy was beginning to soften. So if we use TXU and Southern Company as the benchmarks for well-managed companies, then companies that do not act in similar fashion or in what seems to be a rational manner should be avoided.

PG&E Corporation (NYSE:PCG)

Edison International's intrastate rival, PG&E, was not able to escape the wrath of the California energy crisis. PG&E is really the parent company of Pacific Gas & Electric, the company that filed for bankruptcy in April 2001. The company owed up to $1 billion before the filing. The story is familiar: The company had to buy power in the wholesale market and could not pass on the costs to consumers. As a result, too much debt built up, followed by the need for bankruptcy. But as figure 7.7 shows, the day of the filing proved to be an excellent buying opportunity for those who had

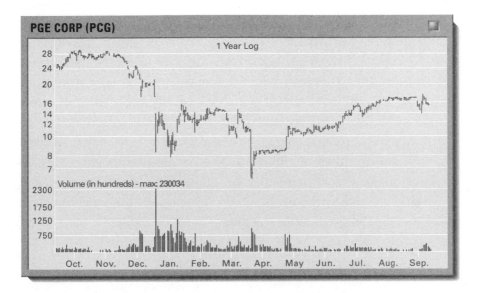

Figure 7.7: *PG&E Corp. (NYSE:PCG), courtesy of Telescan.*

the foresight and the guts to brave the stock on that day. I bought the stock on the announcement for my own account and held it for several days, selling it at a profit.

PG&E did not go out of business, but its subsidiary, Pacific Gas & Electric, did go bankrupt. That was the reason for the rally in PCG, the parent company. When investors saw that the troubled subsidiary was going bankrupt, it became obvious that the parent company could continue to operate. That was the reason for the rally, which, as the chart shows, lasted well into the fall of 2001. This is in direct contrast to the bankruptcy of Enron Corp., where the company in question was not a subsidiary, but a freestanding entity. More important was that little doubt existed that Pacific Gas & Electric had the working infrastructure and personnel to continue to provide electricity for the state of California. Its only problem was that it could not pay its bills, if they continued to mount. Thus, bankruptcy in this case was helpful to the business, not a sign of a need for liquidation. It is important to make these distinctions.

PG&E, the parent company itself, was not in huge trouble as a result of its unfortunate subsidiary, either. A look at the revenues and earnings for 2000 shows that the company brought in over $26 billion for the year, while it declared a huge loss in the final quarter of 2000 and the first quarter of 2001. But by the second quarter of 2001, the company was once again profitable. The lesson here is as pure a contrarian lesson as I've ever seen. And it is one that should be etched into the minds of investors. Let the charts make the decision for you. This was a company in deep trouble, but when the news finally came out, a huge profit opportunity erupted for nimble traders.

AES Corp. (NYSE:AES)

AES Corp., whose full name is Applied Energy Services, illustrates another example of the perils of investing in utilities in the 21st century. Here is a company that is globally diversified and still had a great deal of trouble with its stock price in 2001, even as interest rates fell, which, as I showed earlier, are traditionally a powerful booster to stock prices in the utilities sector. But AES's problems should not have been a surprise, for they were predictable, based on the company's business model and the inherent risks associated with it.

AES is exclusively an international power producer, with power plants in the United States, Asia, Europe, and Latin America, and is in a similar business to that of Calpine. Thus it is subject to the same kinds of market risks, as supply and demand and global economies move the price of power and affect the company's revenues and earnings. Most important is that AES has a significant presence in South America, especially in Brazil, which, along with Argentina, was having currency-related problems in 2001. Here again, a little knowledge of history and past markets is quite helpful. Argentina is a heavily indebted country, which has had a terrible fiscal record for decades. Argentina has also had its share of political instability and in December 2001 was in danger of defaulting on billions of dollars worth of loans. Argentina is also a major trading partner with Brazil, whose economy had actually behaved much more reasonably during the period, due to a more stringent adherence to a semblance of fiscal responsibility. Nevertheless, Brazil's currency—the real—due to its slightly higher standing among global currency traders, is often the butt of heavy selling when problems arise in Argentina.

And Brazil was the reason for the swoon in the shares of AES in September 2001, as the company warned that it would have trouble meeting earnings expectations for the full year due to weakness in the real, as well as to decreasing global economic activity and falling power prices in the U.K. Brazil, however, is not alone in AES's portfolio, because in the late 1990s the company added to its property list electric utility and distribution companies that were located in Argentina and El Salvador. AES also bought properties in India, which made the company look like a powerhouse, with its 70 percent sales growth in 1998. The lesson here for investors is that American companies that own international properties could suffer from political, as well as currency-related, risks, along with the usual risks of supply and demand that go with the power-generating business.

AES, despite its 2001 problems, reiterated its intention to continue its pursuit of Venezuela's largest telecom company. Once again, the company's appetite for expansion, especially during difficult times, could prove to be a double-edged sword, as in the case of Edison International, whose aggressive expansion was nearly a death blow to the company when the California energy crisis hit.

Dominion Resources (NYSE:D)

Dominion Resources is a company that began preparing for deregulation in its primary area of business, Virginia, in 1999, a full five years before the 2004 date of implementation. The company has a long tradition: George Washington and James Madison chartered it in 1781 as the Upper Appomattox Company, a canal operation company, which in 1888 expanded into hydroelectric operations. In 1925, it became the Virginia Electric and Power Company and expanded into North Carolina.

The company involved itself in nuclear power in the early 1970s and was nearly bankrupt in the early 1980s, which is the only real low point in the stock's history. By the early 1990s, the company had regained its footing and in 1997 expanded into the U.K., then branched out into gas and coal exploration in the early 2000s.

While AES fell, in late 2001 Dominion began to show some relative strength and the stock began to hold its ground, even as others fell. This relative strength was due to investors recognizing that Dominion has had a great record of delivering in the past. Furthermore, the company has a sound business base, which includes natural gas reserves and a power plant construction business, with no real major international exposure. Dominion's $9.6 billion in 2000 sales were 51 percent derived from its energy business, but 30 percent and 14 percent came from its energy delivery companies and its natural gas exploration and production, which Dominion enhanced by buying Consolidated Natural Gas. One of the most lucrative areas of the energy sector in the 21st century is likely to be natural gas exploration, which was made clear in December 2001, as the U.S. government opened a sizable chunk of its Rocky Mountain lands for exploration.

Most interesting is that while AES was pursuing a Venezuelan telecom company, Dominion was planning a new power plant in North Carolina. Once again, you could see why Dominion showed relative strength. At the time, Venezuela was starting to show signs of political instability, as its president began to turn his government away from democratic reforms that were previously in place. Nothing fancy here: Venezuela was risky, North Carolina was not. Once again, this is an excellent example of an effective management team continuing to execute a steady-growth business plan based on its domestic strategy. What I like about Dominion is that the company learned its lessons from the early 1980s and continued to concentrate on what it does best: domestic power production and transmission.

Duke Power (NYSE:DUK)

Duke Power is another company that supports the thesis that utility companies can make excellent long-term investments. Duke's major service area is the Carolinas in the United States, but Duke is a massive company with $49 billion in sales. Duke is a major power marketer, with 70 percent of its sales coming from trading and marketing power. Twenty-six percent of its sales in 2000 came from electricity and field services, which is natural gas production. More important is that 98 percent of its sales came from the United States and Canada. Very few utility companies are able to work profitably outside the United States, and the markets applaud companies that do not attempt to move outside their areas of strength.

Duke also operates a 12,000-mile natural gas pipeline that provides service to the northeastern United States, an area of high industrial development and high energy requirements. Duke is excellent at forging partnerships; its trading and marketing arm is a joint venture with Exxon-Mobil, and it has a venture with Fluor, which builds power plants. Duke's international exposure has been smart, because it builds power plants, but does not really operate too many of them. This is about to change, as the company will be buying power-production facilities in the U.K.

American Electric Power (NYSE:AEP)

American Electric Power is based in Columbus, Ohio, but operates utilities in Arkansas, Indiana, Kentucky, Louisiana, Michigan, Ohio, Oklahoma, Tennessee, Texas, Virginia, and West Virginia. AEP also has a significant portion of its business outside of the

United States, with operations in Europe, Australia, and South America. The company is a leading power marketer and produces 78 percent of its power from coal-powered plants, with 14 percent from natural gas and 5 percent from nuclear. However, the stock was weakening in September 2001.

The problem with AEP, as the market saw it, was that the company was getting ready for deregulation. On September 28, the company announced a major management reshuffling, to prepare for the separation of its businesses into deregulated and non-deregulated businesses. But on the day of the announcement, the company also noted that Paul Addis, a high-ranking executive who had been responsible for AEP's highly profitable power-marketing operations, was resigning. Once again, the sudden management change appeared and hurt the stock. The stock fell on the news, as Wall Street hates uncertainty—especially uncertainty in the boardroom at a time when the company is facing a major change, such as splitting into several divisions.

An even more important news item was also released on that day, as the company reassured Wall Street about its upcoming earnings and even predicted further growth in the following year. Earnings and revenues were solid for this company in September 2001. When a stock falls on the day that the company reassures Wall Street about its earnings, especially when earnings are falling all around the market, it says a great deal about investors' concerns about management changes and the company's ability to deliver. That is not a stock to buy on weakness. It is one to avoid.

This is not a knock on the company, whose long-term fundamentals seemed fairly sound, based on publicly available information. It is a situational report, which illustrates key reasons why investors need to do their homework before buying any stock. Learn the nuances of the business, and then apply them to the company. When you combine the fundamentals of the industry with good knowledge of the company and with technical analysis, your results will improve.

Exelon (NYSE:EXC)

Exelon is a huge midwestern U.S. utility that resulted when Philadelphia's Peco Energy bought Chicago's Unicom. The distinguishing characteristic of the combination was that both companies were large operators of nuclear plants. As a result, the merger created a rare company that generates 70 percent of its power from nuclear energy and is the leading nuclear power generator in the United States. Exelon had $7.5 billion in sales in 2000, and 60 percent came from power distribution, while nearly 30 percent came from power generation. The rest came from other enterprises such as the company's wireless venture with AT&T Wireless and voice and data transmission through its fiber-optic network.

Because of Exelon's reliance on nuclear power for its power production, it makes sense to assume that the stock is immune to the volatility of the oil and natural gas markets. But in fact, as figure 7.8 clearly illustrates, the stock got clobbered in September for many of the same reasons that AES did, in addition to falling after the September 11 attack on the World Trade Center—the first gap on the chart. Then on September 27, Exelon announced 450 job cuts and lowered its earnings forecast for the upcoming quarter. Of course, the stock fell dramatically; note the second, and larger, gap on the chart. Exelon's management made it clear that the stock got hurt by several factors: (1) Deregulation led to a glut of power. (2) The slowing economy, combined with the glut, led to lower prices. (3) Factors 1 and 2 were worsened by the effects on the economy of the World Trade Center terrorist attack.

The example is worth exploring further. First, the chart clearly forecast further weakness, as the stock was unable to rise above 70. Earnings and revenue growth rates had already been slowing, and the market was looking at the company not as a dividend play, but as a growth stock. And growth stocks that don't deliver expected growth rates get sold off dramatically. The bottom line here is that the market was not happy with this newly merged

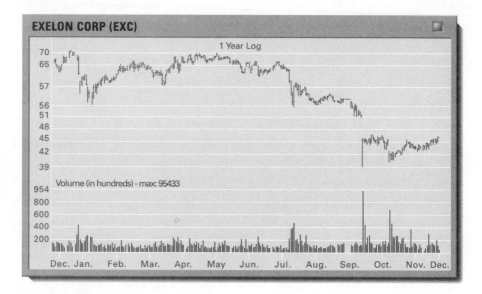

EXELON CORP (EXC)

1 Year Log

Volume (in hundreds) - max: 95433

Dec. Jan.   Feb.   Mar.   Apr.   May   Jun.   Jul.   Aug.   Sep.   Oct.   Nov. Dec.

Figure 7.8: *Exelon (NYSE:EXC), courtesy of Telescan.*

company's inability to deal with a tough market environment. Other stocks in the sector sold off in sympathy.

But by December 2001, as tensions rose between OPEC and Russia over crude oil production cuts, and as the chart shows, the stock began to rise, as investors concerned about global oil and natural gas supplies began to slowly build positions in a company whose nuclear power–generation technology would make it exempt from any potential problems in the oil and natural gas market. This is another example of why you should keep an eye on stocks that break down due to a transient news event, much as with PCG.

This is a great exercise to engage in when investing in stocks. On the day that bad news is reported, Wall Street tends to sell all of the stocks in the sector equally. But this copycat effect is useful, as once the short-term volatility is over, some stocks will recover, while others don't. So, when the market initially reacts in a shotgun fashion, I like to wait. After a few days, when traders and money managers have had a chance to sift through the rubble, some stocks come back, as Exelon did in this example. Knowledge of this company's dominant position on nuclear power–generated electricity was beneficial for investors with very long-term time horizons, who were looking for a low-price entry point into the stock.

The way to turn a difficult situation into a profit is to monitor several stocks in the sector and look for the overwhelming price trend. Once you identify the reason for the rise or fall in price, then look for companies that deviate from the norm. Those that rise when the rest of the sector is falling are worth doing more research on. In this case, the nuclear power angle, during a time of uncertainty in the global oil market, helped investors to spot a potential winner.

Public Service Enterprise Group (NYSE:PEG)

PEG is New Jersey's major utility, with its deregulated power generating utility, PSEG Power, selling electricity to the parent and the wholesale market. In turn, PEG sells power and natural gas to 1.9 and 1.6 million customers, respectively. PEG's revenue sources are well diversified, with natural gas accounting for 31 percent of sales, while power generation produces 33 percent and transmission and distribution 24 percent. As with Exelon, PEG uses nuclear power for 60 percent of its power production, with coal accounting for 31 percent and natural gas for 7 percent.

Nuclear power has not been all rosy for PEG, as its main power source incurred hefty fines in the 1980s and in 1995. And this company's management continued to make interesting acquisitions when in 1999 it bought power plants in Argentina; it also has sizable investments in Chile.

This is a company to watch closely, given its presence in a highly populated and highly industrialized area of the United States and its negative history with its nuclear plants in the past, which casts a slight shadow over it. Other areas of caution are its investment in South America, which makes the company quite

Table 7.6: *Revenues and earnings for PEG, courtesy of* Market Guide.

Revenues (Thousands of U.S. Dollars)

Quarters	1998	1999	2000	2001
March	1,659,000	1,795,000	2,483,000	2,819,000
June	1,362,000	1,436,000	2,159,000	2,171,000
September	1,439,000	1,582,000	1,525,000	
December	1,550,000	1,645,000	681,000	
TOTAL	6,010,000	6,458,000	6,848,000	

Earnings per Share

Quarters	1998	1999	2000	2001
March	0.820	0.840	1.250	1.220
June	0.530	0.825	0.660	0.681
September	0.780	1.010	0.660	
December	0.660	0.610	0.980	
TOTAL	2.790	3.285	3.550	

vulnerable to the potential political and international problems that face other North American utilities in the area, such as AES.

Finally, the revenues and earnings shown in table 7.6 suggest that there was inconsistency of growth throughout the period and a slowing in the rate of growth for revenues and earnings. This was noted in the comparisons of the first and second quarters for 2000 and 2001, which were essentially flat on the earnings front, despite moderate revenue increases. Slowly growing revenues and flat earnings suggest that the company is not very efficiently run or that, at least during the period summarized, it had a great deal of expenses. This was likely a result of the company's large presence in Latin America, the uncertainties created by the exposure, and the increased costs of moving toward a deregulated environment. Once again, uncertainty creates reasons for Wall Street to sell. The flip side is that at some point, the uncertainty is factored in, and the stock can recover.

Reliant Energy (NYSE:REI)

If a picture is worth a thousand words, then the chart of Reliant Energy in figure 7.9 speaks for itself. Here is a huge utility based in Houston, Texas, a company that was established in 1882 and has a long history as a publicly traded stock. And yet its chart is a total disaster. The problem is that REI is a shopaholic. This company loves to buy and sell other companies and take on debt. In September, REI announced a $2.7 billion cash acquisition of Orion Power (NYSE:OP), which would also lead to the assumption of $1.8 billion of Orion debt. That was the killing blow, because REI, as a result of its acquisition binges in the past, had accumulated $26 billion worth of liabilities, which included long-term debt of $9 billion. Note that the company only had $107 million in cash in June 2001. Receivables and asset sales could easily have left the company debt-free and with $6 billion in equity, but the acquisition raised eyebrows and prompted Standard & Poor's to lower Reliant's credit rating.

What I found most interesting in analyzing Reliant was that its earnings and revenues were quite robust, and yet the market ignored this and chose to focus on the company's potential debt problems—a similar perspective that it took with Calpine and worth reinforcing. Note that Wall Street tends to be especially unforgiving if a company has more than one apparent weakness. In this case, the debt problem was obvious. But the international risks made the problem twice as intolerable. Once again, this is a company with a large presence in Latin America, as it has interests in power plants in Argentina, Brazil, Colombia, and El Salvador to go along with its European operations. In 1998, the company bought power plants in California and also made plans to build plants in Arizona and Nevada.

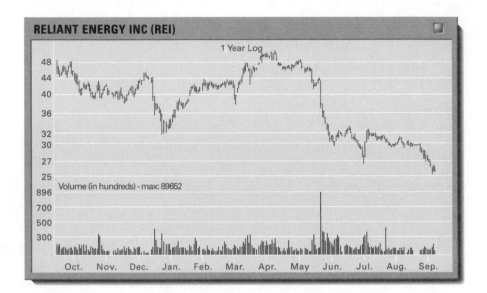

Figure 7.9: *Reliant Energy (NYSE:REI), courtesy of Telescan.*

Another weakness is that Reliant relies on purchased power from other utilities to provide 20 percent of the power it sells to customers. That is another negative, given the Enron disaster and the potential for difficulties in the smooth trading of power between utilities, because the main middleman for the circuit was taken out of the equation. And although Reliant had $29 billion in sales in 2000, its need for power from outside sources was another liability that justified Wall Street's negative opinion of the stock.

First Energy (NYSE:FE)

First Energy replaced Enron in the Dow Jones Utility average in December 2001, and the chart shows an excellent choice by the panel of judges. This is a major player in the midwestern United States; it is based in Akron, Ohio, but is expanding into the East Coast aggressively. Its balance sheet is pristine, with $18 billion in assets and only $8 billion in debt and $13 billion in total liabilities.

Table 7.7: *Growth rates for First Energy, courtesy of* Market Guide.

Growth Rates	1 Year	3 Year	5 Year
Revenue	11.22%	33.40%	23.31%
EPS	7.68%	11.51%	5.60%
Dividend	0.00%	0.00%	0.00%

Its growth rates are all quite acceptable and reachable on a regular basis, meaning that there is little room for disappointment. The company pays no dividend, which means that it is committed to its growth strategy. And the stock has excellent sponsorship on Wall Street, as the chart in figure 7.10 shows.

Perhaps what made First Energy most attractive to the Dow Jones Utility selection panel was that more than 60 percent of the energy produced by FE comes from coal. This makes the company quite able to withstand whipsaws in the energy markets, such as oil and natural gas, given that much of the coal used by utilities comes from the United States and Canada.

First Energy has the usual array of international companies and energy trading operations, but in order to participate in the deregulated marketplace, the company's main business is still in the United States and is largely insulated from the very real threats that others in the sector face more directly.

Summary

This chapter is by no means all-inclusive in the number of companies it profiles, but is quite substantial in providing examples of well-run companies and companies whose business models have led to less-than-stellar performance for their stock. My goal was to look at how companies run their business and extract any trends that Wall Street would view as either positive or negative.

Figure 7.10: *First Energy (NYSE:FE), courtesy of Telescan.*

The message was quite clear. Wall Street views utility companies as both growth and value companies. This means that a great deal of scrutiny is placed on traditional growth parameters, such as revenues and earnings growth rates. At the same time, Wall Street looks at the hard-core fundamentals such as debt ratios, management changes, and business strategies. The final arbiter is price action, and this chapter really gave us some great examples of well-run companies, such as TXU, which the market continued to support during one of the worst bear markets in history.

On the other side, we saw companies whose business strategies were not endorsed by Wall Street. We noted, aside from Enron, other utility companies such as Reliant Energy, whose buying spree of the late 1990s spread into the 21st century and brought misery to its shareholders. I pointed out companies that the market perceived as not reacting well to unexpected problems like the World Trade Center disaster and hinted at the problems caused by Enron's demise, a topic that will be fully explored in the chapter on natural gas.

Perhaps the most underestimated risk when owning utility stocks is to carefully gauge the company's exposure to Latin America, which could well be the next area of major financial and political problems as the 21st century rolls on. Many U.S. and other international companies were sold on the growth prospects of the region and invested heavily in power plants and other infrastructure. In the first part of the new century, this strategy has at the very least been delayed in delivering its promise and has already cost many companies dearly.

The bottom line is that the utility sector offers a broad spectrum of investment opportunities, beginning with dividend yield potential and extending to growth opportunities. Investors who are well versed in top-down analysis, from the trend of interest rates to index and individual stock analysis, are best prepared to profit here.

8

Natural Gas

N atural gas is one of the most important naturally occurring materials in use today. And although this introduction may read like a college textbook, it will give you a sense of what human ingenuity has done with this gift of nature, as well as provide some basic background information that will help you make better investment decisions. Today natural gas is one of the most popular forms of energy, as its ability to burn more cleanly than petroleum and coal make it environmentally attractive. It is extremely versatile and can be used for heating, cooling, producing electricity, and powering vehicles such as cars and buses. The chemical industry uses the chemicals in natural gas to make detergents, drugs, and plastics. Increasingly, natural gas is being mixed with other fuels to improve their environmental performance. As I discussed earlier, natural gas is found in conjunction with crude oil. Both are trapped in pockets of the earth's crust and coexist with other impurities, including water, sand, and often salt.

Natural gas is really methane, a naturally occurring odorless gas that is found either alone in its own natural reservoir or together with crude oil. It is important to note that methane can also coexist with other compounds, such as propane, ethane, and butane, which together are known as natural gas liquids. Propane is also used as a fuel for cars and even to heat and light homes in remote locations. Gas liquids are usually removed before gas enters pipelines. Natural gas is clear and odorless, with the familiar odor that we all recognize resulting from an additive whose purpose is to warn users of a potential leak.

This sector merits its own chapter, not just because of the increasing popularity of natural gas as a global fuel, but because it plays an increasingly pivotal role in the formulation of global energy policy. It is really an industry sector on its own, with its own benchmark index, the AMEX Natural Gas Index (XNG), whose companies are profiled later in the chapter.

I begin with a brief history, then move into the fundamentals of supply and demand. Finally, I'll describe individual benchmark companies, with special emphasis on management, decision making, business models, and, of course, chart analysis.

Where Are the Majority of the World's Natural Gas Reserves?

When I first started to develop, research, and write this book in the winter of 2000 and the spring of 2001, the world was a different place than it became in the fall and early winter of 2001. During those 10 to 12 months much changed, and probably for the next several decades. As I write the concluding chapters, some of the predictions I made in the early pages have already come to pass, even before the book hits the presses. The events of September 11, 2001, at the World Trade Center in New York City will profoundly influence the energy markets. That is a given, with the perpetrators of the tragedy coming from an area in the Middle East—Afghanistan—that is strategic, not because of its energy reserves, but because of its highly charged atmosphere.

If the events of September 11, 2001, and the ensuing and potentially escalating war become a long-lasting global conflict, then regardless of how cooperative OPEC wishes to remain, natural gas is likely to become an increasingly important source of fuel. Thus, it makes sense for investors to know where the largest re-

Table 8.1: *Regional breakdown of global natural gas reserves, adapted from the U.S. Energy Information Administration Web site, www.eia.doe.gov. Reserves expressed in trillion cubic feet.*

Country	Reserves	Country	Reserves
North America		**Central and South America**	
United States	167.4	Venezuela	145.8
Canada	63.5	Argentina	24.3
Mexico	30.4	Total	227.9
Total	261.3		
Western Europe		**Eastern Europe**	
Netherlands	60.0	Russia	1,700.0
Norway	41.0	Turkmenistan	101.0
United Kingdom	26.0	Uzbekistan	66.2
Total	152.7	Kazakhstan	65.0
		Total	1999.2

serves are found and from there to formulate a set of expectations based on political and geographical ideas. Table 8.1 summarizes the major geographical reserve areas for natural gas, with the main reserve countries being listed, as well as the regional totals.

Russia and its former republics are the power of the future in natural gas—at least, for the European continent—and their new-found clout was best displayed when OPEC made several gestures to Russia, Uzbekistan, and others to join the organization. Interestingly, they all declined, another sign that a great deal of back-room action is in progress that will eventually reshape, or at least greatly influence, the natural gas market. In my opinion, table 8.1 drives home the most important message about natural gas and its potential impact on global energy markets: Russia and its former republics have the most reserves of any nations of the developed world, making them the players to be reckoned with in the 21st century. The information provided there is fraught with huge global economic, political, and humanitarian implications, especially in the wake of the September 11 events and the increasing hostilities in the Middle East, as well as in other areas where oil and gas are the main economic force, such as Venezuela and portions of Africa. More important—and a very under-reported fact, which clearly shows how Russia plans to exert its newfound power—was the move that began in the spring of 2001 to re-nationalize the natural gas industry, when in May the government replaced the CEO of Gazprom, the world's largest natural gas company, with the deputy energy minister. Gazprom is publicly traded in Russia, but is 38 percent owned by the government, and its mandate included the provision of natural gas to Russians at a severely discounted rate from global natural gas prices.

The move allowed Gazprom to bully its way through competition, and by October 5, 2001, Gazprom had begun deliveries of natural gas to the Netherlands. According to Stratfor.com (a subscription-based and highly accurate Net-based, private intelligence service), the buzz around Europe at the time had begun to gather steam, with the main point being that Russia was the new go-to energy source.

If Russia can successfully develop the infrastructure and business savvy to turn Gazprom into not just the energy provider of choice for Europe, but a cash cow, the future of the Middle East and OPEC as major providers of crude oil and natural gas will almost surely be diminished. This will create a new set of political and financial variables that investors will have to factor in when making decisions about stocks in this sector. More specifically, I suggest that investors keep a keen eye on which U.S. companies begin to assert and insert themselves aggressively into the Russian natural gas industry.

Note that table 8.1 also shows significant amounts of natural gas reserves in the United States. A good portion of the proven gas reserves are in the southern United States, with Texas and the Gulf of Mexico coast accounting for almost 40 percent of the total. In November 2001, President Bush opened a large area along the Florida coast for exploration, once again supporting the dynamic presented here: The rest of the world is becoming increasingly aggressive in its exploration for gas and oil.

Perhaps the most important fact to remember about natural gas is that the rate of discovery of new, attainable, and economically sensible reserves peaked in 1994. In order to increase exploration and extraction, a rather large increase in price would likely be necessary. And here is where the Russian equation comes into immediate play. Russia is strapped for cash and suddenly has found what could be a way to improve its situation, both financially and politically, with respect to the rest of the world.

In November and December 2001, Russia capped what could be a watershed event in its emergence onto the global scene as a born-again major player. The Crawford, Texas, summit between Presidents Putin and Bush was a prelude to a whirlwind of activity between the two countries, as Russia essentially became a quasi member of NATO; fought a highly publicized battle against OPEC, which kept oil and gas prices from rising during the Afghanistan conflict, despite huge pressure from the oil cartel; and received an important nod from U.S. Energy Secretary Spencer Abraham during his visit to Moscow, when the secretary noted that Russia was on its way to becoming a significant future energy source for the United States. More important, and somewhat off the radar screen, was that Russia completed several pipeline projects to transport oil from its republics to the Caspian and other seaports during this period. At the same time, there were reports in the press of improved shipping lanes for oil in Siberia, which had resulted from global warming and the melting of the ice fields in the area.

When we put all of this together, it suggests that natural gas and oil will be plentiful in years to come and that the companies that prosper will be not only the ones that make big finds, but also the ones that can squeeze the best rates of returns based on efficiency, that have the ability to deliver on their business plans, and that are successful in their association with the emerging new big-time players in Russia and the former republics. As I will discuss further on, the early winner in the race for Russia seems to be Chevron-Texaco, which capped a multiyear investment in a Caspian Sea pipeline in November 2001.

History

The very early history of gas is parallel to that of crude oil. Natural gas is thought to have resulted from the transformation of plankton and other organisms that inhabited the earth in ancient times. As the plankton and organisms died, they sank to the depths of the ocean and were acted upon by heat, bacteria, and the earth's process of rock formation. The resulting mixture oozed into porous rocks, which were covered during the natural progression of the earth's continent formation, and, eventually, oil and gas were trapped in the crevices and natural pockets, where they are found today.

The ancient Chinese are credited with being the first to use natural gas industrially, piping it through bamboo pipelines and using it to heat water in order to extract salt from the water. In 500 A.D., temples in Azerbaijan secretly piped in natural gas from nearby rocky reservoirs to fuel the "eternal fires" of their altars.

In the 1600s scientists in Belgium and England discovered "manufactured gas," a by-product of burning coal. And in 1792, William Murdock, an English engineer, lit his home with gas he had manufactured from coal. He thus extended his workday and next began installing gaslight in cotton mills, an act that earned him the title "Father of Natural Gas." By 1812, a German businessman named Frederick Albert Winsor was able to harness the power of gas on a large-enough scale to be able to light an entire street, London's Pall Mall. He founded the first gas company in 1812. In 1817 the first gas company in the United States was formed in Baltimore. The first U.S. pipeline was built in 1872 in

Rochester, New York. The gas industry did quite well until Edison invented the light bulb; it regained its footing as gas was turned to use in cooking and heating.

In the late 1890s, pipelines were increasingly used for transporting gas over longer distances, but the existing technology, along with the Great Depression and World War II, greatly limited the ability to transport gas across states and across the country. As steel pipes were introduced, gas pipelines flourished after the war and a huge building boom lasted into the 1960s. Along the way, the Natural Gas Act of 1938 was passed, beginning the era of regulation.

In the 1970s, supply shortages resulted from a widely held misperception at the time, that there was a limited supply of natural gas and that the industry was not able to find and process the available supply efficiently. The view inside the industry, which proved to be true, was that there was too much regulation by the government and that the incentive to find new natural gas reserves had been removed. The shortages led to deregulation, which in turn caused a 50 percent increase in supply from the mid-1980s to the early 1990s. The Clean Air Act of 1990 also heightened the popularity of the clean-burning fuel.

As with crude oil, the consensus view of the industry is that enough natural gas is available in all forms to last several generations. The problems are similar to those with oil: that much of the gas is difficult to obtain with the currently available technology. This means that as long as someone is willing to pay more for natural gas, there will be active exploration, due to companies' intense competition as a result of deregulation.

Who Should Own Natural Gas Stocks? And When Is It Best to Own Them?

As with the previously profiled sectors in energy, it is important to define the criteria as to who should own stocks, when to own them, and which approach to take when analyzing them. The integrated oil stocks were more suitable for long-term investors,

Table 8.2: *Highest-yielding gas stocks in the Amex Natural Gas Index, with P/E ratios.*

Stock	Dividend Yield	P/E ratio
Nisource (NYSE:NI)	4.98%	19
National Fuel Gas (NYSE:NFG)	4.39%	11
Questar Corp. (NYSE:STR)	3.47%	11
Williams Companies (NYSE:WMB)	2.64%	12
Apache Corp. (NYSE:APA)	2.61%	6

with a buy-and-hold strategy, whereas the oil service sector was ideally suited to those investors who could time the market. Utility stocks were suited to both styles of investing, but the choices there were more dependent on individual stock criteria and were heavily influenced by the management of individual companies and their ability to execute their business plans. Natural gas stocks are almost identical to electric utility stocks, as they provide both yield-earning and market-timing opportunities.

The buy-and-hold strategy suffered a great deal of punishment in the bear market of 2000–2001, just as market timing suffered during the mega bull market of the 1990s. But the truth is, no strategy will work every time for every person. My own approach is to understand the main points of several strategies and to apply whichever works best at the time to the particular sector I am investing in.

But for those who wish to hold stocks for a very long period of time, such as for many years, dividend yields make the waiting period for capital gains more tolerable, and natural gas utility plays can have excellent yields. Table 8.2 lists the top five yielding stocks in the Amex Natural Gas Index, with their price/earnings (P/E) ratios. The P/E ratio is a classic valuation tool that tells investors how much they are paying for each dollar of earnings by a com-

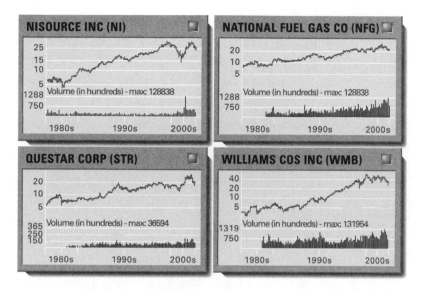

Figure 8.1: *The top four yielding stocks in the Amex Natural Gas Index, a long-term view of each company, courtesy of Telescan.*

pany. Traditionally, P/E ratios below 15 are attractive, whereas P/E ratios of 20 are considered average.

Table 8.2 shows the potential to receive excellent yield in the natural gas sector, just by using blue-chip stocks in the benchmark index. All five stocks also have P/E ratios that are below average. And as the charts in figure 8.1 illustrate, the top four showed excellent long-term trends.

So the answer of who should own natural gas stocks has already been partially answered. Long-term yield-seeking investors who have the patience to withstand the inevitable rise and fall of supply and demand and its influence on the stocks in this sector can find a home here. The key point seems to be that once deregulation was well established, beginning in the 1980s, as the charts clearly show, the natural gas sector and its continuously improving fundamentals, especially its clean-burning profile, have made the stocks very attractive for long-term investors. This is a clear contrast to the electric utility and power sector, where deregulation in the United States is just beginning, and its record in the rest of the world is quite diverse, with great successes and equally dismal disappointments adorning the investment landscape. Part two of the answer is more of a hybrid, as the natural gas sector is also appropriate for short- to intermediate-term investors and active traders who are comfortable with technical analysis, as I will discuss in the next section.

Limited Partnerships: Higher Yield Plays in Natural Gas

For those who are seeking an even higher yield, I suggest looking at limited partnerships. A limited partnership is an investment vehicle that is designed to deliver profits to its partners, both limited partners and managing partners. As a rule, whatever is left after the managing partners have been paid is distributed to the limited partners. And although that may seem unfair, most of the time the managing partners have taken a great deal of risk in establishing the venture before selling stakes to limited partners.

Kinder Morgan Energy Partners (NYSE:KMP) operates petroleum products and natural gas pipelines, as well as 20 storage facilities for the materials. Table 8.3 clearly illustrates the well-honed moneymaking engine that this limited partnership was during the period highlighted in the data. Note that revenues grew consistently, even if not sequentially, during the 14 quarters noted. This was a period in which oil prices were somewhat volatile, and the economy showed periods of both strength and weakness. That means that this company is in a business that is difficult to slow down. No matter what, oil and gas need to move from one place to another, and this company does it well.

More important, this company is well diversified, as its operations include the transport and storage of coal, petroleum coke, and carbon dioxide gas, where KMP is the largest player in the United States. The managing partner for KMP is Kinder Morgan,

Table 8.3: *Earnings and revenues for Kinder Morgan Energy Partners, courtesy of* Market Guide.

Revenues (Thousands of U.S. Dollars)

Quarters	1998	1999	2000	2001
March	36,741	100,049	157,358	1,028,645
June	82,044	102,933	193,758	735,755
September	101,900	104,388	202,575	
December	101,932	121,379	262,751	
TOTAL	322,617	428,749	816,442	

Earnings per Share

Quarters	1998	1999	2000	2001
March	0.260	0.285	0.315	0.445
June	0.250	0.305	0.350	0.360
September	0.260	0.410	0.335	
December	0.275	0.310	0.340	
TOTAL	1.045	1.310	1.340	

a natural gas and exploration company that is a member of the Amex Natural Gas Index, which I will profile later.

Kinder Morgan and another partnership, Kaneb Pipeline Partners (NYSE:KPP), both had excellent performances in the year 2001, as a result of their high yields compared to U.S. Treasury bills and bonds. KMP yielded 6 percent, and KPP yielded 7 percent in October 2001, as the Federal Reserve had lowered interest rates for the seventh time that year. At the same time 90-Day U.S. Treasury Bills were yielding 2.36 percent, while U.S. 30-Year Treasury Bonds were yielding 5.31 percent. Thus, at times of falling interest rates, investors should pay special attention to the natural gas pipeline limited partnerships.

Intermarket Relationships of the Natural Gas Sector

Intermarket analysis was initially described by master technicians John Murphy and Martin Pring. It is the study of what happens to multiple markets in response to similar events. The energy sector is directly influenced by the status of supply and demand for crude oil and related sectors, such as natural gas. Figure 8.2 clearly shows that as the yield on the U.S. 30-Year Treasury Bond fell in May, so did the energy sector, as measured by the oil, oil service, and natural gas indexes. This is a direct result of the market's expectations of falling economic activity as the Internet bubble burst.

Also note that in the month of September, after the September 11 bombing of the World Trade Center, the energy sector bottomed, as the U.S. government and the Federal Reserve together increased fiscal stimuli, lowered interest rates, and increased the money supply, respectively. The message from the charts is unmistakable. Natural gas is an economically sensitive sector, where the expectations of rising demand are an excellent attractive force for money to come back into the sector. In addition, the sensitive nature of the Middle East as a source of oil and natural gas and the beginning of a war in Afghanistan, on October 7, 2001, at 1:00 P.M. Eastern time, made this an important area for investors to focus on during this time period.

Another important relationship is the one between natural gas stocks and natural gas futures. Traditionally, commodity-based stocks lead the commodity higher. And that is precisely what the chart in figure 8.3 shows, as the Amex Natural Gas Index rallied on October 5, prior to the attack on Afghanistan. The key is to watch whether or not the futures confirm the move on the stocks. And a very simple way to check on the futures without having to get a real-time futures-trading system is to visit the New York Mercantile Web site at *www.nymex.com*. The NYMEX runs a ticker on its home page, where the symbol for "natural gas futures" is

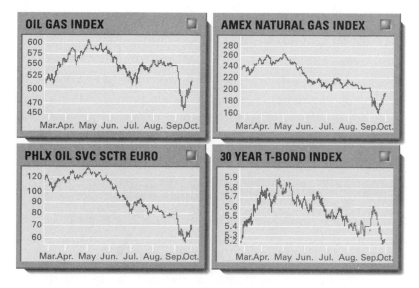

Figure 8.2: *Comparison of integrated oil stocks (XOI; upper left), natural gas stocks (XNG; upper right), oil service stocks (OSX; lower left), and long-term bond yields (TYX; lower right).*

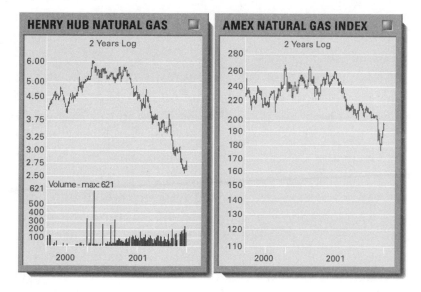

Figure 8.3: *Natural Gas Futures December 2001 (NGZ1; left) and the Amex Natural Gas Index (XNG; right), courtesy of Telescan.*

WA followed by the letter for the month in question and the year. On October 8, 2001, the natural gas contract for December 2001 (WAZ1) was quoted at 2.67, up 0.053 from the October 5 close, offering at least short-term confirmation that the natural gas market was turning higher. The quotes offered by NYMEX on its Web site are 30 minutes delayed, but are quite useful in confirming the major trend of the markets.

What Makes Natural Gas Prices Move?

As with other energy commodities, natural gas moves on supply and demand. And as with other energy sectors, it is fairly easy to gauge supply and demand indirectly by using the active rig count data. As a rule, natural gas prices tend to peak before the number of active rigs, a fact that makes sense. As drilling activity increases supply, the market becomes awash in the commodity and prices drop. When prices fall to a certain level, the market adjusts and the number of active rigs declines. In 2001, the price of natural gas topped out in January, while the number of active rigs topped out in July. This is a similar time range to when natural gas stocks topped out, as in figure 8.3.

The unifying factor is the economy. As economic activity fell in the year 2001, so did the demand for electricity and, as a result, the demand for natural gas. The rig count in this case was a lagging indicator that confirmed what the stock and the futures prices were already telling us. Also important to note was that the respite in the drop in natural gas came as winter was nearing and expectations of increased demand were being built into the price. But a warmer than usual early winter, combined with decreasing economic activity, kept the price from rising too dramatically.

The seasonal component of the price of natural gas is clearly illustrated in table 8.4, which compares the price of six futures contracts, beginning in October 2001 and ending in May 2002. With a falling economy, as the market faced in 2001—a situation

Table 8.4: *Comparison of price in serial futures contracts on October 9, 2001.*

Natural Gas Contract	Price
October 2001	1.83
November 2001	2.34
December 2001	2.69
January 2002	2.90
February 2002	2.90
March 2002	2.80
April 2002	2.70
May 2002	2.77

that worsened as a result of the Word Trade Center attacks—the market was clearly betting that the improvement in gas prices was mostly weather-related. Note that the implied price for the spring months was lower than the price in January and February— historically, the coldest months. Also note that by May 2002, the price had begun to stabilize, as the market was pricing in the potential for some economic improvement, as well as a potential increase in demand for natural gas for summer cooling in California.

The Amex Natural Gas Index

Now that we know the basics of the sector, it's time to get to know the companies. As with prior chapters, I will concentrate on the well-known names and will also include other major companies along the way—either key competitors or niche players, as well as those companies with business practices that have led to either great success or failure.

Anadarko Petroleum (NYSE:APC)

Anadarko Petroleum is an interesting bellwether for the natural gas sector, given its name. But the stock's long-term performance, as seen in figure 8.4, clearly justifies the choice, for Wall Street would not have stuck with a stock for over a decade unless management was doing something right. And a quick look at the history and the business practices of Anadarko shows that the company has made the right moves time and time again.

Anadarko is a well-integrated exploration and facilitation company, as it integrates exploration with the extraction, transport, and marketing of natural gas, providing a one-stop shop for its customers.

Originally a division of Panhandle Eastern, Anadarko was spun off to shareholders in 1986. By then, the company's early exploration and success in the Gulf of Mexico had yielded a huge oil find near the Matagorda Islands, off the Texas coast, a deal that was conducted along with Amoco, which then became part of BP. In the mid-1980s, Anadarko formed a joint venture with SONATRARCH, the Algerian national oil company, and also began exploration in China and Alaska, as well as expanding into West Texas. In the early 1990s, Anadarko was a collaborator in the discovery of the Mahogany field off Louisiana, which began production in 1996.

The key ingredient in Anadarko's success has been that as it forms ventures and makes new larger finds, it sells off pieces of the company that are not working or that don't fit into its main business plan, which is the exploration for and marketing of oil and gas. Perhaps its best move was when it bought Union Pacific, a decision that increased the amount of proven reserves of both oil and gas held by the company. And a short while later, the company sold off its nonperforming assets in Algeria.

Here again, we see a global focus and a significant effort to actively manage its property portfolio in order to stick to its business plan. We don't see Anadarko trying to buy refineries or gas

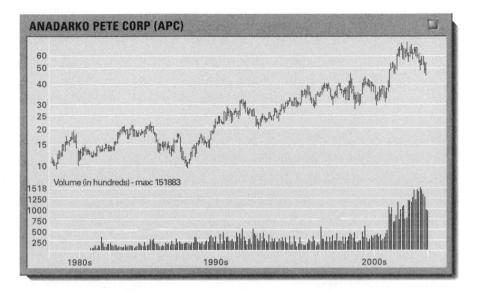

ANADARKO PETE CORP (APC)

Volume (in hundreds) - max: 151883

1980s   1990s   2000s

Figure 8.4: *Anadarko Petroleum Corp. (NYSE:APC), courtesy of Telescan.*

stations. And we don't see this company delving into semiconductor manufacturing. This is a pure play on the front end of the energy market: exploration and marketing.

Anadarko had $5.7 billion of sales in the year 2000, with 93 percent coming from the United States and Canada. Fifty percent of sales were due to marketing, while 28 percent came from gas and 17 percent from oil-related operations.

Field Services
Anadarko operates in four basic segments that it then integrates to provide its customers with a unified solution. Beginning with field services, Anadarko gathers the natural gas as it is pumped out of the ground, then compresses it and processes it to remove impurities. Through its pipeline systems, the company can reroute natural gas, based on supply and demand, as well as on other market conditions.

Producer Services

Here is where Anadarko gathers and stores its natural gas. The company then offers its customers several pricing options, ranging from pricing at the bulkhead to index pricing on a monthly basis. This is all plainly stated on the company Web site at *www.anadarko.com.*

Market Services

Anadarko buys 1 billion cubic feet of natural gas per day and markets 2 billion, making the company a significant player in the open market for the fuel. This is where Anadarko makes its money, which it leverages by adding its transportation and storage services.

Financial Services

The company also provides hedging and risk-management activities to its clients. These are the same techniques that the company uses to protect itself from price swings in the marketplace. And as the company's financial performance shows, this is a significant aspect of its success. Anadarko also provides similar services to the oil industry, serving as both a direct player and an intermediary in oil trading and transport, in the United States and internationally.

Table 8.5 clearly shows the trend for the company's finances, with stout year-over-year growth in revenues and earnings. A great deal of the growth came from the merger with Union Pacific. But that does not take away any of the merit, for it shows that not only can management make acquisitions, but it can integrate the new company into the existing infrastructure and operate it profitably. Note that despite the fall in natural gas prices during 2001, revenues and earnings grew in year-over-year comparisons, although the impressive sequential growth that began in June 1999 and extended until March 2001 finally stopped. This sends a clear message to shareholders that the company is not immune from commodity price swings or the economic cycle, but that it is well positioned to withstand these. More important, the company is

Table 8.5: *Revenues and earnings for Anadarko Petroleum, courtesy of* Market Guide.

Revenues (Thousands of U.S. Dollars)

Quarters	1998	1999	2000	2001
March	147,001	329,000	661,000	3,051,000
June	137,526	419,000	748,000	2,264,000
September	140,191	477,000	1,871,000	
December	135,536	546,000	2,406,000	
TOTAL	560,254	1,771,000	5,686,000	

Earnings per Share

Quarters	1998	1999	2000	2001
March	0.060	–0.190	0.370	2.520
June	0.020	0.060	0.480	1.500
September	–0.020	0.150	1.030	
December	–0.470	0.220	1.750	
TOTAL	–0.410	0.240	3.630	

likely to emerge from down trends in a better position than some of its competitors, which will allow it to buy up more companies.

In summary, just as TXU and Southern Company, Exxon-Mobil and Chevron-Texaco, and Halliburton and Schlumberger, serve as bellwethers for their own sectors of the energy industry, in my opinion the benchmark for the natural gas sector is Anadarko Petroleum, a company whose long-term performance is clearly mirrored in its stock price. Anadarko has an excellent business model, consistently executes its business plan, and continuously assesses its portfolio of properties, discarding noncore and nonperforming assets, thus maintaining its edge.

Apache Corp. (NYSE:APA)

Apache Corp. is in a similar business to Anadarko and had $2.284 billion in sales in the year 2000; its revenue sources and activities were almost equally dependent on oil and gas exploration, with 50 percent of sales pertaining to oil and 48 percent pertaining to natural gas. Sixty percent of Apache's business is in the United States, with 80 percent of its reserves being found in the Gulf of Mexico and North America. This is significant, given what I expect to be a growing dynamic in the future of the energy sector: domestic exploration. Only 15 percent of the business comes equally from operations in Egypt, Canada, and Australia, giving this company a very secure portfolio of properties from a political standpoint. And just like Anadarko, Apache is a frequent evaluator of its properties and business plan, as it continues to be at the top of the heap.

Apache's origins are a true hall of fame story of entrepreneurship, because its founder, Raymond Plank, had an idea of starting a magazine, which eventually evolved into an accounting firm. Although he had no experience in accounting, according to the official story, the company flourished and eventually became a venture capital partnership that also succeeded. In the early 1960s, Plank and his main partner, Truman Anderson, parted ways over a disagreement regarding Apache's real estate ventures, which Plank wanted to sell, in order to focus on the oil business. This is an early but great example of a company that has always been focused on its core business, an attitude that usually works its way into the corporate culture and that in this case has benefited the long-term performance of the stock.

In the 1970s, Apache survived the energy crisis by selling its nonenergy properties. And in the 1980s, the company had a difficult time, as its limited partnership status caused capital losses when tax laws changed. But once again, the company survived by adapting to the new tax laws and concentrating on its core business: oil and gas exploration.

Table 8.6: *Earnings and revenues for Apache Corp., courtesy of* Market Guide.

Revenues (Thousands of U.S. Dollars)

Quarters	1998	1999	2000	2001
March	245,941	163,422	448,191	795,143
June	220,132	246,418	486,413	800,443
September	211,683	340,821	618,513	
December	197,959	395,892	730,787	
TOTAL	875,715	1,146,553	2,283,904	

Earnings per Share

Quarters	1998	1999	2000	2001
March	0.180	−0.040	0.960	2.150
June	0.090	0.280	1.180	1.550
September	0.030	0.590	1.580	
December	−1.640	0.810	1.960	
TOTAL	−1.340	1.640	5.680	

In the 1990s, Apache expanded into Australia, Canada, Poland, and Argentina, always buying good properties and doing the unexpected, as it did in 1991 when it bought wells from Amoco that had 100 million barrels of reserves that were not being extracted. Apache re-opened the wells, an unorthodox and gutsy move that shows the aggressive management style of Mr. Plank, who was still the chairman and CEO in late 2001.

Apache is a pure play on oil and gas exploration and makes it easy to invest in the company's shares, through its dividend reinvestment plan (DRIP), where shareholders can buy stock without paying a broker's commission. The full information is available at the company Web site *(www.apachecorp.com).*

Table 8.7: *Long-term growth rates of earnings (EPS) and revenues for Apache Corp., courtesy of* Market Guide.

Growth Rates	1 Year	3 Year	5 Year
Revenue	99.20%	24.76%	24.92%
EPS	233.26%	51.48%	82.78%

By now, you should be familiar with the quarterly comparisons of revenues and income for the companies profiled in the book. But Apache's are worth looking at because it had a streak of rising revenues that began in 1999 and was still alive in June 2001. Rising revenues are the mark of an aggressive company that is selling its product well. When revenues rise sequentially for a significant period, it means that the company's sales force is doing a good job. Both are excellent signs of sound investments.

Finally, I like to see that the company with great revenues also has great earnings. And Apache clearly passes that test, especially when we look at the year-over-year comparisons, which are presented in table 8.7. The 1-year growth rates are outstanding, but the 3- and 5-year measures are even more impressive, especially in the earnings, which clearly show that the company is well managed and not only grows robustly, but also keeps a good portion of its money in the company's coffers, in order to finance future acquisitions.

El Paso Corp. (NYSE:EPG)

El Paso Corp. is the largest natural gas pipeline operator in the United States, with ownership or interests in 58,000 miles of pipe. The stock, just as with Apache and Anadarko, enjoyed great sponsorship for many years, despite some down times in the early 1990s, thus is another example of a stock that offers investors the opportunity for long-term ownership. The company grew dramat-

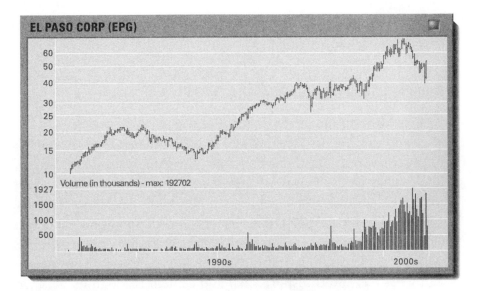

Figure 8.5: *El Paso Corp. (NYSE:EPG), courtesy of Telescan.*

ically through its acquisition of Coastal Corp. and is well diversified, with businesses ranging from power generation and energy
marketing to telecommunications. Internationally, the company
operates power plants and pipelines.

In October 2001, as figure 8.5 shows, the stock rose, when El
Paso Corp. was cleared of major wrongdoing in a price-fixing
lawsuit that was brought against the company by the State of California, as a result of the year 2000 energy crisis. The pipeline
used to transport natural gas to California was built after World
War II. This is a company that has survived much austerity over
the years since its founding in 1928. Most interesting is that in its
old incarnation of El Paso Natural Gas, the company was taken
private by Burlington Resources and then spun off in 1993. After
the spin-off, the company got a new lease on life and has made
the most of it.

This company is well-diversified and is also a possible candidate
for long-term investors to hold in their portfolios. It has applied the

principles of success in the energy patch well: Buy other companies on weakness, and sell noncore and nonperforming assets.

Kinder Morgan Inc. (NYSE:KMI)

Kinder Morgan Inc. is the product of the merger between KN Energy and the Kansas Pipeline and Gas Company. And the stock's long-term chart is a thing of beauty for long-term investors and technical analysts. This is an interesting company whose businesses integrate natural gas pipelines, along with gas power plants, pipelines, and transportation services that the company manages through its Kinder Morgan Energy Partners Limited Partnership, which I profiled earlier in this chapter. Among its other businesses, Kinder stores and transports coal and cement through its bulk terminal unit.

This company has the goal of integrating its storage and transportation operations with the power plants that it expects to have online by 2002. The company got its start in power generation in 1936, when it went against the grain and began to build electric utilities in rural Kansas and Nebraska, a project that many in the business thought would never be profitable. As with most of the large players in natural gas and energy, Kinder Morgan has grown through acquisition, with its biggest acquisition coming in 1998 when it bought MidCon Corp., a move that raised the company's assets to more than $8 billion.

Earnings and revenue growth rates for KMI are not particularly flattering, as shown in table 8.8. That is of concern, given that the company's chart shows exceptional long-term performance. But a comparison of the one-year chart of KMI to Anadarko Petroleum (figure 8.6) shows that on a shorter-term basis, the stock looks attractive. Which stock to buy? It depends on your time frame. For the long term, both companies are fine, as long as they remain in long-term rising trends. In the short term, it makes more sense to buy the company with the best earnings and revenue momentum, because it is the one that will most likely attract the momentum players.

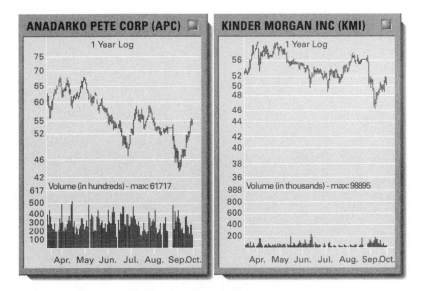

Figure 8.6: *One-year comparison of Anadarko Petroleum (NYSE:APC; left) and Kinder Morgan Inc. (NYSE:KMI; right).*

Table 8.8: *Long-term growth rates of earnings (EPS) and revenues for Kinder Morgan Inc., courtesy of* Market Guide.

Growth Rates	1 Year	3 Year	5 Year
Revenue	47.78%	99.76%	19.55%
EPS	–17.30%	19.71%	5.48%

Enron Corp. (NYSE:ENE) and EOG Resources (NYSE:EOG)

Perhaps the most important market event of the year 2001 in the U.S. energy sector was the swift and complete fall from grace of Enron Corp. (NYSE:ENE). As figure 8.7 clearly shows, the stock was riding high until the bottom fell out. Enron Corp. was the largest wholesale buyer and seller of electrical power in the United States, operating a 25,000-mile gas pipeline system that spans from Texas to the Canadian border and from California to

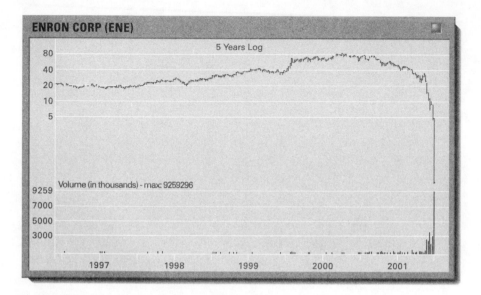

Figure 8.7: *Enron Corp. (NYSE:ENE), courtesy of Telescan.*

Florida, while EOG Resources is a former division of ENE, which was sold off in 1989 as a result of mounting debt for the parent company. In 1999, EOG received Enron Corp.'s remaining interest in the company in exchange for properties in China and India.

This was not only good management, but also very lucky for EOG, as shown in figure 8.8, because the stock acted quite well during the same period in which its former parent imploded.

These two companies are an excellent study in the business of natural gas and of investor perception and management's ability to deliver. And history, as usual, is full of clues as to what will likely happen in the future. Enron Corp. emerged in 1987, as Inter North and Houston Natural Gas merged. Both companies were well established, but had built up a great deal of debt and were forced to sell off assets. By the early 1990s, though, Enron was once again buying assets and in 1997 bought Portland General Electric, a utility, and followed it by buying a U.K. water and wastewater company.

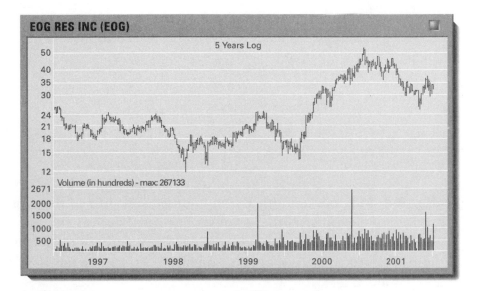

Figure 8.8: *EOG Resources (NYSE:EOG), courtesy of Telescan.*

The spinning off of its Enron Oil & Gas division, which became EOG resources, came after this period of activity. ENE then began to transform itself into an energy-trading powerhouse and in many respects became the market for the trading of electricity and power in the United States. But as it grew in stature, so did it grow in its inability to police itself, as it set itself apart from the rules of the corporate and securities markets, as well as from the rules of common sense and, most of all, the marketplace.

Table 8.9 summarizes the key detail that initially spooked the markets in 2001, as the company posted huge revenue growth, but a monstrous fall in earnings growth. In fact, what Enron did was to turn an energy company into more or less a financial services company, because all that was truly left of ENE were trading and hedging operations in the commodity markets. In effect, Enron became a hedge fund that posed as an energy company. And while the company operated the leading wholesale energy exchange in the United States, with its Internet-based operations, it

Table 8.9: *Growth rates for Enron Corp., courtesy of* Market Guide.

Growth Rates	1 Year	3 Year	5 Year
Revenue	151.27%	70.67%	61.45%
EPS	–11.51%	91.81%	2.98%
Dividend	0.00%	3.10%	4.24%

also traded in coal and other commodities and offered hedging services to its clients via the use of sophisticated derivative strategies, a trio of words that should make most investors shudder, as these have been the cause of many financial disasters in the 1980s and beyond.

The straw that broke the camel's back came when the company revealed that it had several "off balance sheet" partnerships in operation, which were guaranteed by the company and which had directly benefited company officers, especially its chief financial officer, Andrew Fastow. Fastow resigned, and it was subsequently revealed that he had made $30 million personally from the partnerships, while the company had lost over $1.2 billion in its own equity. The SEC began a probe, the company's debt was downgraded to junk, and the rest was grim history.

It seems perversely fitting that this sad event in corporate history came to a head at a time when the global economy was beginning to show signs of recovery and as the implications for stable energy prices were appearing, due to the increased rivalry between OPEC and Russia, two opposing forces in the supply-and-demand equation in the world's energy sector and a story that is well detailed elsewhere in this book.

To be well understood, the story of Enron's downfall must be properly set up by details of its rise. Perhaps the most important aspect of the story is that ENE had created a very smooth way for power companies to find both buyers and sellers for excess production, in effect becoming a marketplace through its Internet trading platform. Prior to ENE's Web-based platform, a much more complex and inefficient system was in place, in which companies dealt either directly with each other or through more cumbersome means. Thus, the smooth marketplace that Enron had created, even if ENE re-emerges after bankruptcy, will take years to rebuild and could keep the U.S. market from enjoying the impressive customer savings for power that seemed possible from the creation of the new market.

But the real problem with ENE and its partnerships was that the company's problems were perceived by the market as possibly spreading to the rest of the natural gas and utility sector, a perception that in many cases was well founded, given that Enron was a central player in power trading. As a result, many other companies, including major banks that had loans and deals with Enron, such as J. P. Morgan and Citigroup, had their stocks affected.

The clue that something was terribly wrong with ENE came with the initial shake-up, as key members of the management team—including the newly appointed CEO, Jeffrey Skilling—resigned in 2001. At the center of why the company fell off the face of the earth was the arrogance reportedly displayed by Skilling and what was described as a small group of "whiz kid" traders, who were at the helm of the ship when it hit the iceberg called the economic cycle. As global economies slowed, power trading slowed, and the company's huge debt load and off-the-books flim-flam caught up to it, as these things always do. The result was fairly predictable. When we compare this company's "off the books" deals and "we know something that the market can't grasp" attitude to the very-well-thought-out and focused methods of Anadarko and Apache, it is clear why the company went bankrupt and is unlikely to rise from the ashes in any semblance of its former self. The selling in Enron was also typical investor behavior in a momentum stock. When the company stumbles, investors sell without mercy.

EOG, the spin-off, is a more traditional exploration company with a great deal of activity in North and South America, especially

Table 8.10: *Growth rates for EOG, courtesy of* Market Guide.

Growth Rates	1 Year	3 Year	5 Year
Revenue	76.93%	23.89%	18.09%
EPS	–18.88%	61.37%	29.72%
Dividend	12.50%	4.00%	2.38%

from its major positions in Trinidad and the Appalachian basin. The Trinidad project accounts for 6 percent of sales, while the U.S. operations are worth 82 percent, and Canada accounts for 12 percent. Seventy-eight percent of the $1.5 billion of sales came from gas exploration, while 22 percent came from crude oil and natural gas liquids. By contrast, ENE had $100 million in sales in 2000, with 93 percent coming from wholesale trading of energy and commodities, and 4 percent coming from retail energy sales.

Both stocks mirrored each other's performance over the longer term, but the market was more inclined to buy EOG on the rebound, despite the company's decreased growth rate, which is displayed in table 8.10. The keys here are twofold. First, EOG is an exploration company with strong reserves and no management properties. This means that its assets are more tangible and more easily manageable, as well as potentially liquid. ENE was in many ways a huge hedge fund, which also operated an Internet-based sales exchange. It is important to note that for the June 2001 quarter, ENE and EOG were both profitable, as was originally reported, even if their earnings growth rates fell. But by September, ENE had to declare a $638 million loss, due to its "off the books" dealings. More important was that despite its tangible assets, such as power plants in China and a water management company in the U.K., ENE was a trading company that got badly hurt when the economy slowed down and energy and power prices fell.

As a result, this comparison of two entities, which were once part of the same company, illustrates some important aspects of trading and investing in the natural gas sector. This is a sector where the fundamentals matter. Actual proven reserves and other assets, such as functional pipelines, matter. And management's actions and ability to maneuver and deliver during difficult times are paramount, as from those achievements all other results stem. ENE's management problems and the gross "cooking of the books" led to its underperformance and eventual downfall.

Also note that in the future, in the natural gas sector, investors may be more likely to favor companies in the exploration and production side—at least in the early part of the cycle, where supply is greater than demand as companies gear up for a rise in the business cycle. This favors companies like EOG, Anadarko, and Apache. Companies like Enron Corp., whose business was trading commodities, are likely to be more attractive to investors late in the cycle, where demand is outstripping supply.

Burlington Resources (NYSE:BR)

Burlington Resources is a major producer of natural gas, with huge reserves in North America. The company had over $3 billion in sales in the year 2000, with 82 percent of its reserves and sales having to do with natural gas and 18 percent with oil. The company's origins go back to 1864. Burlington also owns the largest coal reserves in the United States, as well as 12.5 million acres of forest and significant oil and gas reserves. In the 1980s, the company split into the Burlington Northern Railroad and Burlington Resources.

Burlington is almost a pure commodity play, with its forests and coal reserves. But it also became an exploration company, with its purchase of Louisiana Land and Exploration in the late 1990s. Global diversification came from deals and agreements the company signed in Algeria and Canada. The missing piece here, as with many of these companies, is a position in Russia.

It seems ironic, but this descendant of a very old company is still in its infancy and is taking its first major steps in a tough new world. For that reason, this company bears watching, for its

Table 8.11: *Growth rates for Burlington Resources, courtesy of* Market Guide.

Growth Rates	1 Year	3 Year	5 Year
Revenue	36.06%	9.84%	12.66%
EPS	NM%	23.28%	13.52%
Dividend	19.57%	6.14%	4.56%

management seems to be moving cautiously, concentrating on growing its business in Canada—a move that may prove to be quite intelligent, given the potential for a prolonged global conflict as a result of the September 11 events.

Table 8.11 shows steady but unspectacular growth rates in revenues and earnings, but a rise in the dividend paid out. This could be misleading, given that the yield was only 1.51 percent at the time. Wall Street has not been that impressed with Burlington's slow and steady pace over the years, as the stock has been in a very broad trading range, rather than in a steadily rising trend like Anadarko and Apache. Our analysis once again proves that this is an average stock and not a huge winner for long-term investors.

Williams Companies (NYSE:WMB)

Williams Companies is a well-diversified gas exploration and production company that operates 27,500 miles of pipelines in the United States, as well as running over 60 truck stops, refineries, and ethanol plants. The company refocused its operations on natural gas by spinning off its 33,000-mile fiber-optic line and Williams Communications, along with its energy-trading operations. Had it not done this spin-off, the company quite possibly could have run into problems similar to those of Enron, as the telecom sector imploded. But the ability to recognize mistakes in time and to act ac-

Table 8.12: *Growth rates for Williams Companies, courtesy of* Market Guide.

Growth Rates	1 Year	3 Year	5 Year
Revenue	44.99%	8.02%	12.95%
EPS	405.99%	24.25%	17.79%
Dividend	0.00%	3.57%	10.76%

cordingly are what separate good management from bad. A perfect example of good management came when Williams tripled its natural gas reserves as it beat out Royal Dutch/Shell for Barrett Resources, a highly publicized merger battle in 2001.

This is a huge company along the lines of El Paso Corp., with $10 billion in sales for the year 2000, 74 percent of it coming from energy services and 18 percent from its gas pipeline operations. Eight percent came from its telecommunications operations, which the company entered in 1985 and of which it sold a significant portion to LDDS, the company that became Worldcom and merged with MCI to form the familiar MCI Worldcom.

Prior to Enron, Wall Street liked the way this company did business. This is borne out by the company's humble origins, when its founders, David and Miller Williams, established Williams Brothers, the predecessor company, by forming the company when their employer abandoned the project during a road construction contract. This kind of storied beginning often builds incredible success in the business world, as we saw with Texaco and Halliburton previously.

Table 8.12 shows that Williams grew impressively in the most recent year. That was mostly due to the purchase of Barrett Resources. So, what the table tells you is that the company is poised for some impressive gains, after rather lackluster growth rates, where only the dividends were worth noting. Otherwise, Williams is a reliable company, which seems to make up for what it lacks in flash by having a very well-run set of businesses. It is an excellent candidate for long-term stock holders. The only caveat is that CEO Keith E. Bailey, who presided over the restructuring, will retire in 2002. A poor follow-up in management could cost this company some Wall Street confidence, as could its exposure to the telecom market.

Dynegy Inc. (NYSE:DYN)

Dynegy became the apparent heir to Enron's wholesale middleman empire in power trading. It is a well-diversified energy company, with businesses ranging from energy trading to marketing, power generation, natural gas liquids production, electricity and natural gas transmission and distribution, and telecommunications. Dynegy also benefited from a 27 percent stake in the company from the increasingly well-positioned Chevron-Texaco. This company is proof that what Enron tried to do for many years—to incorporate generation, marketing, and trading of power—is possible and can be done in a way that produces impressive revenue and profit growth, as shown in table 8.13, which summarizes the 3-year period of 1998–2000 for Dynegy.

The company started as a wholesale trader of natural gas after the deregulation of the industry and began providing hedging services to its clients, also trading in natural gas futures for its own account. This was followed by the creation of an electric power clearinghouse, as the company bought several gas properties, including Chevron's natural gas operations. This gave Chevron—now Chevron-Texaco—its stake in Dynegy, which in itself is an excellent vote of confidence, because Dynegy is still a young company. Dynegy continued its aggressive foray into diversification by buying Illinova, a major utility in Illinois, after it had bought Destec Energy and sold that company's international operations. And that was followed by the purchase of a telecommunications company and power plants in the Northeast and Arizona.

Dynegy is a classic growth play, which is also its potential downfall, as it has a heavy debt burden from its acquisition binge.

Table 8.13: *Revenue and earnings summary for Dynegy, courtesy* of Market Guide.

Revenues (Thousands of U.S. Dollars)

Year	1998	1999	2000
TOTAL	14,257,997	15,429,976	29,445,000

Earnings per Share

Year	1998	1999	2000
TOTAL	0.330	0.650	1.470

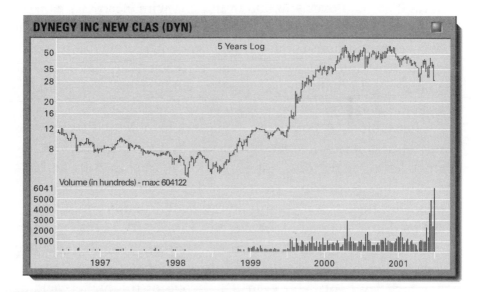

Figure 8.9: *Dynegy Inc. (NYSE:DYN), courtesy of Telescan.*

Wall Street is likely to be forgiving, as long as the company can deliver reasonable growth rates. But the fall of Enron saddled Dynegy with a $10 billion lawsuit, as it ended a takeover for Enron in those final chaotic days of November 2001, and Enron alleged that Dynegy was not allowed to end the merger without some kind of payoff. As I write, it is the early stages of pre-litigation and only time will tell what happens. I suspect that Dynegy will survive, given its association with Chevron-Texaco and the fact that, in a pinch, the company could even be bought by its largest shareholder.

Nisource (NYSE:NI)

Nisource uses a business model similar to other diversified utility companies like TXU, with a focus on natural gas. The company owns utilities in Indiana, the Northeast, the Mid-Atlantic, and the midwestern United States. It serves 3.2 million customers with natural gas and over 400,000 in Indiana with electricity as well. The company had $6 billion in sales in the year 2000, with relatively equal portions coming from energy marketing (32 percent), gas distribution (30 percent), and electricity (26 percent). The company's 16,000-mile gas pipeline and its associated underground storage system provided 6 percent of sales.

But table 8.14 points out some serious potential trouble for this huge company, which was noted by the market, where the stock fell along with the rest of the bear market in 2001 and had a hard time recovering. This was a direct contrast to Anadarko, the bellwether, a stock that bounced better than Nisource, when the market attempted to recover in October 2001. More important, look at the growth rates for Nisource, which are excellent for revenues and dividends, but not for earnings, as the company has high levels of debt, even if it is one of the higher-yielding stocks in the Amex Natural Gas Index.

The message here is that even if this is a high-yielding stock, it is a risky stock. If the company's earnings don't begin to grow, the dividend could be cut to improve earnings growth. In fact, Nisource lost money in the June 2001 quarter, due to its acquisition of Columbia Gas, which it financed by increasing debt. I looked at Nisource's balance sheet and also found something alarming: This huge company had only $142 million worth of

Table 8.14: *Growth rates for Nisource, courtesy of* Market Guide.

Growth Rates	1 Year	3 Year	5 Year
Revenue	84.23%	32.60%	27.80%
EPS	–11.81%	–11.00%	–4.45%
Dividend	5.88%	5.68%	6.32%

cash in June 2001, while carrying $8 billion worth of debt and $14 billion worth of current liabilities.

The bottom line is that this highly leveraged company is using a high dividend yield to attract investors, at the cost of its earnings growth rates. Unless that kind of strategy is short term—which it doesn't seem to be for Nisource, given that its decreasing earnings growth rates have been in place for several years—this could lead to trouble. Look for companies with a cleaner balance sheet and that are chock full of cash, along with better growth rates, even if there is no dividend or lower dividend growth rates.

Questar Corp. (NYSE:STR)

Questar Corp. is a high-yielding natural gas stock with a different picture from that of Nisource. It is a well-diversified exploration, gathering, storage, and distribution company, with 705,000 customers in the Rocky Mountain region of the United States.

Table 8.15 shows that the 3- and 5-year growth rates for revenues and earnings are steady and thus likely to be sustainable. A visit to Questar's Web site *(www.questar.com)* and a quick read of the company's financial report show that the company had slowly but surely built itself up for the unregulated environment. This means that as gas prices rise, so should profits for this company, due to its leveraging of its product to match the new environment, such as was seen in the California energy crisis.

Table 8.15: *Growth rates for Questar Corp., courtesy of* Market Guide.

Growth Rates	1 Year	3 Year	5 Year
Revenue	37.00%	10.58%	14.29%
EPS	62.09%	15.26%	13.60%
Dividend	2.24%	3.38%	3.38%

National Fuel Gas Company (NYSE:NFG)

National Fuel Gas is a company similar to others that I have profiled, with a vertically integrated and diversified business model that includes exploration, gathering, marketing, storage, and transportation of natural gas. This is a smaller company than El Paso Corp. and others in the sector, having $100 million in sales for the year 2000, with 55 percent coming from its National Fuel Gas Distribution utility, which serves the Buffalo, New York, area. Another 26 percent comes from energy marketing and pipeline and storage operations.

The stock enjoys a good deal of Wall Street sponsorship, but—similar to Nisource—had only $57 million in cash in June 2001, while carrying $1.5 billion worth of debt on its balance sheet. To this company's credit, its acquisitions have been on a smaller scale than those of its rivals, and its international exposure is mostly in Canada. This stock is best invested in with the aid of chart analysis and by those who seek reasonably high yields and who have a long-term time horizon of several years.

Noble Affiliates (NYSE:NBL)

Noble Affiliates is another natural gas powerhouse with an excellent long-term performance. The company spun off Noble Drilling in 1985 and has excellent short- and long-term growth rates, as shown in table 8.16. The company explores for and mar-

Table 8.16: *Growth rates for Noble Affiliates, courtesy of* Market Guide.

Growth Rates	1 Year	3 Year	5 Year
Revenue	53.17%	7.67%	23.40%
EPS	291.19%	24.99%	110.86%
Dividend	0.00%	0.00%	0.00%

kets natural gas and oil. It has operations both in the United States and internationally, but no real ties in Russia. The stock has a very steady long-term up trend, which was most impressive toward 2000–2001, as the company's huge growth rates captured Wall Street's imagination.

Especially impressive was the 1-year growth rate in revenues and earnings, which came from higher prices and the ability to extract higher profit margins from those higher prices. A great deal of that growth came despite reasonably high debt levels and low cash levels. The key is that there is a very low dividend of only 16 cents per year. This means that all of the money earned goes back into the company. More important is that Noble was able to turn around from a point of huge losses in 1998 to huge profits in the year 2000. That kind of rapid turnaround is usually a money magnet for momentum managers. The flip side is that one bad quarter could lead to a huge decline in the stock, as momentum players abandon it. This stock is not for long-term holders, but is well suited for those with intermediate-term time horizons.

Ocean Energy Inc. (NYSE:OEI)

Ocean Energy is a pure exploration and production play, with no utility, marketing, or trading businesses. That accounts for the overall volatility of the price of the stock and also for its excellent performance in the late 1990s and into 2000–2001. The combination of natural gas's increasing popularity as a fuel and the global uncertainty in the energy markets makes this a stock to keep a close eye on. The company has both U.S. and international properties, including some in Egypt, Pakistan, and Russia. The Russian project is a 50-50 joint venture in the republic of Tatarstan, north of Kazakhstan, where OEI had 350 existing oil wells in the year 2001 and was expecting to drill another 40. The Russian wells already contribute to OEI's bottom line and continue to position the company well for the future.

This is significant, given that aside from major players, it is not easy to find companies that are doing business in Russia. The Russian involvement may be the one single feature of this company that separates it from the rest of the pack, as this shows that management is thinking way ahead of its peers or had the necessary connections to be able to cut through all the red tape needed to establish itself in Russia.

Pogo Producing Company (NYSE:PPP)

Pogo Producing is another exploration and production company in the natural gas index. This is a timing vehicle, which has had a well-defined trading range over the 20-plus years highlighted in the chart. But the right side of figure 8.10 points out something quite notable. The stock did not break below 25 in the year 2000 and actually shows an increase in volume during the consolidation phase. The increase in volume is the mark of institutional investors, who like to buy stocks as they consolidate. This suggests that Wall Street likes something that is going on with the company. And table 8.17 provides the answer: explosive growth.

My point here is that Pogo is showing some relative strength, which means that it is not falling in a market that was still in a down trend, as measured by the major averages during the autumn of 2001. Relative strength is a clue that more research is

Table 8.17: *Growth rates for Pogo Producing, courtesy of* Market Guide.

Growth Rates	1 Year	3 Year	5 Year
Revenue	81.01%	20.26%	25.88%
EPS	261.86%	23.37%	48.35%
Dividend	0.00%	0.00%	0.00%

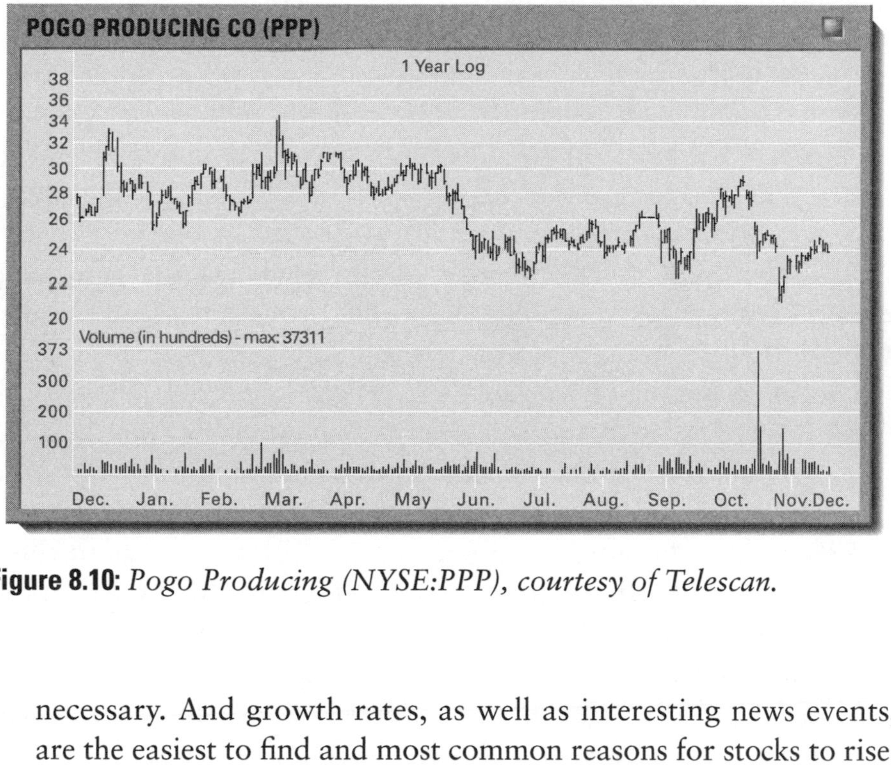

Figure 8.10: *Pogo Producing (NYSE:PPP), courtesy of Telescan.*

necessary. And growth rates, as well as interesting news events, are the easiest to find and most common reasons for stocks to rise.

Pogo is also well positioned, with most of its properties—except for those in Thailand—being found in the United States, where it has Gulf of Mexico positions, as well as in Canada and the U.K. There is no risk from Middle Eastern politics here. And as the chart clearly shows, this stock follows the general trend of the natural gas sector.

Summary

Natural gas may well be the fuel of choice for the world in the near and intermediate future, as OPEC's hold on the oil market showed some signs of slippage in 2001. In my opinion, this may be the most important chapter in the book, because the sleeping giant in both global politics and natural gas reserves—Russia—has begun to make its moves onto the world stage, and much of its strength comes from its vast energy resources, especially natural gas. This—Russia's sudden rise in prominence as a major player in global politics and energy—along with Enron's fall from grace were, in my opinion, the most important nonwar developments of the year 2001 in the energy sector. The combination has the potential to turn the energy world upside-down and to move markets in both directions because of the tug-of-war in the news coverage and in fundamental developments. Global warming, along with possible ongoing skirmishes between the United States and its allies and the increasingly militant terrorist groups in the world, will undoubtedly cause natural gas stocks to be in the thick of things.

I spent a great deal of time discussing long-term charts and revenue and earnings growth rates in this chapter. And while some readers may find the repetition irksome, my intent was to show you that this kind of information is not just readily available, but is the major underlying reason for portfolio managers buying and selling stocks. Each example had subtle aspects that on the surface may have seemed similar. But a closer look usually revealed that company's own peculiar singularity of character.

The bottom line in natural gas is that aside from the supply-and-demand fundamentals of the market, individual companies that are growing rapidly get the benefit of the doubt from investment communities—whether they make bad decisions or not—as long as the growth rates are delivered. When growth rates fall, the stocks get clobbered. More important, those companies with huge debt loads and bad management are eventually hammered, such as Enron Corp., where everything went wrong seemingly all at once. In fact, though, things had been wrong for some time and had been concealed by management. A careful analysis shows that the company made bad decisions over a long period of time, a pattern of behavior that finally caught up to management and cost the shareholders a great deal of money and suffering.

9

Alternative Energy Companies

Although this is the shortest chapter in the book, it was among the toughest to research and write. The material is a hodgepodge of information, partly based on the alternative fuel thesis, as well as just a general grab bag. But this wastebasket does contain some interesting data that can be used to build a file for the future, as the less-recognized fuel sources and the companies depicted here may indeed have their day in the sun.

Contrary to popular belief, science is not particularly advanced when it comes to alternative energy, as most power is still created by coal-powered electricity-generating plants. But because coal gets little respect from either the public or Wall Street, I include it in this chapter to offer you a composite picture of the nonglamorous, but important, energy sources that are available. And although some may not agree, hydroelectric and nuclear power aren't really alternative power sources, with the former powering nearly 10 percent of the electricity in the United States and the latter providing over 20 percent. These two sectors have had a long history of being used to generate electricity, and although nuclear power is also a military fuel and has had a storied past, due to problems with contamination of the environment, it is still responsible for generating a significant amount of electricity. Therefore, this chapter provides a window into the future, as scientists continue their attempt to decipher the mysteries of fusion, the sun's source of nuclear power.

If we look at the current state of the art in alternative power sources, while taking into consideration global politics, it seems that governments and private industry should become increasingly serious about alternative power sources. There is plenty of oil and natural gas left to recover, not to mention some still to be discovered. But because the recoverable oil and gas are largely found in unfriendly environments, both physical and political, and are thus expensive to recover, there is increased evidence of a slow migration to solar and wind power, which has not yet truly invaded the mindset of the private sector or Wall Street.

As I drove from Dallas to El Paso in November 2001, it was hard to miss the wind turbines that dotted the landscape near Abilene, the transitional area in Texas where the lush green north and east Texas hills give way to the more arid expanse of west Texas. Here, companies like TXU are slowly but surely becoming involved with wind power.

So, even though plenty of private and government projects are available, none of them seem to be getting the media attention that the average publicly held integrated or oil exploration company receives in its efforts to find, extract, and market oil and natural gas. And the reasons for the lack of interest are quite simple. Oil and gas are known quantities. Furthermore, the global economy is built around them. So, as long as businesses and consumers are willing to pay for gas and other traditional power sources, oil companies will travel to the ends of the earth to find them, extract them, process them, and put them in a form that can be used to light and heat homes and businesses and power transportation.

Finally, it is not easy to find information on alternative power companies, and this was by far the most challenging of chapters to produce. My conclusion—and I hope, yours—will likely be inevitable. Energy investors should keep an eye on the alternative power sector, but any substantial investment should be kept in the traditional four sectors.

Power Cells

On January 8, 2002, General Motors unveiled a new energy-efficient car at the Detroit Auto Show. The car, named the Autonomy, would use fuel cell technology powered by hydrogen. And on January 9, 2002, U.S. Energy Secretary Spencer Abraham announced that the U.S. government, in partnership with the automobile industry, would fund research aimed at producing fuel cell–powered cars. On January 9, the fuel cell stocks all rallied, only to give back much of the gain on the same day. That is an accurate representation of what investors can expect in this sector of the market for several years to come: short-lived rallies based on news developments.

Power cells function by converting fuels, such as ethanol, petroleum, and natural gas, into energy with water and heat as the by-products. But even here, although the energy is environmentally friendly, it still requires a fuel source, such as the fossil fuels that we are dependent on now. The key is that fuel cells are a way to convert conventional fuel sources into hydrogen, which can then be used to power conventional combustion engines. That is why this is a very attractive alternative fuel, especially for automobile engines and the generation of electricity. The main difference between fuel cells and batteries is that fuel cells don't run out of power, as long as a power source is available. The key component of fuel cells is the proton exchange membrane that allows the chemical reaction to take place. A great summary and great source of information is *www.fuelcells.org*.

The leading publicly traded fuel cell companies are Ballard Power (NASDAQ:BLDP) and Fuel Cell (NASDAQ:FCEL). The performance of both companies is charted in figure 9.1, which

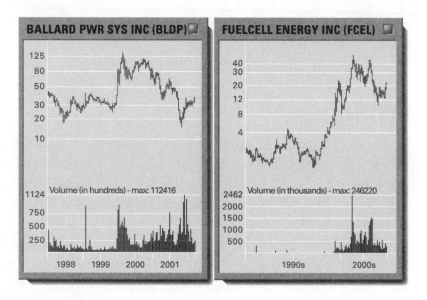

Figure 9.1: *Ballard Power Systems (NASDAQ:BLDP; left) and Fuel Cell Energy Inc. (NASDAQ:FCEL; right), courtesy of Telescan.*

shows that of the two, Fuel Cell has been around longer. Ballard is partly owned by Ford and Daimler-Chrysler, which each own 18 percent of the company, and it has stable revenues from its research partnerships and sales, but had only one profitable quarter in the 1998–2001 period. The best part about Ballard, aside from its corporate partners, is that it had $250 million in cash and only $54 million in liabilities in June 2001, with a total of over $600 million in assets. This tells us that the company is well run and has enough money, as well as deep pockets behind it, to continue its research. The stock's long-term performance, as shown in figure 9.1, suggests that it is a stock to watch, but not to own. The stock, for which figure 9.1 provides a long-term picture, actually did best on the day following the entire run up in the sector that occurred on January 8, 2002. This suggests that the market is beginning to apply a certain premium to Ballard, and that it may be a stock that investors could include in their portfolios as a speculative play.

Fuel Cell's financial performance has been quite similar, with small revenues being offset by continuing losses. The difference between the two companies is that each emphasizes different aspects of fuel cell technology. Fuel Cell is working on a fuel cell power plant for the city of Los Angeles and is also in a partnership with Daimler-Chrysler. Fuel Cell had $48 million in cash in April 2001, with only $10 million in liabilities. But the chart is far more attractive from a long-term perspective than that of Ballard's. My approach to both of these companies is the same. Keep them on the radar screen, but don't put money into them unless the technicals are in excellent shape, or unless you can afford to lose money for a long time in hopes that this technology will pay off handsomely in a decade or more. Consistent results are still many years away.

Coal

Coal is not an alternative fuel, because it is the fuel most commonly used to make electricity in the United States. But the two major coal companies are as unknown to most investors as if they were alternative fuel producers. For that reason, I have included them here to highlight potential investment vehicles, not esoteric science projects.

Peabody is the largest, while Arch is number two, in terms of sales for coal. Both are conventional companies that have had profits and losses due to the supply-and-demand cycle for coal, which is governed by similar external factors to those that move oil and natural gas. The type of analysis I highlighted earlier in the book can be applied here: focusing on the supply-and-demand scenario and then applying the analysis to growth rates and other company fundamentals. Neither company had favorable growth rates during the period I checked, and the volatility of the charts (figure 9.2) attests to the fact, especially when compared to other

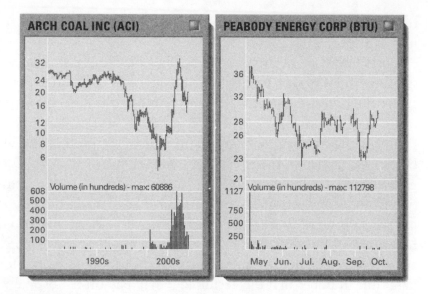

Figure 9.2: *Arch Coal Inc. (NYSE:ACI; left) and Peabody Energy (NYSE: BTU; right), courtesy of Telescan.*

energy stocks in the more conventional sectors. Once again, in energy, size does matter, and there is no reason to go looking for out-of-the-way small stocks, when the institutional money flow is usually to the well-known blue chips.

Solar Power

If we lived in a perfect world, then wind and solar power would be the most sensible energy sources. They are already present, and one or both energy sources are readily available most of the time, to provide clean energy. But no one has been able to make a solar power cell or a windmill that can enable cars to travel 100 miles per hour or all the other sexy things that are possible with fossil fuels.

Figure 9.3 shows that two major companies are in the solar cell business. But these are really specialized chip companies, as solar cells are specialized semiconductors that convert the sun's light energy into electricity. And although solar energy is not used

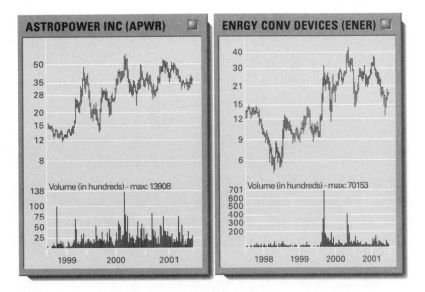

Figure 9.3: *Astropower Inc. (NASDAQ:APWR; left) and Energy Conversion Devices Inc. (NASDAQ:ENER; right).*

to power major industries in most cases, it does have a wide appeal among individuals and small businesses to power niche applications like water heaters for homes and swimming pools, electrical gate motors, and other small applications. But there is a growing interest in both solar and wind energy, as the Green Energy Network developed by the U.S. government continues to expand, especially in the southwestern United States, where Austin, Texas, is the leading recipient of wind-powered electricity.

Astropower is the stronger of the two leading companies, with relatively stable revenues and earnings. And the charts clearly show that investors prefer its shares to those of Energy Conversion Devices.

Wind Power

Wind power is one of the oldest forms of fuel known to humanity, and old-fashioned windmills have given way to wind turbines, which often dot the landscape in places such as the southwestern United States desert areas, where the naturally occurring fuel is plentiful. Wind turbines are often combined with solar power cells to increase the yield and provide a nearly continuous power source, which can be used for charging batteries, producing electricity, grinding grain, or pumping water. Most interesting is that due to government support and improved technology, the cost of producing electricity by the use of wind power has dropped over 80 percent, according to the U.S. Department of Energy. An excellent pair of sources of information about wind energy in general is *The World Directory of Renewable Energy (www.jxj.com/yearbook/wdress/)* and "The Source for Renewable Energy" *(http://energy.sourceguides.com/index.shtml).*

I spent a great deal of time looking for companies in wind power to profile on this subject and was not able to locate a single publicly traded company where the personnel I spoke to had any knowledge of their company's involvement with wind power, even though sources indicated that these companies were involved in making the products. That is not particularly encouraging, although, undoubtedly, many operational turbines exist in the United States and other countries around the world. If you can prove me wrong, e-mail me with the details at *support@joe-duarte.com.*

My lack of results in producing a publicly traded company that makes anything that has to do with wind power clearly speaks to the infancy of the sector.

Nuclear Power

The U.S. Energy Information Agency lists over 60 active nuclear power plants in the United States, which together produce over 20 percent of the total electricity used in the country. Thus nuclear power is the second most commonly used power source in the world's biggest economy, behind coal. It is a clean-burning fuel, but highly controversial, due to major accidents such as those at Chernobyl and Three Mile Island, as well as to uranium's well-documented use in World War II as a weapon of mass destruction, its use during the Cold War as a deterrent, and the potential dangers of an atomic bomb falling in the hands of terrorists as the 21st century grinds on.

Nuclear energy is naturally found in the sun, where extreme heat leads to the combination of pairs of hydrogen ions, in order to form helium. It is that union, or fusion, that scientists hope to use someday to produce power. Contrary to popular belief, nuclear electric plants are not much different in concept from conventional power plants and use a very similar process to that used by conventional power plants to create the steam that turns the turbines to produce electricity. And while most plants use coal to heat the water needed to create steam, in nuclear power plants the heat comes from uranium atoms, whose splitting, or fission, releases heat and begins the process.

There are no real direct ways to invest in companies that make nuclear reactors, other than General Electric (NYSE:GE), the huge conglomerate, which is really more of an entertainment play because it owns NBC and related networks, as well as a financial play with GE Capital. GE makes boiling-water reactors, where the water boils in the reactor. A second kind of reactor, called a pressurized-water reactor, is made by Westinghouse Electric, which was spun off from Westinghouse when it became the predecessor of CBS, which was then bought by Viacom (NYSE:VIA). In this kind of reactor the water is pressurized, but does not boil. The hot water is then pumped into another tank where the steam is created.

In the utility chapter, I described major utility companies that already provide a significant portion of the United States' energy supply. In this chapter I will describe a company that is central to the nuclear energy industry, USEC (NYSE:USU).

USEC is a very interesting company, as it is the leader in the field of converting nuclear power, especially from old weapons, to fuel used in power plants. The company has 75 percent of the U.S. market and one-third of the European market. The company was a

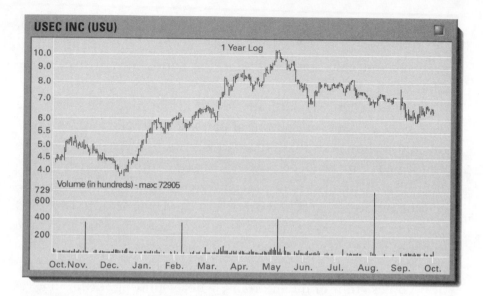

Figure 9.4: *USEC Inc. (NYSE:USU), courtesy of Telescan.*

spin-off from the U.S. government to the public, which raised $1.4 billion in its IPO, but which faces a market that is stagnant at best, given the danger of the potential problems with the fuel and a technology base that makes it very difficult to convert weapons-grade nuclear matter to the grade required to create electricity.

As an ongoing concern, the company is in no real danger of falling away, as it has steady revenues and no short-term debt, with $500 million of long-term debt and twice as many assets as liabilities. The stock did rise in 2000, as the California energy crisis brought nuclear energy into the debate. But as oil prices fell, nuclear power once again faded to the background, and the stock fell. This is not a stock that should be held by investors who are not technically oriented.

Hydroelectric Power

I described major publicly traded utilities with hydroelectric-generating capacity in the utility chapter. Otherwise, hydroelectric power is still the province of the federal government in the United States. The federal system consists of 29 dams under the control of the Department of Energy and its Power Management Administration (PMA). The PMA is an electricity wholesaler divided into five regions: Bonneville, which operates in the Northwestern continental United States; and the others are Southeast, Southwest, Western Area, and Alaska power administrations. These operations are not designed to be profitable and thus make it very difficult—unless they are someday sold to the private sector—for major involvement from Wall Street.

An interesting investment somewhat beyond the scope of this book that could be a play on hydroelectric power would be the purchase of bonds issued by some of these government agencies or their subsidiaries, such as the Tennessee Valley Authority. The TVA made headlines in the mid-1990s when it offered 100-year bonds.

Biofuels

Biofuels are the by-products of plants and woody fibers, such as alcohols and esters. Relax, this isn't organic chemistry class 101. The most commonly used fuel in this category is bioethanol, while others are known as biodiesel and biomethanol. These are useful in two ways. First, much of the material used would otherwise be discarded, because it is composed of woodchips and other plant residues. And second, biofuels tend to burn cleaner than gasoline and other fossil fuels. Bioethanol is a common additive to gasoline, while biodiesel, a product of plant oils, is used as an additive to common diesel.

I personally like the idea of biofuels, because they may provide the United States and the rest of the world with a reasonable, yet familiar, alternative to fossil fuels and may be a good transitional fuel prior to what may be a more aggressive conversion in the next 20 to 30 years to more environmentally friendly fuels, such as those provided by fuel cells.

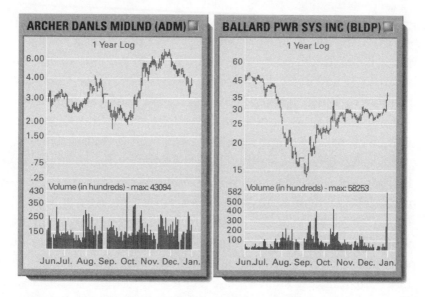

Figure 9.5: *Archer-Daniels Midland Co. (NYSE:ADM) and Ballard Power (NASDAQ:BLDP), courtesy of Telescan.*

The best direct play on biofuels is Archer-Daniels Midland, the large American farming company that produces a significant portion of the world's grain products. Archer-Daniels had its legal troubles in the past, as a result of a price-fixing scheme, but is a well-run company otherwise, with steady revenues and earnings. It can be a core long-term holding for a well-diversified portfolio.

But note the response on January 9 to the announcement by the U.S. government of its intention to fund fuel cell research. ADM shares rallied initially, but then fell. In fact, if you compare both stocks, you can see that in September, they both bottomed and began to rally. But by December, ADM had begun to fall, as BLDP continued to form a nice base. That suggests that smart money was going into Ballard and coming out of ADM. Much of this kind of action is the result of fund managers carefully monitoring what happens in congressional hearings and also of their having access to better and faster information than do individual investors.

A perfect place to find useful information is *www.energywashington.com,* a premium Web site that covers the action in Congress better than just about anybody with regard to energy. Fund managers often subscribe to sites such as this one, while large fund families have dedicated personnel and consultants whom they use to gather this kind of information. Even if you don't subscribe to the service, a visit to the site will let you glimpse the headlines, which on their own merit will often provide the gist of the story and allow you to make more informed decisions.

Summary

Well, that does it for the wide world of energy in nine easy chapters. This was the last chapter to cover individual companies and how they do business. In chapter 10, I organize all of the book's concepts into a trading and investing system that you can use for short-, intermediate-, and long-term investing.

Because of the September 11 attacks and the increasingly hostile world of the early 21st century, global governments and energy companies now have little choice but to diversify their energy policies to include non-OPEC sources of fossil fuels and also to increasingly fund and support alternative fuels.

CHAPTER

10

Technical and Fundamental Analysis

Instead of devoting this chapter to countless esoteric indicators, I'd like to take you through my trading routine, in a real-time trade that I made in Anadarko Petroleum in October 2001. I do this, realizing full well that it might not be everyone's cup of tea, because not everyone is willing to wake up at 4:00 A.M. every morning and begin scouring the Internet for news and data with which to make decisions. But, as John Bollinger described in *Bollinger on Bollinger Bands,* by the time you read this chapter and either discard its teachings or incorporate them into your own plan, a great deal of change to the methods described will have already taken place. Most of it will come from the way you process and organize data in your own mind, as well as from the amount of work you are willing to put into making better trading and investing decisions. So, I have no fear that you will steal my trade secrets. And if you do, congratulations, because you got your money's worth after buying this book. I wish you the best results possible.

Thus, my goal is to give you some perspective, in a blow-by-blow fashion, about what kinds of steps you might want to take if you are serious about being a successful investor, in energy or in any other sector. The key is to develop a checklist, which turns into a routine that you can follow automatically and in which you do not miss any steps. You should write it down and paste it on your bulletin board, on the side of your PC, or anywhere else that you can see it.

But before I move on to my routine, I will say that the comments that follow are strictly related to the energy sector. As a professional money manager, I monitor all of the major sectors of the market on a daily basis, and I begin all of my analysis with a scan of the interest rate picture and the prospects for any changes there. Finally, it is important to realize that because the energy markets are so interconnected to global politics, we must follow the flow of the news, especially as it comes out of OPEC.

Although much of this chapter deals with technical analysis, prior to my making this trade in Anadarko Petroleum, I had gone through the same rigorous analysis of earnings and revenue trends, as well as the company's balance sheet, that I described earlier in the book. As a courtesy to you, I did not repeat that information here. The trading period I am concentrating on began Monday, October 22, and ran to Friday, October 26.

Gathering Background Information

The first step in my Monday routine is to see the background for the coming week. So I began getting ready for October 22 on the prior Saturday, October 20. The weekend gives me a little extra time to think about things and creates a mindset for Monday. This was a textbook period in the energy markets, which combined high-drama political factors along with seasonal and technical aspects of the market, and which well illustrates how to put together all of the information in this book. This time period is very representative of my routine. On Saturday, I pored over *Barron's* magazine and *Barron's* online *(www.barrons.com)*, looking for any consensus in emerging market opinion. This is where I check what the Fed is doing, by looking at an indicator called the average maturity of money market funds to determine the growth rate of money supply and what the market's perception of interest rates is. And while money supply analysis is out of context here, please understand that the process is important. I like to see money supply growing, as it means that the amount of money available for buying stocks is rising. On the weekend I am concentrating on, money supply growth was adequate, and the average maturities were stable. I won't describe the average maturities indicator in detail here because I did this in both *After-Hours Trading Made Easy* and *Successful Biotech Investing,* but the indicator is easy to find in *Barron's* and works well. If the average maturities are rising, investors expect lower rates. If the maturities are falling, the market expects interest rates to fall.

This is because maturities measure how long money market mutual fund managers are willing to hold short-term commercial paper. If they are not willing to hold it for a long time, it means that they know that rates are going to rise, and they could get a higher yield next week or even tomorrow. The indicator has a very high correlation to the U.S. 30-Year Treasury Bond Yield. On October 22, 2001, the indicator was at 54 days, where it had been for three of the previous five weeks, and signaled that rates were stable. The indicator had been at 46 days in January 2001, when the Fed became very aggressive by lowering interest rates, and bonds began to rally, as the expectations for a slower economy began to build.

In this scenario, stable maturities told us that the market was not expecting the Fed to ease too many more times and by default was trying to tell us that the economy had bottomed. At the same time, money supply growth was still rising, although not at such a pace that inflation was a worry. This told me that the Fed was on the market's and the economy's side and that the market was being comforted, both good things. From previous chapters, this should ring a bell, because stable economies are often a prelude to rising economies and thus rising demand for goods and services and, eventually, higher energy prices. So the very first pass over the macro data was positive for energy stocks. In fact, during the prior week, Ford Motor Company went into the corporate credit markets and had a huge bond placement. The average maturities were telling us that the market was ripe for increasing credit demand.

I scan articles in *Barron's,* but unless something really catches my eye, I go straight to data that is in "Barron's Market Laboratory," where the print is small—which means that most people will ignore it and that you have the advantage.

What I specifically look for in *Barron's* regarding energy is the action in the index options for the natural gas index (XNG), the oil index (XOI), and the oil service index. I then use them to calculate a modified put/call ratio, called the Hines ratio because it was developed by Ray Hines, and originally published in *Technical Analysis of Stocks and Commodities* magazine *(www.trader.com).* But before discussing the Hines ratio, I should give you an overview of what the put/call ratio is, because the Hines ratio is a variation of that theme.

The original put/call ratio was invented by Marty Zweig and is a pure contrarian market sentiment indicator. The CBOE put/call ratio is published daily at the close at *www.cboe.com,* as well as every half hour during the trading day, as I'll expand on soon. Just to set the record straight, put options allow the holder to sell an underlying asset in the future at a predetermined price. Call options allow the holder to buy something in the future at a certain price. Put option buyers are betting that the underlying asset will fall, while call option buyers are hoping that the underlying asset will rise in price.

As I wrote in *Active Investor* magazine *(www.activeinvestor-mag.com),* conventional put/call ratios above 0.7—meaning seven calls for every 10 puts—suggest that pessimism is increasing. Significant market bottoms tend to occur when the put/call ratio rises above 1. An average reading is in the 0.5–0.6 range, and cautionary readings occur when the ratio falls below 0.4–0.5. In 2001, significant trading bottoms in the S&P 500 came in the March–April period and in the September–October period. The

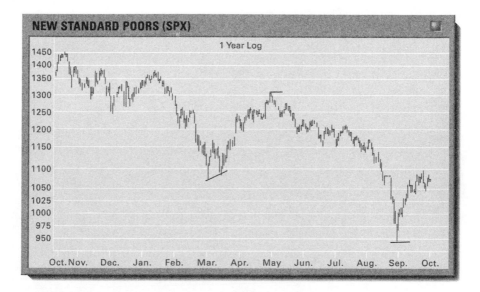

Figure 10.1: *The S&P 500 Index (marked) and the put/call ratio offered important trading opportunities in 2001. The lines mark important market trading points. Courtesy of Telescan.*

put/call ratio registered a reading of 1.08, on March 16, just one day prior to the intraday reversal day on March 19, which was what traders call a momentum bottom. The panic bottom, or the second half of the "W," came on April 3, when the put/call ratio was 0.99. These were excellent indications, as figure 10.1 illustrates. More important, on May 18 and 21, the put/call ratios at the close of the market were 0.47 on both days. The market had had a huge bounce, and too many people turned bullish. The chart speaks for itself, as the market fell until late September. The last and very dramatic portion of the fall came as a result of the September 11 disaster.

The right side of figure 10.1 shows the second significant trading opportunity in 2001, at the accelerated sell-off due to the September 11 events. The big spike on the chart came on September 21, when the market finally bottomed. But the CBOE put/call ratio was flashing a bullish signal as early as September 17, when

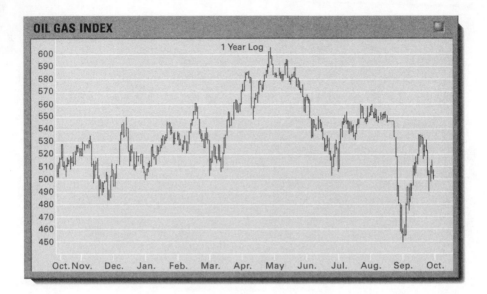

Figure 10.2: *The Amex Oil Index (XOI) also bottomed in March 2001 and September 2001. Courtesy of Telescan.*

it ended the day at 1.14. This was followed by bullish readings of 1.13, 0.89, 1.27, and 1.23 in the next four trading sessions. The 1.27 and 1.23 came on September 20 and 21 and officially marked the bottom.

What does the put/call ratio have to do with energy stocks? Figure 10.2 clearly shows that the Amex Oil Index bottomed during similar time frames in 2001 and offered investors two excellent opportunities. The key to the S&P 500 is to recognize market turning points based on both the charts and the market sentiment. If the sentiment is telling you something, but the market does not respond, then the relationship is malfunctioning and trading during that period is dangerous. But in these two instances, the relationship between market sentiment indicators and the charts was intact, both at key bottoms and at the May top. I discuss the put/call ratios and other sentiment indicators at length on a daily basis at *www.joe-duarte.com*.

Table 10.1 is modeled after the information posted on the CBOE, the Chicago Board of Options Exchange, on a nightly basis.

Table 10.1: *The CBOE put/call ratio. Table modeled after nightly data published at* www.cboe.com.

CBOE Market Summary for 10/19/2001

Put/Call Ratio: 0.80

Equity Option

Total Equity Call Volume: 986,135

Total Equity Put Volume: 670,978

Total Volume: 1,657,113

Index Option

Total Index Call Volume: 118,865

Total Index Put Volume: 215,651

Total Volume: 334,516

Note that two other divisions are in the data that follow the put/call ratio. The reason is that the put/call ratio adds all of the equity options and all of the index options in order to calculate the ratio. In this case you would add all of the puts, which would equal 1,105,000, and all of the calls, which would equal 886,629. The equation would then be expressed in a fraction, as in figure 10.3.

The CBOE Index put/call ratio is a measure of professional action in the options market. This is useful, but has slightly different parameters. Because professionals—meaning hedge funds, mutual funds, and big traders—often hedge bets, there is always some activity in the put option side of the ledger. So a bullish number here is considered to be 1.1, while a bearish number occurs when the ratio falls below 0.90. Any reading above 1.3 is very bullish, while numbers above 1.80 are almost certain signs that at least a short-term bottom is in. This was very clear in March–April of 2001, when the time period ranging from March 28 to April 3 gave us index put/call ratio readings of 2.33, 2.24, 1.93, 1.84, and 2.43.

$$\frac{\text{Equity + Index Puts}}{\text{Equity + Index Calls}} = \frac{1,105,000}{0.80} = 886,629$$

Figure 10.3: *Method for calculating the CBOE put/call ratio.*

Hines ratios for OSX =

$$\frac{\text{Puts/Put Open Interest}}{\text{Calls/Call Open Interest}} = \frac{46128 / 91529}{15550 / 62138} = \frac{0.50}{0.25} = 2.00$$

Hines ratio for XOI on 10/19/01 = 1.27

Hines ratio for XNG on 10/19/01 = 1.49

Figure 10.4: *The Hines ratio for the week of October 19, 2001.*

These bullish readings came when the S&P 500 was making the second V of the W bottom, seen in figure 10.1, and marked total panic on the part of the big money. The point is that it pays to keep tabs on market sentiment, if you know what you are looking for, and make sure that the charts confirm what the sentiment is telling you.

The Hines ratio is a variation on the put/call ratio, as it includes open interest or the amount of active positions in a set of options. Figure 10.4 lists the equation and the calculation from October 19, based on the data published in *Barron's* under the heading of "Stock Index Options: Weekly Summary," which can be found in "Barron's Market Lab," for the Philadelphia Oil Service Index (OSX). The data for the Amex Oil Index (XOI) and XNG are also shown.

The inclusion of open interest in the put/call ratio makes the data more reliable because it also measures how much commitment each side has on its bets. I like to see a great deal of put option buying with falling open interest. This means that people are so fearful that they aren't even willing to bet against the market.

By the same token, when call open interest shrinks and call option volume rises, it means that the bulls are getting cocky. The extreme in open interest is what makes the ratio an excellent signal.

What the data in figure 10.4 show is that traders were reasonably fearful of a continuation in the fall of crude oil prices that was in place in the autumn of 2001. These data were not showing panic, but also were not telling us that a huge sell-off was in the offing. When I looked at the news in the oil sector, I noted that Venezuelan President Hugo Chavez was on a 21-day global tour, trying to convince OPEC and non-OPEC oil producers to cut back production, but he was having little success. No real shock, given what we know about OPEC countries and their sole dependence on oil for income. Other news surfaced on October 23, when the API inventory report showed a larger-than-expected surplus of crude and gasoline inventories.

At this point, I was getting somewhat concerned about rising supplies possibly sending oil prices and stocks plummeting. But concern does not mean panic. And as Mark Seleznov, of Trend Trader.com *(www.trendtrader.com),* always says, "Trade the chart." So, rather than panicking, I reviewed my open energy position at the time in Anadarko Petroleum, which I had bought a few days earlier, based on a combination of the company's leadership role, its excellent management, and its good-looking chart, which is featured in figure 10.5.

My favorite Web-based charting site is AskResearch, whose charts I feature in my daily columns on my Web site *(www .joe-duarte.com).* AskResearch offers both delayed (free) and real-time (premium) charting services. Figure 10.5 is an example of the free delayed charts. What I like about AskResearch's charts is that I can layer my favorite technical indicators on top of each other and look at them simultaneously, which gives me a better idea about what is happening with the stock for the intermediate term.

In this case, I saw a stock in a consolidation pattern, after having made a sizable up move that added 14 points to the stock in a few weeks, following the September bottom. My decision was to

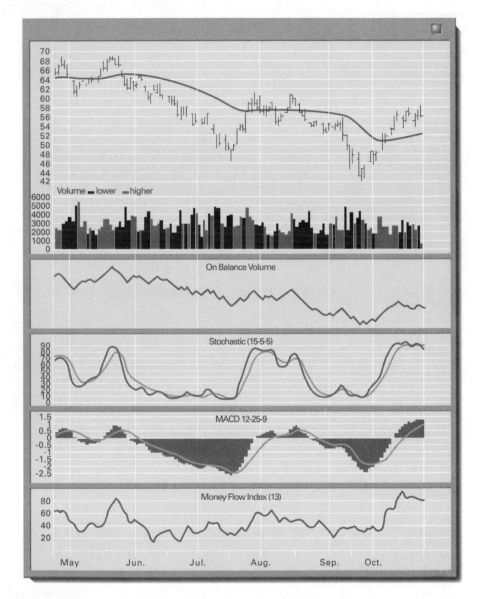

Figure 10.5: *Anadarko Petroleum and technical indicators on October 24, 2001, courtesy of AskResearch,* www.askresearch.com.

hold onto the stock, based on the response of the stock to what should have been very bad news. To the casual observer, OPEC's failure to act when Chavez was touring the world could have seemed like a certain reason to sell. But the chart said that the stock was overbought and consolidating.

Here is what I saw and why I didn't sell the stock. First, APC was above its 50-day moving average, the line that traversed the middle of the chart, and was near 53 on October 24, as I wrote. The 50-day average is a nice intermediate-term gauge that tells you the basic trend of the stock for the past 50 days and is calculated by averaging the last 50 days of trading and plotting the point on the graph. Note the slight up slope of the line in the month of October. Note also that the stock's price dropped to the 50-day moving average several times and did not fall below during the period. This is called support and means that buyers are waiting to buy the stock at that level.

Next, I noted that the stock had not been able to rise above the 56–57 area on several attempts. That is what is known as resistance and means that sellers are waiting there to sell the stock. Only when the selling is exhausted can the stock move higher. Also note that the stock had trouble rising above 60 in August, and that it could well have trouble there again if it broke above 56. I bought at 54 with a target of 60, based on that information. My expectations were to sell half of my position at 60, and keep the other half in play if the stock convinced me that it would go higher. By using targets and selling some of my position when they are hit, I always have a better chance of minimizing losses. Another way to minimize losses is to use sell stops. In this case, I placed my sell stop at 51.50, limiting my loss to less than 5 percent and staying with the trend, because the stock would have to fall below the 50-day moving average to trigger my sell stop.

It's also important to note volume as a stock moves, and APC's volume action was constructive. First, note the rise in volume as the stock hit bottom in late September. A precipitous fall on rising volume is a sign of capitulation and fear. Next, note that the rally off the bottom and to the area of consolidation came on rising volume, a sign of good buying action. And finally, note that the volume trailed off as the stock consolidated—another good sign, telling us that the selling is orderly and that strong hands are holding the stock.

This brings us to *on balance volume,* which is the first indicator under the volume portion of the chart. On balance volume measures net buying and selling in a stock by using a formula beyond our scope here. The indicator was developed by Joe Granville and measures accumulation or distribution. Note that the indicator bottomed in July, along with the stock, but did not make a new high along the way, and the stock fell. Also note that the overall slope of the indicator was negative until September, when it finally hit bottom. Finally, I saw that the indicator was not very robust coming off the bottom in October, but that it was only moving sideways. This is something to watch and a reason for my tight stop, in case on balance volume gave a sell signal by turning down. When stocks are rising, you want to see on balance volume rising. This indicator sometimes turns up or down before a stock and can be an early warning signal of a change in trend.

The next indicator is the stochastics oscillator, developed by George Lane, which measures whether a stock is overbought or oversold. Overbought stocks either consolidate or fall, while oversold stocks tend to make bottoms and eventually rally. In this case, APC is overbought, as measured by stochastics, because it is above 80. Buy signals in stochastics come when the dark line crosses above the lighter line. And sell signals occur when the reverse takes place. In this case, stochastics is overbought and has given a negative crossover. Reason to sell? Not until the chart says so. In many cases stochastics sell signals lead only to consolidations, as this stock looks to be doing. Note the action in July and August, when the stochastics gave an oversold reading, and the stock rallied. But also note that on balance volume kept falling, telling us that the rally was not likely to last. In October, on balance volume was moving sideways when the stochastics was overbought, telling us again that this was a consolidation pattern.

The moving average convergence divergence indicator (MACD) was developed by Gerald Appel and measures momentum. I like to use it to mark significant bottoms and to follow the progress of rising stocks. A buy signal is triggered when the bars of the histogram cross over the line. And momentum is signaled by the direction of the bars and the lines. In October, this indicator told me that momentum in APC was just fine. The indicator was above the zero line, which is a signal that momentum is acting well, and even as the stochastics was overbought, MACD still had room to rise a bit. Note that when APC made a bottom in July, MACD rallied, but made lower peaks than it did when it came off the bottom in September. This tells us that the momentum was stronger in October. Also note that the September bottom did not take MACD to lower lows, compared to August, despite the stock making a new low. This is known as a positive divergence and is a mark that the selling has truly been exhausted.

Finally, I like to use the money flow index, which is also a volume-derived indicator and which measures accumulation distribution, as well as momentum and, indirectly, overbought and oversold states. The latter two are slightly unorthodox uses of the indicator, but I have found them to work well. Note how money flow was weak as the stock sold off in the spring. This coincided with a down trend in on balance volume, the indicator to which I always defer when analyzing whether a stock is under accumulation or distribution. But also note that money flow did not make a new low in September along with the stock. This is the same indication given by MACD and confirmed that the stock was oversold and likely to rally. And the best use of money flow is its ability to show you out-of-the-ordinary strength in a stock, as it did when it shot up to a reading above 80, as APC rallied. The indicator also rolled over during the consolidation, but that is not a big negative, as it would have been if MACD and on balance volume rolled over as well.

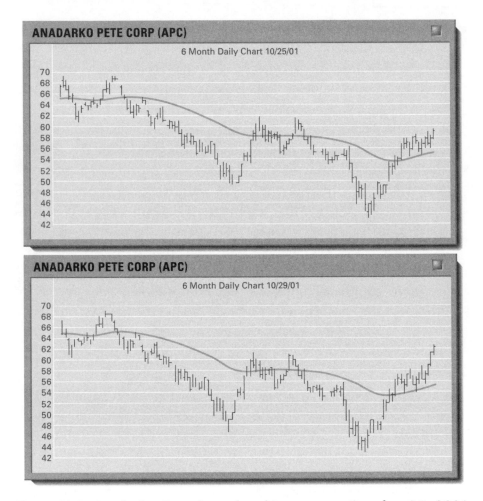

Figure 10.6: *Anadarko Petroleum breaking out on October 25, 2001, and continuing on October 29, 2001, courtesy of AskResearch,* www.askresearch.com.

Figure 10.6 shows that on October 25, 2001, the stock broke out above 56, proving that my decision to hold the stock based on the analysis method described here was correct. And by the next day it had moved to 59 on an intraday basis. The market's excuse on October 25, 2001, was that an unexpected blizzard hit the Dakotas and that the East Coast of the United States was next;

thus, natural gas consumption and prices could rise, due to a potentially early and unexpectedly cold winter. By October 26, 2001, Venezuelan President Hugo Chavez had been able to extract conciliatory comments, but no real promises, from both Russia and Canada. Yet his efforts brought out more OPEC members, who began to chorus his call for production cutbacks. And while these were not the bloodthirsty battle cries of yore, the news kept the price of crude oil from falling and extended OPEC members' support for production cuts into the natural gas market. So, while the war in Afghanistan was raging, OPEC slowly but surely regrouped as winter drew near, and a nice set of fundamental developments coalesced to boost a stock that was ripe for a breakout. And by October 29, 2001, the stock had broken above 60. But even with the fundamental and news-driven move, the stock was telling us, way before the news, that the strength for a nice move up was building. And that's the message of this whole exercise. Pick the best stocks based on management, earnings, and revenue growth. Then get a grip on the external factors of OPEC and supply and demand. Finally, learn to interpret the language of the charts. By combining all three aspects of analysis, you should be able to pick winners consistently.

Time-Frame Issues

Now that I've discussed the actual trade, it's important to fill in the details. One of the most important aspects of successful investing is to understand your time frame or how you view the action in the stock. I like to see the market in many time frames, and figure 10.7 shows a comparison of Anadarko Petroleum to the oil service index (OSX; top left), the natural gas index (XNG, top right), and the oil index (XOI; bottom left). This is a long-term look that shows us that the sectors have been in a down trend, and that they are fighting to turn that down trend into an up trend after bottoming. It also shows us that the oil service index looks the best of the three indexes, and that APC looks better

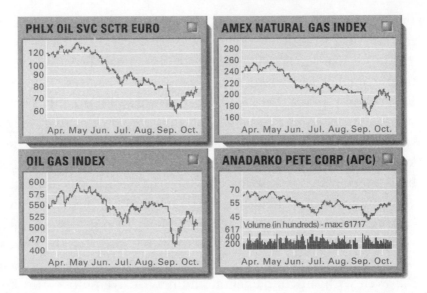

Figure 10.7: *Long-term view of the energy complex and Anadarko Petro-leum on October 24, 2001, courtesy of Telescan.*

than any of them. This is a sign of relative strength on the part of the stock, which is clearly in a strong rebound phase.

But figure 10.8 shows a different view. All of the indexes have rallied off their intraday bottoms, even in the face of potentially negative news, such as comfortable inventories and potential disarray within OPEC—both items that could drop oil and energy prices and cut into company profits. Also note that Anadarko is showing the most strength on an intraday basis, having crossed above the resistance at the 56 area.

Finally, I like to look at the 10-day trend in the sector, which is visible in figure 10.9. Once again, we see that Anadarko is a very strong stock, as the rest of the complex looks to be weakening. This is both a positive, because the stock is showing relative strength, and also a potential negative, as the 10-day trend was increasingly top-heavy for the energy sector, a sign that the weakness could spread to Anadarko. The natural gas index was particularly

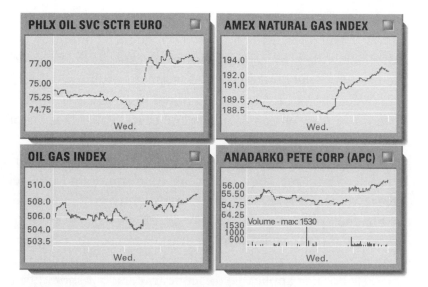

Figure 10.8: *Intraday view of the energy complex and Anadarko Petroleum on October 24, 2001, courtesy of Telescan.*

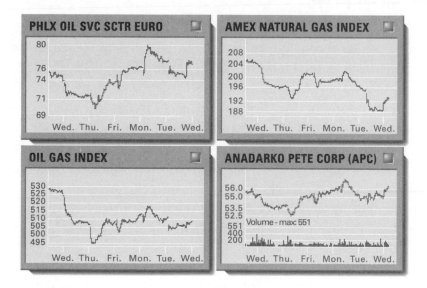

Figure 10.9: *Ten-day view of the energy complex and Anadarko Petroleum on October 24, 2001, courtesy of Telescan.*

weak on that day, due to bad news for Enron Corp., which at the time was being investigated for potential financial improprieties, as well as facing the prospect of having to increase its float of stock to raise money to pay off debt. This was quite satisfying for me from an analytical point of view, since I noted in an earlier chapter that Enron was not a well-run company and that it could face big problems as a result of its management style and high debt level.

What I've done in this section is put together both fundamental and technical methods, including time frame and intersector analysis, to decide whether to stay in a slightly profitable position that I had held for several days. My decision was to keep the position, knowing full well that it could go against me. I hedged my decision by placing a sell stop under the stock. This multifaceted analysis is not just applicable to active traders, but should be used by long-term investors as well.

The Sector Plays

The next area of trading I'd like to discuss is that of sector-related plays, either through open-ended mutual funds or exchange-traded funds, such as the HOLDRS and I-shares. Exchange-traded funds are offered by Merrill Lynch (HOLDRS) and by Barclays (I-shares). Many mutual fund companies offer sector funds as well, but there are details that separate them, which make one set of sector funds more easily traded than the rest. The advantage of trading sector funds is that your analysis stops once you decide the basic trend of the market—meaning interest rates and overall supply and demand of the cycle—making this approach ideal for those who don't have time to pick stocks or to do the painstaking search through earnings reports or online databases.

The HOLDRS and I-shares trade like individual stocks, making them ideal for short-term trading strategies, such as the Energy Timing Portfolio, featured on my Web site at *www.joe-duarte.com*. In this timing portfolio I use HOLDRS trusts, individual stocks,

Table 10.2: *Selected sector-trading opportunities in the energy sector.*

Sector Vehicle	Symbol	Category	Exchange
Oil Service HOLDRS	OIH	exchange-traded	AMEX
Sector Spyder Energy I-Shares Trust	XLE	exchange-traded	AMEX
Dow Jones U.S. Energy	IYE	exchange-traded	AMEX
Fidelity Select Energy Fidelity Select	FSENX	sector fund	Fidelity Inv.
Energy Service Fidelity Select	FSESX	sector fund	Fidelity Inv.
Natural Gas Fidelity Select	FSNGX	sector fund	Fidelity Inv.
Natural Resources	FNARX	sector fund	Fidelity Inv.

and I-shares, based on the underlying performance of the sectors they represent.

In my own accounts and my managed client accounts, I use stocks, exchange-traded funds, and sector funds. My favorite sector fund family is Fidelity, because it is the biggest, offers the most variety, and features hourly pricing on its sector funds. My client and personal accounts are housed at Fidelity, and I receive no compensation from this firm. Table 10.2 summarizes my favorite vehicles.

Table 10.2 does not include sector offerings from Vanguard, Invesco, or many other mutual fund companies that market these trading vehicles, for one specific reason. Only Fidelity caters to mutual fund switchers. Both Vanguard and Invesco discourage frequent switching, while Fidelity gets around the problem by charging fees. But Fidelity's 3 percent load on the Select funds is not as big a problem as it seems, once you look at the particulars. The fee is only charged once for a specific amount of money.

For example, if you opened an account at Fidelity for $10,000 and decided to buy Fidelity Select Natural Resources, Fidelity would charge you $300 the first time you went into the fund. But if you sold the fund in six weeks and made a 20 percent gain, then you would have paid the 3 percent on $11,640, the initial amount minus the fee, which was $9,700, and your profit of $1,940. If you hold the fund for 30 days or longer and trade online, Fidelity would charge you $7.50 to sell. If you use its toll-free number after holding the fund for 30 days or longer, Fidelity charges $15.00 to sell. If you sell in less than 30 days, the firm charges 0.75 percent of the amount you sell. All in all, if you hold the funds for 30 days or longer, your fees are minimal, and you can steadily build the amount of money you've paid the fees on if you are a good trader, without ever having to pay the load again. This is preferable to being penalized and harassed by fund companies just because you want to manage your money actively.

Otherwise, you can trade the HOLDRS or I-shares by using a discount broker online and paying a commission, which is anywhere from as little as $5 to as much as $20.95, with somewhere around $14 being the average online commission. If you use a full-service broker, your commission will be higher.

How to Use Sector Funds

The analysis used to trade sector vehicles is exactly the same that you would use to trade stocks. You must keep up with the supply-and-demand scenario, political developments, and earnings and revenue trends for the individual sectors. And you must know which vehicle closely matches which sector index. Figure 10.10 shows the close relationship between the Philadelphia Oil Service Sector (OSX; top left), the Oil Service HOLDRS trust (OIH; top right), the Fidelity Select Energy Service Fund (FSESX; bottom left), and the Crude Oil December futures (CLZ1; bottom right). The charts clearly show that both OIH and FSESX move in tandem to the trend in the OSX index. The crude oil futures are di-

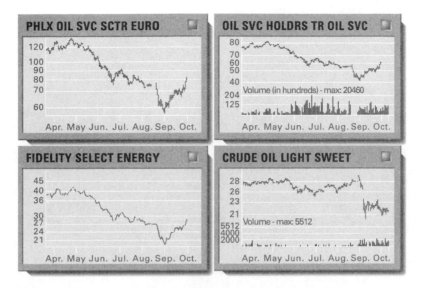

Figure 10.10: *Close relationship between sector vehicles, commodity prices, and sector indexes in the oil service sector, courtesy of Telescan.*

verging from the rising trend. From a trading standpoint, this does suggest that the rally in the oil service stocks may be limited, because the oil futures are clearly not participating. This is a cautionary sign that must be taken into consideration, especially as the trading vehicles reach resistance areas, such as the 90 area on the OSX and the 30 and 70 areas on the FSESX and OIH. The point here is that by keeping an eye on the index and the trading vehicles simultaneously, you could make better bets.

Figure 10.11 shows that the correlation between crude oil futures (CLZ1; top left) and the Amex Oil Index (XOI; top right), as well as the Sector Spyder Trust for Energy (XLE; bottom left) and the Fidelity Select Energy Fund (FSENX; bottom right), is also quite impressive. Here we see that this sector, which is heavily weighted toward the large multinational integrated oil companies, is having a more subdued reaction to the factors I described earlier. This makes sense, since this rally was primarily brought on by cold weather, which drives up natural gas prices more than

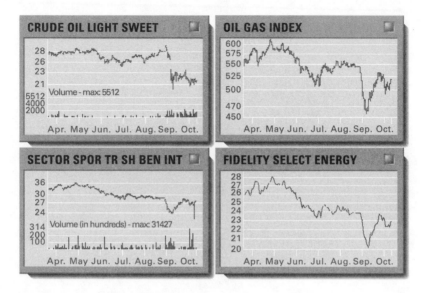

Figure 10.11: *Close relationship between sector vehicles, commodity prices, and sector indexes in the oil sector, courtesy of Telescan.*

crude oil, unless there is a shortage of heating oil—which was the case in 2000, but not in 2001, due to the decrease in demand on airplane fuel as a result of the September 11 events. Also, remember that crude oil supplies were more than adequate and could easily be driven into heating oil if needed.

Finally, figure 10.12 looks at the natural gas sector, where the Amex Natural Gas Index (XNG; top left) is compared to the Fidelity Select Natural Gas Portfolio (FSNGX; top right), natural gas futures (NGZ1; bottom left), and my favorite stock at the time, which had risen to 59.23 by October 26, 2001. Although I was happy with the Anadarko trade, my reason for including it here was that of the trading options at the time, it was clearly the best one. The sector fund was lagging, more than likely due to the fund manager owning Enron, a stock that continued to fall due to its problems with management during this time. Note that the price of natural gas futures began creeping up in September. Also note that APC bottomed in September, along with the index

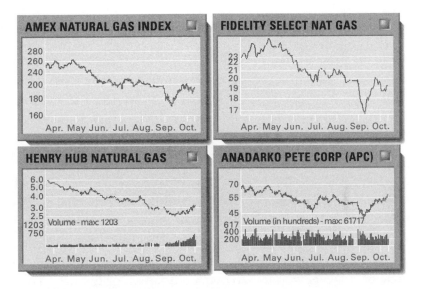

Figure 10.12: *Close relationship between sector vehicles, commodity prices, stocks, and sector indexes in the natural gas sector, courtesy of Telescan.*

and the fund. This is the kind of confirmation that you should look for before buying into the energy sector. Compare this convergence of the trend with the divergence offered by the crude oil futures in figures 10.10 and 10.11. At this time, the best bet was to buy the service stocks or the natural gas stocks because the prospect for crude, according to the message of the futures markets, was not as positive.

The moving-average method and oscillator methods that I described for my trade in Anadarko are easily applicable to the sector plays with both the exchange-traded and the open-ended sector funds. All of these indicators are available free at Web sites like AskResearch, Wall Street City *(www.wallstreetcity)*, Prophet Charts *(www.prophetfinance.com)*, and Big Charts *(www.bigcharts.com)*. Most online charting services also offer access to real-time quotes and charting for reasonable monthly fees for individual investors. I highly recommend that you become well versed in reading charts and in the use of oscillators.

Long-Term Strategies

While the previous section has a great deal of detail about short- to intermediate-term trading, equal time is reserved for those who have a 10- to 15-year time horizon. If history is any guide about what the potential is for the energy sector, figure 10.13 suggests that the 2001 dip in the oil and gas sector indexes is a potential buying opportunity for long-term investors in the sector funds. Both Fidelity Select Energy (FSENX) and Fidelity Select Natural Gas (FSNGX) have come back to long-term support levels, meaning that there are likely to be buyers in the stocks owned in the portfolios at these levels. Remember that integrated oil stocks and natural gas utilities tend to pay nice dividends. That makes them ideal for value-oriented institutional money managers who like to own companies for decades. This kind of dip in a sector with an excellent long-term record is what they often consider a gift from the gods.

Investors who use a dollar–cost averaging method could use this pause to buy more shares at a lower price. This method works best if you have a very long time frame and is ideal for college money, as well as 401(k) plans and IRAs. It is not something I would recommend for anyone over 35–40 years of age or for college funds for teenagers.

What to Do to Protect Yourself

No chapter on technical analysis would be complete without telling you what to do if you make a mistake. When I described my Anadarko trade earlier in this chapter, I noted that I used a sell stop. This means that after my trade had been executed, I placed a limit order that would be triggered if the stock fell to the level I specified.

I bought the stock at 54 and set the stop at 51.50, initially. This was about 5 percent below the initial purchase. When I am trading for the intermediate term—meaning that I expect to be in the position for several weeks to months—I will usually place a

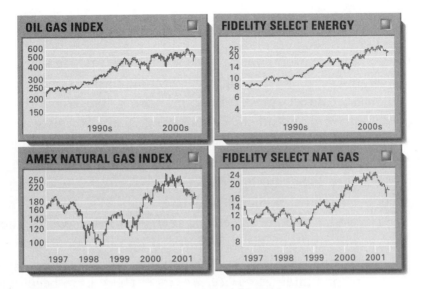

Figure 10.13: *Long-term chart analysis, courtesy of Telescan.*

stop 5 to 10 percent below my purchase price. That range is based on the work of William O'Neil, the founder of *Investor's Business Daily* and the author of *How To Make Money in Stocks* and other trading bestsellers. O'Neil and *Investor's Business Daily* have redefined the art of momentum trading, and over the years I have been saved a great deal of trouble by using their sell stop limits. Even if you don't actually put in the stop order, you should always mentally know where your sell stop is and apply it to sector funds as well.

Your Trading Tools

Finally, I'd like to add a small section on your trading tools. If you're going to seriously trade online, I suggest a fast computer, with a chip that is no more than one or, at most, two generations behind the most current one. As I write, I am due for an upgrade, because my Pentium II 333 is at least two turns behind the Pentium 4s, which have more than 1 gigabyte of processing speed.

Max out your random access memory (RAM), because trading software takes up a lot of room, and you may often have it going along with several open browser windows, as you scan news sources and keep up with online accounting information.

Consider direct-access trading platforms, like Trend Trader's TORS software and others. If you are very active, this will save you time and money. Most trading sites have reasonably good charting software with the indicators I described here, but you may want to look into other excellent packages like those provided by MetaStock, e-Signal, and Telescan.

Above all, if you are an active trader, your results will be much more adequate if you use a high-speed Internet connection like DSL, broadband wireless, or cable modem. Also, consider having more than one Internet service provider. There have been many times when my main network has fallen during the trading day, and I have been able to get around it by logging on to my back-up network.

Finally, you may want to have a laptop set up with a back-up system, in case you have to travel or your main network goes down. If worse comes to worse, you may have to succumb to the old dial-up modem. What a horrible thought.

Summary

This chapter was designed to put it all together. I used a trading example of a real trade I made in Anadarko Petroleum in October 2001, to illustrate how I combine analysis of market sentiment, the trend of interest rates, the status of supply and demand in the energy sector, global politics, company fundamentals, and technical analysis to generate profitable trades. I also illustrated the use of intermarket analysis to pick which energy sector to enter by using sector-oriented exchange-traded and open-ended mutual funds.

If you made it this far, this is a chapter to review and to use as a reference when you make your own trading and investment decisions. Do not deviate from the principles here or you are likely to get hurt. You may add your own wrinkles, which is great, as you must customize this information to suit your needs. But if you try to force your will on stocks or sectors, or trade energy stocks on a whim, without first carefully analyzing the fundamentals and the technicals, you are likely to lose money quite often.

Conclusion

For those who made it this far, I thank you for your patience and sincerely hope that you are ready to make better investments and trades in the energy markets. I tried to make the concepts accessible to a wide audience. This book is unique in its scope, given its intense focus on both fundamental and technical stock analysis. But even though my focus was on stocks, I could not completely tear myself away from the serious game of hardball taking place in the global political scene and the central role that energy plays in every aspect of our lives, politically and otherwise. For as in no other sector, politics and energy go hand-in-hand, beginning with deregulation issues in the United States and ranging to the ever-increasing focus on the Middle East and the war on terrorism.

When I began this book, the United States was reeling from the sad and trying events of the 2000 presidential election. Those events scarred the nation's psyche. The public and extremely high-stakes legal and political battles were fought on global television, with 24-hour news channels providing blow-by-blow coverage and analysis of the events. In my introduction, I also noted that the election of President Bush was pivotal, because of his own pedigree and the energy-related expertise of his cabinet, especially of Vice President Dick Cheney, the former CEO of Halliburton.

But nothing that I saw in the election or in the contentious first eight months of President Bush's first term could have prepared me for the events of September 11 and their effects on the global markets, as well as what I believe is yet to come—a significant change in the dynamics not just of life, but of the energy sector.

When writing the initial chapters, I already possessed a pro's knowledge of the technical analysis of the energy markets, because I had traded and invested in the sector with good results for many years. I had a working, but shallow, concept of supply-and-demand fundamentals and a fair knowledge of the politics involved, in the classic sense—in other words, OPEC rules the oil world. But as I researched the book, a whole new exciting world of information opened up.

I became acquainted with geographical and geological notions that had faded into the depths of my memory. I began to enjoy reading about far-off places like Russia and its former republics. And I emerged with a newfound feeling of academic accomplishment.

Most interesting was the discovery that despite the ubiquitous nature of the sun and the wind, little has been done to harness these clean fuels for energy. Instead, companies prefer to travel to the hottest deserts, the most malaria-infested rain forests, as well as the deepest wave- and shark-filled oceans, the most hostile and politically unstable countries, and the coldest of tundras, to dig for oil and natural gas. Some people are driven by the challenge to do these things. Most are motivated by the knowledge that crude oil and natural gas rule the energy world. But as it becomes more difficult to navigate the political waters and the pay-off for going to all that trouble decreases, I suspect that alternative energy sources will have their day. And although that makes little sense right now, the attitude toward alternative fuel sources could well change due to the unfortunate events of September 11, 2001. Even as I write, oil companies are very discreetly beginning to increase their interest in non-OPEC and non–crude oil fuel and energy solutions, such as wind and solar power, as well as fuel cells. And more important, companies like General Motors, Ford, and

Chrysler are stepping up their interest in fuel cell technology as a method to power cars.

As I uncovered each new layer of information, a great deal about how the world works and how the energy market is truly pivotal became increasingly apparent. Sure, everyone knows we need oil and natural gas to power our homes, cars, and businesses. But what researching this book gave me, and what I hope I transferred to these pages, is a serious and very applicable database of information, with a significant shelf life, that has already made me a better trader and investor. I hope it does the same for you. The information I uncovered—such as Web sites like *www.energyeconomist.com* and *www.dismal.com,* as well as the bevy of Department of Energy sites that I repeatedly quote in the book—is useful on a daily basis to help me make money. I encourage you to become familiar with these sites as well.

In the past, I was an opportunistic analyst of the energy markets, as they pertained to the rest of the markets, and a participant when the technicals of the sector were right. I am now an avid follower of the industry and its subsectors, having become a full-time analyst of the stocks in the industry. I also write an energy-timing column on my Web site, *www.joe-duarte.com.* Most important, because of the political research that I had to undertake, I now have a much better understanding of the world in which we live and can apply that knowledge both inside and outside of the markets.

The events of September 11, 2001, were pivotal in the production of this book, for the permanent changes engendered there can already be seen in the financial markets. The cost of doing business will rise as a result of higher insurance premiums. Entertainment companies will be greatly challenged to fill movie theaters with violent, terror-based films. And if I had to make a long-term and perhaps wild prediction, I would say that the beginning of the end for OPEC might have been on that fateful day.

I am not saying that OPEC will cease to exist—certainly not right away—for it still has most of the world's oil and the infrastructure and relationships to remain in business for the near future. But its reign of power, as we once knew and recognized it, through its ability to move the markets with threats of cutting off oil supplies, may have truly been eradicated—ironically, by the same country that President Ronald Reagan once called the "evil empire."

For as the world wept and sat in shocked silence in the aftermath of the World Trade Center attacks, Russia took the bull by the horns and became everyone's best friend. I am not being sarcastic here. Russia did what any country in its right mind would do when presented with a once-in-a-lifetime opportunity: Russia came out of nowhere to lend stability and, more subtly, to put its natural resources where the rest of the world could see them and quietly wonder, Maybe we can diversify our oil and gas purchasing, just a little, in case OPEC decides to play hardball again.

And indeed, in many parts of the book I noted that OPEC was not using its clout as often to threaten the West. Initially, I concluded that OPEC had begun to behave like a responsible business, taking care of its customers while trying to get a reasonable price for itself. And I still believe that this is partially true, for OPEC does have a business to run, and it has become increasingly savvy in the way it conducts itself. But the crisis widened, the price of oil kept dropping, and it became quite clear that OPEC was not in any position to do more than jaw-bone the markets and quietly panic. Although the West may have fallen into recession in the few months before and after the September 11 catastrophe, unlike OPEC countries the West has a more diverse economic base and can withstand protracted downturns better.

Most OPEC countries are not democratic, do not have well-diversified economies, and are almost totally dependent on the price of crude oil for their gross domestic products. And perhaps a deeper reason for the world to question its dependence on OPEC is that because of their geography and political structure, several, if not all, members of OPEC have either directly or indirectly supported, still support, or allegedly have associations with terrorism—the new preeminent evil in the world against which everyone now shares a common dread. Although that feeling might not have reached a fever pitch just yet, politics and people are strange. Thus, for all those reasons, OPEC is vulnerable.

A great example of OPEC's vulnerability and lack of leadership is that it took three weeks of intense in-person lobbying by Venezuelan President Hugo Chavez, in October 2001, to get OPEC members to agree in principle to production cutbacks as the price of oil sank. In the past, Saudi Arabia, Iran, Iraq, and even Libya would have been pounding the table for cutbacks before Chavez could get his suitcases packed. Chavez also traveled to Russia, England, Canada, and Mexico to try to gain concessions from non-OPEC producers, who all paid courteous lip service, but offered no real tangible assurances of assistance. This lack of unity in OPEC and the lukewarm response from the competing non-OPEC crowd support my thesis that OPEC's days as the dominant player in crude oil are numbered.

OPEC's demise—or, at least, its reduction in the oil markets—may be slow in developing, but it is almost certain because the member countries' inability to deal with internal political and demographic problems will eventually overwhelm their ability to hold the world hostage to their fading monopoly. According to *www.stratfor.com,* as I wrote these final comments, Saudi Arabia was a hotbed of Islamic fundamentalism, and Venezuela's own Chavez was in deep political trouble because his communist tendencies and their proclivity to cause more domestic economic problems at a time when oil prices were falling could lead to his early demise as president. If we extend this kind of analysis to all of the OPEC countries, we could find festering political unrest and discontent in all of them. With their internal problems threatening their nondemocratic governments, coupled with the growing maldistribution of wealth, members of the cartel will have to cheat on their quotas to bring in as much money as possible into their countries and keep their monolithic governments in power. As their cheating continues, so will the finger-pointing and internal bickering increase, and so will their ability to control the price of oil decrease. This is not new, except this time it is slightly different, given what could be a decade or longer of intermittent war against terrorism waged by the United States and most likely some combination of countries in Europe and the U.K.

Meanwhile, Russia's new friendly pro-Europe, pro-NATO, and pro–United States stance will boost international investment in that country's vast oil and gas reserves, finally making it a significant power in natural resources—not just on paper and in potential, but in its ability to generate real money that could actually make its way to the economy. When a major corporation like Exxon-Mobil is faced with having to make a multibillion-dollar investment overseas, it will almost certainly have to weigh the increased risk to its employees and equipment from unfriendly OPEC nations. Major global oil companies will likely decide to go to a more friendly—and, indeed, needy—place, where bargain-basement deals are more possible than in well-established OPEC-type countries.

China's potential as a major player is also growing, as U.S. and European oil companies increase their presence there. My prediction for China is slightly different. I would expect the next decade to cast China as a major participant in global joint venture–type operations with the major oil companies, as political and terrorist risks are likely to increase and companies begin to spread their risk aversion.

Not many analysts are discussing this emerging dynamic yet. Thus, it is still a subtle change in the supply-and-demand scenario. But in my opinion, this is the beginning of a major new set of circumstances in the energy game. In fact, I believe that this is the small straw that could not only break the proverbial camel's back, but could also change the fundamentals in the energy market, as we know them. And if you glean nothing else from this book, keep your eyes peeled on Russia and China, for the bear and the dragon are coming out of hibernation. Our world will never be the same again. Happy hunting.

Appendix A:
World Oil Reserves

Country	Oil (billions of barrels)	Gas (trillions of cubic feet)
North America		
United States	28.4	167.4
Mexico	21.8	30.1
Canada	4.9	63.9
Central and South America		
Brazil	7.4	8
Argentina	2.8	24.2
Colombia	2.6	6.9
Ecuador	2.1	3.7
Trinidad & Tobago	0.6	19.8
Guatemala	0.5	0.1
Peru	0.4	9
Cuba	0.3	0.6
Chile	0.2	5.5
Bolivia	0.1	4.3
Suriname	0.1	0
Barbados	0	0

Country	Oil (billions of barrels)	Gas (trillions of cubic feet)
Western Europe		
Norway	10.8	41.4
U.K.	5.2	26.7
Denmark	1.1	3.4
Italy	0.6	8.1
Germany	0.4	12
Turkey	0.3	0.3
Austria	0.1	0.9
Croatia	0.1	1.2
France	0.1	0.5
Netherlands	0.1	62.5
Serbia & Montenegro	0.1	1.7
Greece	0	0
Ireland	0	0.7
Spain	0	0.1
Eastern Europe and the Former U.S.S.R.		
Russia	48.6	1,700
Kazahkstan	5.4	65
Romania	1.4	13.2
Azerbaijan	1.2	4.4
Uzbekistan	0.6	66.2
Turkmenistan	0.5	101
Ukraine	0.4	39.6
Albania	0.2	0.1
Hungary	0.1	2.9
Poland	0.1	5.1
Bulgaria	0	0.2
The Czech Republic	0	0.1
Slovakia	0	0.5

Country	Oil (billions of barrels)	Gas (trillions of cubic feet)
Middle East		
Saudi Arabia*	263.5	204.5
Iraq*	112.5	109.8
U.A.E.*	97.8	212
Kuwait*	96.5	52.7
Iran*	89.7	812.3
Oman	5.3	28.4
Yemen	4	16.9
Quatar*	3.7	3
Syria	2.5	8.5
Bahrain	0.1	3.9
Israel	0	0
Jordan	0	0.2
Africa		
Libya*	29.5	46.4
Nigeria*	22.5	124
Algeria*	9.2	159.7
Angola	5.4	1.6
Egypt	2.9	35.2
Gabon	2.5	1.2
Congo (Brazzaville)	1.5	3.2
Cameroon	0.4	3.9
Sudan	0.3	3
Tunisia	0.3	2.8
Congo (Kinshasa)	0.2	0
Ivory Coast	0.1	1.1
Benin	0	0
Equatorial Guinea	0	1.3
Ethiopia	0	0.9
Ghana	0	0.8

Country	Oil (billions of barrels)	Gas (trillions of cubic feet)
Madagascar	0	0.1
Morocco	0	0
Mozambique	0	2
Namibia	0	3
Rwanda	0	2
Somalia	0	0.2
South Africa	0	0.8
Tanzania	0	1

*OPEC *member countries*

Appendix B: Electric Utilities
Best Performing for 1998–2001

This appendix provides investment leads beyond those companies already highlighted in the text, as well as contact information.

Company	Symbol	% Change
Company	*Symbol*	*% Change*

Calpine Corporation   CPN   759.94%
50 West San Fernando Street
San Jose, CA 95113
Tel: 408-995-5115
Fax: 408-995-0505
Web site: www.calpine.com
Business Summary: Calpine acquires, develops, owns, and operates power-generation facilities and sells electricity and its by-product—thermal energy, in the form of steam—predominantly in the United States and Canada. Calpine has ownership interests in and operates gas-fired cogeneration facilities, gas fields, gathering systems and gas pipelines, geothermal steam fields, and geothermal power-generation facilities in the United States and Canada.

Company	Symbol	% Change

U.S. Energy Systems Inc. **USEY** 311.00%
One North Lexington Avenue, 4th Floor
White Plains, NY 10601
Tel: 914-993-6443
Fax: 914-993-5190
Web site: www.usenergysystems.com
Business Summary: U.S. Energy Systems owns, develops, and operates cogeneration and independent power plants through its subsidiaries. U.S. Energy also provides environmental and remedial services, including the collection and recycling of motor and industrial oils and water. Its power plants produce and sell electricity to both direct end users and regulated public electric utility companies. Its primary energy facilities are two geothermal power plants in Nevada. The environmental services division provides services that include consultation, remediation, recovery, and utilities services in the midwestern United States.

Bangor Hydro-Electric Company **BGR** 176.26%
33 State Street
Bangor, ME 04401
Tel: 207-945-5621
Fax: n/a
Web site: www.bhe.com
Business Summary: Bangor Hydro-Electric Company is a public utility engaged in the generation, purchase, transmission, distribution, and sale of electric energy and other energy-related services. Bangor serves an area of approximately 5,275 square miles and a population of approximately 192,000 people.

Company	Symbol	% Change

Dynegy Incorporated   DYN   151.29%
    1000 Louisiana, Suite 5800
    Houston, TX 77002
    Tel: 713-507-6400
    Fax: 713-507-3871
    Web site: www.dynegy.com
Business Summary: Dynegy markets and trades natural gas, power, coal, emission allowances, and weather derivatives. Dynegy also generates electricity and gathers and processes natural gas liquids. The company has operations in the transmission and distribution of electricity and natural gas and provides retail service to electric and gas consumers. The company provides services to customers in North America, the United Kingdom, and Continental Europe.

Huaneng Power International   HNP   122.79%
    2C Fuxingmennan Street, West Wing Building C
    Tianyin Mansion, Beijing, China 100031
    Tel: +86-10-6649-1999
    Fax: +86-10-6649-1860
    Web site: www.hpi.com.cn
Business Summary: Huaneng Power International develops, constructs, owns, and operates large thermal power plants throughout China. Huaneng owns 13 power plants in 6 of China's coastal regions.

Company	Symbol	% Change

Maine Public Service Company   MAP   93.89%
209 State Street
Presque Isle, ME 04769
Tel: 207-768-5811
Fax: 207-764-6586
Web site: www.mainepublicservice.com
Business Summary: Maine Public Service Company supplies electricity to retail and wholesale customers in northern Maine. The company has a Canadian subsidiary, Maine and New Brunswick Electrical Power Company Limited, that is primarily a hydroelectric generating company.

Baycorp Holdings, Ltd.   MWH   63.81%
222 International Drive, Suite 125
Portsmouth, NH 03801-6819
Tel: 603-431-6600
Fax: n/a
Web site: n/a
Business Summary: Baycorp Holdings operates through its subsidiaries in generation and trading businesses and an Internet-based energy trading and information business. The subsidiaries of the company are Great Bay Power Corporation and Little Bay Power Corporation.

Company	*Symbol*	*% Change*

Central Vermont Public Service   CV   62.33%
    Corporation
77 Grove Street
Rutland, VT 05701
Tel: 802-773-2711
Fax: 802-747-2199
Web site: www.cvps.com
Business Summary: Central Vermont Public Service Corporation purchases, produces, transmits, distributes, and sells electricity in New Hampshire and Vermont. The company also has real estate and investments. It serves 142,000 customers in nearly three-fourths of the towns, villages, and cities in Vermont.

Otter Tail Power Company   OTTR   49.55%
215 South Cascade Street
Fergus Falls, MN 56538-0496
Tel: 218-739-8200
Fax: 218-739-8770
Web site: www.ottertail.com
Business Summary: Otter Tail Corporation produces polyvinyl chloride pipe, agricultural equipment, automobile and truck frame straightening equipment, and accessories for the auto body shop industry. Otter Tail also does contract machining, metal parts stamping, fabrication sales, service, rentals, refurbishing, and operations of medical imaging equipment. The company sells products related to medical imaging supplies and accessories. The company is involved with electric operations, electrical and telephone construction, contracting, transportation, telecommunications, entertainment, and energy services and natural gas marketing.

Company	Symbol	% Change

Green Mountain Power Corporation   **GMP**   **43.91%**
163 Acorn Lane
Colchester, VT 05446
Tel: 802-864-5731
Fax: n/a
Web site: www.gmpvt.com
Business Summary: Green Mountain Power supplies electrical power to residential, small commercial, and industrial customers. Green Mountain's primary service area is north central Vermont. Green Mountain is a wholesaler to municipalities and cooperatives.

Appendix C: Gas Utilities
Best Performing for 1998–2001

This appendix was produced to provide a broader investment database and to provide contact information for investors.

Company	Symbol	% Change
Southern Union Company	SUG	13.07%

504 Lavaca Street, Suite 800
Austin, TX 78701
Tel: 512-477-5852
Fax: 512-477-3879
Web site: www.southernunionco.com

Business Summary: Southern Union Company distributes natural gas as a public utility through Southern Union Gas and Missouri Gas Energy. Southern Union Gas serves 511,000 customers in Texas; Missouri Gas Energy, headquartered in Kansas City, serves 482,000 customers in central and western Missouri. The company markets natural gas to end users, operates natural gas pipeline systems, distributes propane, and markets commercial gas air conditioning and other gas-fired engine-driven applications.

Company	*Symbol*	*% Change*

Cascade Natural Gas Corporation   CGC   2.20%
   222 Fairview Avenue North
   Seattle, WA 98109
   Tel: 206-624-3900
   Fax: 206-654-4024
   Web site: n/a
   Business Summary: Cascade Natural Gas distributes natural gas to customers in the states of Washington and Oregon. The company has about 185,000 customers. Cascade also refines crude oil, produces chemicals, generates electricity, and processes forest products.

Energy West Inc.   EWST   1.64%
   1 First Avenue South
   Great Falls, MT 59401-2229
   Tel: 406-791-7500
   Fax: 406-791-7560
   Web site: www.ewst.com
   Business Summary: Energy West distributes and sells natural gas and propane. The company operates three wholly owned subsidiaries: Energy West Propane, Inc.; Energy West Resources, Inc.; and Energy West Development, Inc.

RGC Resources, Inc.   RGCO   1.32%
   519 Kimball Ave N.E.
   Roanoke, VA 24016
   Tel: 540-777-4427
   Fax: 540-777-3855
   Web site: www.rgcresources.com
   Business Summary: RGC Resources distributes and sells repurchased natural gas.

Company	Symbol	% Change

NICOR INC.   GAS   0.96%
 1844 Ferry Road
 Naperville, IL 60563-9600
 Tel: 630-305-9500
 Fax: 630-983-9328
 Web site: www.nicorinc.com
 Business Summary: Nicor distributes gas, transports containerized freight in the Caribbean, and provides unregulated energy products and services. The company obtains its supply through long-term contracts and on-the-spot markets. The gas distribution segment serves nearly 2 million customers in a service area that includes most of the northern third of Illinois, except Chicago.

UGI Corporation   UGI   0.41%
 460 North Gulph Road
 King of Prussia, PA 19406
 Tel: 610-337-1000
 Fax: n/a
 Web site: www.ugicorp.com
 Business Summary: UGI is a holding company that provides propane, as well as markets gas and electric utility businesses through subsidiaries. The gas division is a medium-sized local natural gas distributor. The electric division is a small electric utility. UGI operates through its subsidiaries: AmeriGas Propane Inc.; UGI Utilities, Inc.; UGI Enterprises, Inc.; and UTI Energy Services Inc.

Company	Symbol	% Change

People's Energy Corporation   PGL   –1.30%
130 East Randolph Drive, 24th Floor
Chicago, IL 60601-6207
Tel: 312-240-4000
Fax: n/a
Web site: www.pecorp.com
Business Summary: People's Energy has six business segments, including gas distribution, power generation, midstream services, retail energy services, oil and gas production, and other activities, such as district heating, cooling, and the development of natural gas fueling stations for natural gas vehicles.

Chesapeake Utilities Corporation   CPK   –1.96%
909 Silver Lake Boulevard
Dover, DE 19904
Tel: 302-734-6799
Fax: n/a
Web site: www.chpk.com
Business Summary: Chesapeake Utilities is a diversified utility company that provides natural gas distribution and transmission, propane distribution, and information technology services. The company serves more than 34,700 residential, commercial, and industrial customers in southern Delaware, Maryland's Eastern Shore, and Central Florida.

Company	*Symbol*	*% Change*

South Jersey Industries   SJI   –2.40%
1 South Jersey Plaza
Folsom, NJ 08037
Tel: 609-561-9000
Fax: n/a
Web site: www.sjindustries.com
Business Summary: South Jersey Industries is a diversified holding company whose major subsidiary is South Jersey Gas Company. South Jersey Industries serves 112 municipalities throughout Atlantic, Cape May, and Salem Counties and portions of Burlington, Camden, and Gloucester Counties. The company serves about 1.2 million customers.

EnergySouth Inc.   ENSI   –2.68%
2828 Dauphin Street
Mobile, AL 36606
Tel: 334-450-4774
Fax: n/a
Web site: www.energysouth.com
Business Summary: EnergySouth distributes and transports natural gas to residential, commercial, and industrial customers in Southwest Alabama. The company's primary business areas are natural gas distribution and natural gas storage.

Appendix D: Integrated Oil and Gas Companies

This appendix expands and supplements information already presented in the main text.

Amerada Hess Corporation
1185 Avenue of the Americas
New York, NY 10036
Tel: 212-997-8500
Fax: 212-536-8390
Web site: www.hess.com
Symbol: AHC
Business Summary: Amerada Hess is an integrated oil and gas company that conducts exploration and production in Denmark, Gabon, Norway, the U.K., and the United States. It also operates in Azerbaijan, Indonesia, Thailand, and other countries. Amerada Hess has proven reserves totaling more than 1.1 billion barrels of oil equivalent. The company operates a refinery in the U.S. Virgin Islands and in New Jersey. It sells gas at its 1,180 HESS gas stations in the eastern United States.

BP plc

Britannic House, 1 Finsbury Circus
London EC2M 7BA, U.K.
Tel: +44-20-7496-4000
Fax: +44-20-7496-4630
Web site: www.bp.com
Symbol: BP
Business Summary: Formerly known as BP Amoco, BP is the world's third-largest integrated oil company. The company has grown by buying Atlantic Richfield Company (ARCO). It has proven reserves of 15 billion barrels, with large holdings in Alaska and the North Sea. BP is the largest producer of oil and gas in America. BP is also one of the top refiners, with capacity of 2.9 million barrels of oil per day. BP operates 29,000 gas stations worldwide.

Exxon-Mobil Corporation

5959 Las Colinas Boulevard
Irving, TX 75039
Tel: 972-444-1000
Fax: 972-444-1350
Web site: www.exxon.mobil.com
Symbol: XOM
Business Summary: Exxon-Mobil is the largest integrated oil company, with proven reserves of almost 21 billion barrels of oil. Its refineries have a capacity of 6 million barrels per day. Exxon-Mobil supplies in excess of 40,000 service stations in over 100 countries, operating as Exxon, Esso, and Mobil brands. It produces and sells petrochemicals and has interests in coal mining, minerals, and electric power generation.

Royal Dutch/Shell Group

30, Carel van Bylandtlaan 2596 HR
The Hague, The Netherlands
Tel: +31-70-377-6655
Fax: +31-70-377-3115
Web site: www.shell.com
Symbol: SC
Business Summary: Royal Dutch/Shell Group is the world's number-two oil and gas group, with proven reserves of 9.7 million barrels of oil and 56.2 trillion cubic feet of gas. It has operations in more than 135 countries. In addition to operating 46,000 gas stations worldwide, the group also makes chemicals and develops renewable energy sources.

Total Fina Elf S.A.

2 Place de la Coupole, 92400 Courbevoie
La Défense 6, France
Tel: +33-1-47-44-45-46
Fax: +33-1-47-44-78-78
Web site: www.totalfinaelf.com
Symbol: TOT
Business Summary: Total Fina Elf has operations in more than 100 countries and proven reserves of 10.8 billion barrels of oil equivalent. It operates 26 refineries and more than 17,600 service stations. The company is a major chemical producer.

Chevron Corporation

575 Market Street
San Francisco, CA 94105
Tel: 415-894-7700
Fax: 415-894-0583
Web site: www.chevron.com
Symbol: CHV
Business Summary: Chevron is the number-three U.S. integrated oil company, runs more than 8,100 gas stations, and has proven

reserves of 5 billion barrels of oil and 9.5 trillion cubic feet of natural gas. It will expand even further by buying Texaco, and the new Chevron-Texaco will be the world's fourth-largest integrated oil company. Chevron holds a 50 percent stake in global refiner and marketer Caltex and has combined its chemicals operations with those of Phillips Petroleum.

Conoco Inc.

600 N. Dairy Ashford
Houston, TX 77079
Tel: 281-293-1000
Fax: 281-293-1440
Web site: www.conoco.com
Symbol: COC
Business Summary: Conoco explores for oil and gas in 20 countries. It has proven reserves of 3.7 billion barrels of oil. Conoco runs about 6,000 miles of U.S. pipeline and either owns or has stakes in nine refineries in the United States, Europe, and Asia. The company operates more than 7,000 gas stations and markets, trades electricity and gas, and develops and builds power plants.

Equitable Resources, Inc.

One Oxford Centre, Suite 3300
Pittsburgh, PA 15219
Tel: 412-553-5700
Fax: 412-553-7781
Web site: www.eqt.com
Symbol: EQT
Business Summary: Oil and gas development, marketing, and distribution company Equitable Resources, Inc. (ERI), hopes all its customers get a fair share. ERI's utility unit (Equitable Gas) serves 275,000 customers in southwestern Pennsylvania (including Pittsburgh) and northern West Virginia. Focusing on Appalachian production, ERI's Equitable Production bought Statoil's Appalachian properties and sold its own Gulf of Mexico assets to Westport Oil

and Gas for $50 million and a 36 percent stake in Westport. ERI has proven reserves of 2.2 trillion cubic feet of gas. It also provides natural gas transmission and storage through NORESCO and offers energy services such as international infrastructure management and financing.

Phillips Petroleum Company

Phillips Building
Bartlesville, OK 74004
Tel: 918-661-6600
Fax: 918-661-6279
Web site: www.phillips66.com
Symbol: P
Business Summary: Phillips is one of the largest U.S.-based integrated oil companies, with proven reserves of 5 billion barrels of oil. Phillips has merged its gas-gathering and processing business with that of Duke Energy, and it has combined its chemicals division with that of Chevron. Phillips refineries have a combined capacity of 1.7 million barrels per day. Phillips sells fuel at more than 12,000 stations.

Shell Oil Company

One Shell Plaza
Houston, TX 77002
Tel: 713-241-6161
Fax: 713-241-4044
Web site: www.shellus.com
Symbol: SHEL
Business Summary: Shell Oil doesn't shilly-shally around. It explores for, produces, and markets oil, natural gas, and chemicals. The company focuses its exploration on the Gulf of Mexico and has proven reserves of 1.2 billion barrels of oil and 1.9 trillion cubic feet of natural gas. Leading an industry trend toward alliances, Shell has partnered with Texaco and Saudi Aramco in U.S. refining and marketing ventures and with Exxon-Mobil in production

in California. Shell is also a major producer of petrochemical products (Shell Chemical). The company markets natural gas and electricity through its Coral Energy unit. Shell's parent, Royal Dutch/Shell Group, is the world's number-two petroleum company (behind Exxon-Mobil).

Texaco Inc.
2000 Westchester Avenue
White Plains, NY 10650
Tel: 914-253-4000
Fax: 914-253-7753
Web site: www.texaco.com
Symbol: TX
Business Summary: To keep its star rising, Texaco has agreed to be acquired by Chevron. The number-two U.S. integrated oil company (after Exxon-Mobil), Texaco has reserves of 4.9 billion barrels of oil equivalent. With a refining capacity of 3.1 million barrels per day, the company and its affiliates market fuel and lubricants at more than 39,000 gas stations worldwide. To gain approval for the Chevron deal, Texaco has agreed to sell its stakes in two joint ventures that hold the company's U.S. refineries and service stations: Equilon (44 percent, with Shell) and Motiva (33 percent, with Shell and Saudi Aramco). Texaco owns half of Caltex, its international refining and marketing joint venture with Chevron.

Appendix E: Majors
Best Performing for 1998–2001

This appendix expands on information presented in the main text and offers leads into other major companies in the energy sector.

Company	Symbol	% Change
A.O. Tatneft	TNT	507.17%

A.O. Tatneft
Ul. Lenina 75
Almetyevsk, Tatarstan 423400
Tel: +7 85512 5-5856
Fax: +7 85512 5-6865
Web site: www.tatneft.ru

Business Summary: Tatneft is an exploration, development, production, refining, and marketing company. Tatneft's reserves are in the Volga-Urals basin in the Tatarstan Republic. Tatneft exports to both the Commonwealth Independent States and the non-Commonwealth Independent States, like Germany, France, and Poland.

Company	Symbol	% Change

Imperial Oil Limited   IMO   80.42%
111 St. Clair Avenue West
Toronto, Ontario, Canada M5W 1K3
Tel: 416-968-4713
Fax: 416-968-4095
Web site: www.imperialoil.ca
Business Summary: Imperial Oil Limited is a refiner of petroleum products and producer of crude oil and natural gas.

Phillips Petroleum Company   P   19.95%
Phillips Building
Bartlesville, OK 74004
Tel: 918-661-6600
Fax: n/a
Web site: www.phillips66.com
Business Summary: Phillips Petroleum has four business segments: exploration and production; gas gathering, processing, and marketing; refining, marketing, and transportation; and chemicals.

The Shell Transport and   SC   18.23%
Trading Company
Shell Centre
London, England SE1 7NA
Tel: +44 20 7934-3363
Fax: +44 20 7934-5153
Web site: www.shell.com
Business Summary: Shell's main businesses include exploration and production, downstream gas and power generation, oil products, chemicals, and renewables.

Company	*Symbol*	*% Change*

Exxon-Mobil Corp   XOM   10.05%
   5959 Las Colinas Boulevard
   Irving, TX 75039-2298
   Tel: 972-444-1000
   Fax: 972-444-1350
   Web site: www.exxon.mobil.com
   Business Summary: Exxon-Mobil is primarily involved in the exploration for and the production, transportation, and sale of crude oil and natural gas and in the manufacture, transportation, and sale of petroleum products. The company manufactures and markets petrochemicals and participates in coal and mineral mining and electric power generation worldwide. The company and its affiliates operate or market products in the United States and about 200 other countries and territories.

BP Plc   BP   9.10%
   1 Finsbury Circus, Britannic House
   London, England EC2M 7BA
   Tel: +44 020 7496-5200
   Fax: +44 020 7496-5806
   Web site: www.bpamaco.com
   Business Summary: BP's main businesses are exploration and production, gas and power, refining and marketing, and chemicals. The group has major operations in Europe, North and South America, Australasia, and parts of Africa.

Company	Symbol	% Change

Total Fina Elf S.A.   TOT   9.09%
2, Place de la Coupole la Defense Cedex 92078
Paris, France
Tel: +33-1-47-44-45-46
Fax: +33-1-47-44-78-78
Web site: www.totalfinaelf.com
Business Summary: Total Fina Elf has operations in more than 100 countries and proven reserves of 10.8 billion barrels of oil equivalent. It operates 26 refineries and more than 17,600 service stations. The company is a major chemical producer.

Texaco Inc.   TX   5.24%
2000 Westchester Avenue
White Plains, NY 10650
Tel: 914-253-4000
Fax: 914-253-6286
Web site: n/a
Business Summary: Texaco's business is worldwide in exploration for and production, transportation, refining, and marketing of crude oil, natural gas liquids, natural gas and petroleum products, power generation, and gasification.

Company	*Symbol*	*% Change*

Repsol, S.A.   REP   3.84%
Paseo de la Castellana 278
Madrid, Spain
Tel: +34 91 348 8-1 00
Fax: +34 91 348 2-8 21
Web site: www.repsol.com
Business Summary: Repsol explores for, develops, and produces crude oil and natural gas. The company transports petroleum products, liquefied petroleum gas (LPG), and natural gas. Repsol also produces a wide range of petrochemicals and markets petroleum products, petroleum derivatives, petrochemicals, LPG, and natural gas.

ENI S.P.A.   E   0.57%
Piazzale Enrico Mattei 1, 00144
Rome, Italy
Tel: +39 06 59 82 2-6 24
Fax: +39 06 59 82 2-6 31
Web site: www.Eni.it/English/home.html
Business Summary: Ente Nazionale Idrocarburi explores for and produces oil and natural gas; supplies, transports, and distributes natural gas; and refines and distributes oil-derived products and petrochemicals. The company has operations in 69 countries worldwide.

Appendix F: Oil & Gas

Best Performing for 1998—2001

This appendix is designed to supplement and expand on the main text.

Company	Symbol	% Change
Petroquest Energy Inc.	PQUE	526.67%

    400 E. Kaliste Saloom Road, Suite 3000
Lafayette, LA 70508
Tel: 337-232-7028
Fax: n/a
Web site: n/a
Business Summary: Petroquest generates, explores for, develops, acquires, and operates oil and gas properties. The company operates oil and gas properties both onshore and offshore in the Gulf Coast region.

Company	*Symbol*	*% Change*

A.O. Tatneft   TNT   507.17%
UL. Lenina 75, 423400
Almetyevsk, Tatarstan
Tel: +7-85512-5-5856
Fax: +7-85512-5-6865
Web site: www.tatneft.ru
Business Summary: Tatneft is an exploration, development, production, refining, and marketing company. Tatneft's reserves are in the Volga-Urals basin in the Tatarstan Republic. Tatneft exports to both the Commonwealth Independent States and the non-Commonwealth Independent States, like Germany, France, and Poland.

Chesapeake Energy Corporation   CHK   397.78%
6100 North Western Avenue
Oklahoma City, OK 73118
Tel: 405-848-8000
Fax: 405-843-0573
Web site: www.chesapeake-energy.com
Business Summary: Chesapeake Energy acquires, explores for, and develops properties for the production of crude oil and natural gas from underground reservoirs. The properties of the company are located in Oklahoma, Texas, Arkansas, Louisiana, Kansas, Montana, Colorado, North Dakota, and New Mexico, as well as in British Columbia and Saskatchewan, Canada.

Company	Symbol	% Change

Patina Oil & Gas Corporation   POG   387.67%
  1625 Broadway
  Denver, CO 80202
  Tel: 303-389-3600
  Fax: 303-389-3680
  Web site: www.patinaoil.com
  Business Summary: Patina acquires, develops, explores for, and produces oil and natural gas. Patina operates its own exploration and production waste management, which enables it to dispose of tank sludge and contaminated soil. Patina sells its products to end users, refiners, marketers, and others through intrastate and inter-state pipelines.

Mitchell Energy & Dev Corp   MND   308.93%
  2001 Timberloch Place
  The Woodlands, TX 77387-4000
  Tel: 713-377-5500
  Fax: n/a
  Web site: www.mitchellenergy.com
  Business Summary: Mitchell Energy is involved in the exploration for and production of natural gas, natural gas liquids, crude oil, and condensate; operation of natural gas gathering systems; and marketing of natural gas through purchase and resale activities. Mitchell owns or operates about 9,100 miles of natural gas–gathering systems located in Texas.

Company	Symbol	% Change

PYR Energy Corp   PYR   274.00%
1675 Broadway, Suite 2540
Denver, CO 80202
Tel: 303-825-3748
Fax: 303-825-3768
Web site: www.pyrenergy.com
Business Summary: PYR Energy is a development-stage company that explores for and exploits onshore natural gas and oil accumulations. The company uses 3-D seismic and computer-aided technology for the systematic exploration of oil and gas. Its exploration activities are located in the western United States.

Prima Energy Corporation   PENG   227.22%
1099 18th Street, Suite 400
Denver, CO 80202
Tel: 303-297-2100
Fax: n/a
Web site: www.primaenergy.com
Business Summary: Prima Energy explores for, acquires, develops, and operates oil and gas properties. Prima provides oilfield services and markets for natural gas.

Company	*Symbol*	*% Change*

Remington Oil & Gas Corp   ROIL   225.75%
8201 Preston Road, Suite 600
Dallas, TX 75225-6211
Tel: 214-210-2650
Fax: 214-210-2643
Web site: www.remoil.com
Business Summary: Remington Oil & Gas engages in exploration for, development of, and production of oil and gas reserves in the offshore Gulf of Mexico and onshore Gulf Coast areas. The company identifies prospective oil- and gas-producing properties by seismic technology and drills exploratory wells after acquiring an interest in the prospective property.

Western Gas Resources, Incorporated   WGR   193.86%
12200 N. Pecos Street
Denver, CO 80234-3439
Tel: 303-452-5603
Fax: n/a
Web site: www.westerngas.com
Business Summary: Western Gas Resources designs, constructs, owns, and operates natural gas–gathering systems and facilities for the processing and treating of natural gas and NGLs.

Company	Symbol	% Change
Frontier Oil Corp	FTO	181.12%

Frontier Oil Corp
10000 Memorial Drive, Suite 600
Houston, TX 77024-3411
Tel: 713-688-9600
Fax: 713-688-0616
Web site: www.frontieroil.com
Business Summary: Frontier Oil Corporation has crude oil refineries and sells refined petroleum products to the wholesale market. Frontier operates total crude oil capacity of over 150,000 barrels per day. The company operates refineries in Cheyenne, Wyoming, and El Dorado, Kansas. The company sells refined products from the Cheyenne refineries to independent retailers, jobbers, and major oil companies.

Appendix G:
Oil Drilling Companies
Best Performing for 1998–2001

This appendix expands company information beyond that provided in the main text.

Company	Symbol	% Change

Credo Petroleum Corporation   CRED   168.69%
1801 Broadway, Suite 900
Denver, CO 80202
Tel: 303-297-2200
Fax: n/a
Web site: www.credopetroleum.com
Business Summary: Credo Petroleum explores for, acquires, develops, and produces oil and gas in the Mid-Continent and Rocky Mountain regions of the United States. The company actively drills for, acquires, and operates oil and gas properties.

Company	Symbol	% Change

Daugherty Resources Inc.   NGAS   124.00%
120 Prosperous Place, Suite 201
Lexington, KY 40509-1844
Tel: 859-263-3948
Fax: 606-263-4228
Web site: n/a
Business Summary: Daugherty Resources has assets in oil and gas, as well as gold and silver properties. The company engages in exploration for and development of oil and gas. The company operates approximately 136 natural gas wells and 5 oil wells in the Appalachian Basin and 45 oil wells in the Illinois Basin.

Smedvig A S   SMVB   111.50%
Finnestadveien 28
Stavanger 4001, Sweden
Tel: +47 51 50 9-9 00
Fax: +47 51 50 9-6 88
Web site: n/a
Business Summary: Smedvig is an offshore drilling contractor with mobile deepwater drilling rigs and self-erecting tender rigs. The company also contracts to do drilling, maintenance, modification, and well abandonment on fixed installations.

Swift Energy Company   SFY   111.43%
16825 Northchase Drive, Suite 400
Houston, TX 77060
Tel: 281-874-2700
Fax: 281-874-2726
Web site: www.swiftenergy.com
Business Summary: Swift Energy develops, explores for, acquires, and operates oil and gas properties, with a special emphasis on onshore natural gas reserves. The company focuses on domestic activities in specific regions. Swift operates over 800 wells. The company has oil and gas interests in New Zealand, Venezuela, and Russia.

Company	*Symbol*	*% Change*

Exploration Company (The)   **TXCO**   107.11%
    500 North Loop 1604, East Suite 250
    San Antonio, TX 78232
    Tel: 210-496-5300
    Fax: n/a
    Web site: n/a
    Business Summary: The Exploration Company of Delaware explores for, develops, and produces oil, natural gas, and minerals. The operations of the company are conducted primarily in Texas, North Dakota, South Dakota, and Montana.

Patterson-UTI Energy Inc.   **PTEN**   100.58%
    4510 Lamesa Highway
    Snyder, TX 79550
    Tel: 915-573-1104
    Fax: 915-573-0281
    Web site: www.patenergy.com
    Business Summary: Patterson-UTI Energy provides domestic land-based drilling services to independent oil and natural gas companies. The company focuses its operations in Texas, New Mexico, Oklahoma, Louisiana, Mississippi, and Utah. The group has 152 drilling rigs.

Daleco Resources Corp.   **DLOV**   98.21%
    120 North Church Street, Suite 615
    West Chester, PA 19380
    Tel: 610-429-0181
    Fax: 610-429-0818
    Web site: n/a
    Business Summary: Daleco Resources explores for, develops, and produces oil and gas properties, harvests timber concessions, and holds mineral interests.

Company	*Symbol*	*% Change*

Smedvig A S SMVA 91.80%
Finnestadveien 28
Stavanger 4001, Sweden
Tel: +47 51 50 9-9 00
Fax: +47 51 50 9-6 88
Web site: n/a
Business Summary: Smedvig contracts for offshore drilling. The company has mobile deepwater drilling rigs, has self-erecting tender rigs, and contracts for drilling, maintenance, modification and well abandonment on fixed installations.

Precision Drilling Corp. PDS 80.99%
150 6th Avenue SW, 4200 Petro-Centre
Calgary, Alberta, Canada T2P 3Y7
Tel: 403-716-4500
Fax: 403-264-0251
Web site: www.precisiondrilling.com
Business Summary: Precision Drilling is an integrated oilfield drilling and energy service company, providing technologically advanced equipment and quality service to the oil, gas, and industrial businesses. It also provides land drilling services to oil and gas exploration and production companies, logging and measurement while drilling, technology and services, underbalanced drilling technology and production testing, industrial maintenance, and turnaround services.

Company	*Symbol*	*% Change*

TMBR/Sharp Drilling Inc.   TBDI   80.77%
4607 West Industrial Blvd.
Midland, TX 79703
Tel: 915-699-5050
Fax: 915-699-5828
Web site: n/a
Business Summary: TMBR/Sharp Drilling provides domestic on-shore contract drilling services of oil and gas to major and independent oil and gas companies. The company also acquires, explores for, develops, produces, and sells oil and natural gas. The company's drilling activities are primarily conducted in the Permian Basin of west Texas and eastern Mexico, utilizing its 18 drilling rigs.

Appendix H: Oilfield Equipment and Services
Best Performing for 1998—2001

This appendix provides additional information and supplements and expands on information in the main text.

Company	Symbol	% Change
Company	*Symbol*	*% Change*

Coflexip S.A.   CXIPY   124.16%
23 Avenue de Neuilly
Paris, France
Tel: +33-1-40-67-6-0 00
Fax: +33-1-40-67-6-0 03
Web site: www.coflexip.com
Business Summary: Coflexip provides oil and gas field development solutions, engineering and project management, and off-shore services from installation to abandonment. These activities include sub-sea product manufacturing and operations.

Company	Symbol	% Change

BJ Services Company **BJS** **119.14%**
5500 Northwest Central Drive
Houston, TX 77092
Tel: 713-462-4239
Fax: 713-895-5603
Web site: www.bjservices.com
Business Summary: BJ Services Company provides pressure pumping and other oilfield services worldwide. These services are used in the completion of new oil and natural gas wells and in remedial work with onshore and offshore wells. The company also provides product and equipment sales to local service companies, tubular services, and process and pipeline services in the United States, Canada, the Gulf of Mexico, Latin America, Europe, Asia, Africa, and the Middle East.

Cal Dive International Inc. **CDIS** **82.13%**
400 N. Sam Houston Parkway E., Suite 400
Houston, TX 77060
Tel: 281-618-0400
Fax: 281-618-0501
Web site: www.caldive.com
Business Summary: Cal Dive International provides a full range of services to offshore oil and gas exploration, production, and pipeline companies, including underwater construction, well operations, maintenance and repair of pipelines and platforms, and salvage operations. The company acquires selected mature, noncore offshore natural gas and oil properties from operators and provides them with a cost-effective alternative to decommissioning.

Company	Symbol	% Change

Weatherford International Inc.   WFT   79.13%
515 Post Oak Boulevard, Suite 600
Houston TX 77027-3415
Tel: 713-693-4000
Fax: 713-693-4294
Web site: www.weatherford.com
Business Summary: Weatherford International drills, completes, and produces oil and natural gas wells. Drilling and intervention services provide fishing and rental services, well installation, cementing products, and underbalanced drilling and specialty pipeline services. The company utilizes leading proprietary and patented technologies to maximize production.

Hanover Compressor Co.   HC   71.67%
12001 North Houston Rosslyn
Houston, TX 77086
Tel: 281-447-8787
Fax: 281-447-8781
Web site: www.hanover.com
Business Summary: Hanover Compressor provides natural gas compression, gas handling, and related services in the United States and international markets. The company also provides compressor and oil and gas production equipment fabrication operations. Hanover's products and services are necessary to the production, processing, transportation, and storage of natural gas.

Company	Symbol	% Change

Superior Energy Services Inc. SPN 65.05%
1105 Peters Road
Harvey, LA 70058
Tel: 504-362-4321
Fax: 504-362-1430
Web site: www.superiorenergy.com
Business Summary: Superior Energy Services provides specialized oilfield services and equipment to oil and gas companies in the exploration for, production of, and development of oil and gas properties. The company's development activities of oil and gas properties offshore are located in the Gulf of Mexico and throughout the Gulf Coast region. The company provides services to stimulate oil and gas production.

Offshore Logistics Inc. OLOG 57.45%
224 Rue De Jean
Lafayette, LA 70505
Tel: 337-233-1221
Fax: 318-235-6678
Web site: n/a
Business Summary: Offshore Logistics provides helicopter transportation services worldwide to the offshore oil and gas industry and is a production management services business. The group also provides personnel and medical support services worldwide to the oil and gas industry.

Company	Symbol	% Change

Bouygues Offshore S.A.   BWG   54.59%
3 rue Stephenson
Montigny-le-Bretonneux, France 78884
Tel: +33-1-30-60-8-8-88
Fax: +33-30-64-5-6-75
Web site: www.bouygues-offshore.com
Business Summary: Bouygues Offshore provides oil and gas project management; financial engineering; equipment procurement; and design, construction, installation, and operation of offshore and onshore fields. The company also does cryogenic storage and construction of import and export terminals and turnkey plants. Bouygues designs and constructs oil and gas terminals, as well as refining and petrochemical, steel, and metal-processing plants.

Team, Inc.   TMI   51.43%
200 Hermann Drive
Alvin, TX 77511
Tel: 281-331-6154
Fax: 281-331-4107
Web site: www.teamindustrialservices.com
Business Summary: Team provides industrial repair services and designs, manufactures, sells, and rents portable machine tools. Its customers include chemical, petrochemical, refining, pulp and paper, power, steel, and other industries.

Appendix I: Pipeline Companies
Best Performing for 1998–2001

This appendix expands on the companies described in the main text.

Company	Symbol	% Change
Western Gas Resources, Incorporated	WGR	193.86%

Western Gas Resources, Incorporated
12200 N. Pecos Street
Denver, CO 80234-3439
Tel: 303-452-5603
Fax: n/a
Web site: www.westerngas.com
Business Summary: Western Gas Resources designs, constructs, owns, and operates natural gas–gathering systems and facilities for the processing and treating of natural gas and NGLs.

Company	Symbol	% Change

Penn Octane Corporation   POCC   166.67%
77-530 Enfield Lane, Bldg. D
Palm Desert, CA 92211
Tel: 760-772-9080
Fax: n/a
Web site: www.pennwilsoncng.com
Business Summary: Penn Octane purchases, transports, and sells liquefied petroleum gas (LPG). The company sells LPG primarily to P.M.I. Trading Limited, the subsidiary of the state-owned Mexican oil company, for distribution in the northeast region of Mexico. The major supplier of the company is Exxon Company, U.S.A.

Kinder Morgan Energy Partners   KMP   110.24%
500 Dallas Street, Suite 1000
Houston, TX 77002
Tel: 713-369-9000
Fax: n/a
Web site: www.kindermorgan.com
Business Summary: Kinder Morgan Energy Partners, L.P., owns and manages a diversified portfolio of midstream energy assets. The operations are carried through four operating limited partnerships. The partnership's operations are grouped into three business segments: Pacific operations, mid-continent operations, and bulk terminals operations.

Company	Symbol	% Change

Kinder Morgan Inc. KMI 53.51%
500 Dallas Street, Suite 1000
Houston, TX 77002
Tel: 713-369-9000
Fax: n/a
Web site: www.kindermorgan.com
Business Summary: Kinder Morgan Incorporated is an integrated energy services provider with operations that include producing, gathering, processing, storage, transportation, and marketing of natural gas. The company serves residential, commercial, agricultural, and industrial customers.

El Paso Energy Partners L.P. EPN 43.02%
1001 Louisiana Street
El Paso Building
Houston, TX 77002
Tel: 713-420-2131
Fax: n/a
Web site: www.elpasopartners.com
Business Summary: El Paso Energy Partners produces natural gas and crude oil in the Gulf of Mexico. El Paso Energy owns interests in gas pipelines located offshore of Louisiana and eastern Texas to gather and transport natural gas.

Company	Symbol	% Change

Westcoast Energy Inc.   **WE**   **40.84%**
1333 West Georgia Street
Vancouver, British Columbia, Canada V6E 3K9
Tel: 604-488-8000
Fax: 604-488-8500
Web site: www.westcoastenergy.com
Business Summary: Westcoast Energy operates international transmission and field services, as well as gas distribution and power-generation services. Other business activities include natural gas gathering, processing, and transmission; natural gas distribution, storage, and transmission; electrical and thermal energy generated from natural gas; energy marketing; retail energy services, and information technology and financial services.

El Paso Corp.   **EPG**   **28.80%**
1001 Louisiana Street
El Paso Building
Houston, TX 77002
Tel: 713-420-2131
Fax: n/a
Web site: www.epenergy.com
Business Summary: The principal activities of El Paso Corporation are the provision of interstate and intrastate pipeline transportation; gathering, processing, and storage of natural gas, power, and other energy-related commodities; power generation; the development and operation of energy infrastructure facilities worldwide; and the domestic exploration for and production of natural gas and oil.

Company	Symbol	% Change

Buckeye Partners, L.P.   BPL   24.46%
100 Matsonford Road, Suite 500
5 Radnor Corporate Center
Radnor, PA 19087
Tel: 484-232-4000
Fax: 610-770-4541
Web site: www.buckeye.com
Business Summary: Buckeye Partners is an independent pipeline carrier of refined petroleum products in the United States. Buckeye's refined petroleum products are carried from refineries to other locations through 2,970 miles of pipeline in nine states.

TEPPCO Partners, L.P.   TPP   23.41%
2929 Allen Parkway
Houston, TX 77252-2521
Tel: 713-759-3636
Fax: n/a
Web site: www.teppco.com
Business Summary: Teppco Partners is one of the pipeline common carriers of refined petroleum products and LPGs in the United States. Teppco owns and operates approximately 4,300 miles of pipeline from southeast Texas through the central, midwestern, and northeastern United States. The pipeline system includes delivery terminals along the pipeline for distribution to other pipelines, tank trucks, and rail cars or barges.

Appendix J: Oil Companies
Secondary 1998—2001

This appendix provides information not contained in the main text.

Company	Symbol	% Change
Petroquest Energy Inc.	PQUE	526.67%

Petroquest Energy Inc.
400 E. Kaliste Saloom Road, Suite 3000
Lafayette, LA 70508
Tel: 337-232-7028
Fax: n/a
Web site: n/a
Business Summary: Petroquest Energy generates, explores for, develops, acquires, and operates oil and gas properties. The company operates oil and gas properties both onshore and offshore in the Gulf Coast region.

Company	*Symbol*	*% Change*
Chesapeake Energy Corporation	CHK	397.78%

6100 North Western Avenue
Oklahoma City, OK 73118
Tel: 405-848-8000
Fax: 405-843-0573
Web site: www.chesapeake-energy.com
Business Summary: Chesapeake Energy acquires, explores for, and develops properties for the production of crude oil and natural gas from underground reservoirs. Its properties are located in Oklahoma, Texas, Arkansas, Louisiana, Kansas, Montana, Colorado, North Dakota, New Mexico, and British Columbia and Saskatchewan, Canada.

Patina Oil & Gas Corporation	POG	387.67%

1625 Broadway
Denver, CO 80202
Tel: 303-389-3600
Fax: 303-389-3680
Web site: www.patinaoil.com
Business Summary: Patina Oil & Gas acquires, develops, exploits, and produces oil and natural gas. The company operates its own exploration and production waste management, enabling it to dispose of tank sludge and contaminated soil. The company's products are sold to end users, refiners, marketers, and others through intrastate and interstate pipelines.

Company	*Symbol*	*% Change*

Mitchell Energy & Development Corp. MND 308.93%
2001 Timberloch Place
The Woodlands, TX 77387-4000
Tel: 713-377-5500
Fax: n/a
Web site: www.mitchellenergy.com
Business Summary: Mitchell Energy explores for and produces natural gas, natural gas liquids, crude oil, and condensate; it operates natural gas–gathering systems and markets natural gas through purchase and resale activities. Mitchell owns or operates approximately 9,100 miles of natural gas–gathering systems, which are located in Texas.

PYR Energy Corp. PYR 274.00%
1675 Broadway, Suite 2540
Denver, CO 80202
Tel: 303-825-3748
Fax: 303-825-3768
Web site: www.pyrenergy.com
Business Summary: PYR Energy is a development-stage company that explores for and exploits onshore natural gas and oil accumulations. The company uses 3-D seismic and computer-aided technology for the systematic exploration of oil and gas.

Company	Symbol	% Change

Prima Energy Corporation   PENG   227.22%
   1099 18th Street, Suite 400
   Denver, CO 80202
   Tel: 303-297-2100
   Fax: n/a
   Web site: www.primaenergy.com
Business Summary: Prima Energy explores for, acquires, develops, and operates oil and gas properties. The company develops, sells, and provides oil and natural gas for wells that it operates for third parties.

Frontier Oil Corp.   FTO   181.12%
   10000 Memorial Drive, Suite 600
   Houston, TX 77024-3411
   Tel: 713-688-9600
   Fax: 713-688-0616
   Web site: www.frontieroil.com
Business Summary: Frontier Oil Corporation operates crude oil refineries and does wholesale marketing of refined petroleum products, including various grades of gasoline, diesel fuel, jet fuel, asphalt, chemicals, and petroleum coke. The company operates refineries in Cheyenne, Wyoming, and El Dorado, Kansas.

Company	*Symbol*	*% Change*

Louis Dreyfus Natural Gas Corporation   LD   169.71%
14000 Quail Springs Parkway, Suite 600
Oklahoma City, OK 73134
Tel: 405-749-1300
Fax: 405-749-9382
Web site: www.ldng.com
Business Summary: Louis Dreyfus Natural Gas Corporation acquires, develops, explores for, produces, and markets natural gas and crude oil. The activities of the company are carried on in Texas, New Mexico, Oklahoma, Kansas, Arkansas, and Louisiana. The company has entered into fixed-price natural gas delivery contracts with natural gas pipeline marketing affiliates, a municipality, an independent power producer, and other end users, basically to reduce exposure to decreases in oil and natural gas prices due to volatile fluctuation.

Enterprise Products Partners   EPD   165.82%
2727 North Loop West
Houston, TX 77008-1037
Tel: 713-880-6500
Fax: n/a
Web site: n/a
Business Summary: Enterprise Products provides processing and transportation services to producers of natural gas liquids and consumers of natural gas liquid products. Enterprise Products has long-term fractionation agreements with Burlington Resources, Texaco, and Union Pacific Resources.

Selected Bibliography

Batra, Ravi. *The Downfall of Capitalism & Communism: Can Capitalism Be Saved?* Second Edition. Venus Books, 1990.

Batra, Ravi. *The Great Depression of 1990.* Simon & Schuster, 1985.

Beckner, Steven K. *Back from the Brink—The Greenspan Years.* John Wiley & Sons, 1996.

Burke, Gibbons. "Getting Connected." *Active Trader Magazine,* Volume 1 (2000).

Duarte, Joe. "A 10-Year Overview of Market Sentiment." *Technical Analysis of Stocks and Commodities Magazine,* Volume 16 (1998).

Duarte, Joe. "Combining Sentiment Indicators for Timing Mutual Funds." *Technical Analysis of Stocks and Commodities Magazine,* Volume 10 (January 1992).

Duarte, Joe. "Trading the Mood of the Market." *Active Trader Magazine,* Volume 2:9 (2001).

Elder, Alexander. *Trading for a Living.* John Wiley & Sons, 1993.

Galbraith, John Kenneth. *A Short History of Financial Euphoria.* Penguin Books, 1993.

Greider, William. *Secrets of the Temple.* Simon & Schuster, 1987.

Lefevre, Edwin. *Reminiscences of a Stock Operator.* Fraser Publishing, 1980.

Murphy, John J. *Technical Analysis of the Financial Markets.* New York Institute of Finance, 1999.

Nassar, David S. *How to Get Started in Electronic Day Trading.* McGraw-Hill, 1999.

O'Neil, William J. *24 Essential Lessons for Investment Success.* McGraw-Hill, 2000.

Sperandeo, Victor, and Brown T. Sullivan. *Trader Vic—Methods of a Wall Street Master.* John Wiley & Sons, 1991.

Yergin, Daniel. *The Prize: The Epic Quest for Oil, Money & Power,* Touchstone Books, 1991.

Zweig, Martin, and Morrie Goldfisher. *Winning on Wall Street.* Warner Books, 1986.

Index